Debunking the Myth of Job Fit in Higher Education and Student Affairs

ACPA Books Contact Information

ACPA International Office

Tricia A. Fechter Gates
Deputy Executive Director
One Dupont Circle, NW, Suite 300
Washington, DC 20036-1110
(202) 759-4825
FAX (202) 827-0601
pfechter@acpa.nche.edu

ACPA Books Series Editor

Robert T. Palmer
Chair, Department of Educational Leadership
and Policy Studies
Howard University
(202) 806-7347
robert.palmer@Howard.edu

Debunking the Myth of Job Fit in Higher Education and Student Affairs

Edited by
Brian J. Reece, Vu T. Tran,
Elliott N. DeVore, and Gabby Porcaro

Foreword by
Stephen John Quaye

ACPA
College Student
Educators International

Stylus

STERLING, VIRGINIA

Published by Stylus Publishing, LLC.
22883 Quicksilver Drive
Sterling, Virginia 20166-2019

Library of Congress Cataloging-in-Publication Data

Names: Reece, Brian J., editor.
Title: Debunking the myth of job fit in student affairs / edited by Brian J. Reece,
Vu T. Tran, Elliott N. DeVore, and Gabby Porcaro ; foreword by Stephen Quaye.
Description: Sterling, Virginia : Stylus Publishing, 2018. |
Includes bibliographical references and index.
Identifiers: LCCN 2018017198 (print) | LCCN 2018034151 (ebook) |
ISBN 9781620367896 (uPDF) | ISBN 9781620367902 (mobi, ePub) |
ISBN 9781620367872 (cloth : alk. paper) | ISBN 9781620367889
(pbk. : alk. paper) | ISBN 9781620367896 (library networkable e-edition) |
ISBN 9781620367902 (consumer e-edition)
Subjects: LCSH: Student affairs services–Social aspects–United States. | Student
counselors–Employment–United States. | Minorities in higher education–
United States. | Women in higher education–United States.
Classification: LCC LB2342.92 (ebook) | LCC LB2342.92 .D43 2018 (print) |
DDC 378.1/97–dc23
LC record available at https://lccn.loc.gov/2018017198

13-digit ISBN: 978-1-62036-787-2 (cloth)
13-digit ISBN: 978-1-62036-788-9 (paperback)
13-digit ISBN: 978-1-62036-789-6 (library networkable e-edition)
13-digit ISBN: 978-1-62036-790-2 (consumer e-edition)

Printed in the United States of America

All first editions printed on acid-free paper
that meets the American National Standards Institute
Z39-48 Standard.

Bulk Purchases
Quantity discounts are available for use in workshops and for
staff development.
Call 1-800-232-0223

First Edition, 2019

To our CSJE family. And to those of us who have ever felt something less than true belonging.

Contents

Figures and Tables   ix

Foreword   xi
    Stephen John Quaye

Acknowledgments   xv

1 FROM FIT TO BELONGING   1
New Dialogues on the Student Affairs Job Search
    Brian J. Reece, Vu T. Tran, Elliott N. DeVore, and Gabby Porcaro

2 INNOCENT UNTIL PROVEN GUILTY   27
**A Critical Interrogation of the Legal Aspects
of Job Fit in Higher Education**
    David Hòa Khoa Nguyễn and LaWanda W.M. Ward

3 EMPLOYER DEFINITIONS OF AND REFLECTIONS ON *FIT* IN HIRING PROCESSES   49
    Léna Kavaliauskas Crain and Mathew J.L. Shepard

4 HOLOGRAMS, MISFITS, AND AUTHENTIC SELVES   67
Fit as Narrative Agency Through Inequality Regimes
    *Jessica Bennett, Travis T. York, Van Bailey, Marshall Habermann-Guthrie,
Luis Jimenez Inoa, Meghan Gaffney Wells, and Akiko Yamaguchi*

5 NO, I CAN'T MEET YOU FOR AN $8 COFFEE   97
How Class Shows Up in Workspaces
    Sonja Ardoin and becky martinez

6 FINDING FIT AS AN "OUTSIDER WITHIN"   119
**A Critical Exploration of Black Women Navigating
the Workplace in Higher Education**
    Stacey D. Garrett and Natasha T. Turman

7 CODE WORD *FIT*   147
   **Exploring the Systemic Exclusion of Professionals of
   Color in Predominantly White Institutions**
   Heather O. Browning and Patrice M. Palmer

8 NEGOTIATING FIT WHILE "MISFIT"   167
   Three Ways Trans Professionals Navigate Student Affairs
   C.J. Venable, Kyle Inselman, and Nick Thuot

9 "YOU'LL FIT RIGHT IN"   193
   **Fit as a Euphemism for Whiteness in Higher
   Education Hiring Practices**
   Kyle C. Ashlee

10 (RE)VIEWING AND (RE)MOVING THE MYSTIQUE SURROUNDING "FIT" IN
   STUDENT AFFAIRS   217
   A Challenge to Our Field
   Walter P. Parrish III

   Editors and Contributors   231

   Index   241

Figures and Tables

FIGURES

Figure 2.1   EEOC charge-filing process.   34
Figure 2.2   Filing employment discrimination charges with
              the EEOC.   35

TABLES

Table 4.1   Self-Reported Characteristics of Coauthors   74
Table 5.1   Yosso's (2005) Community Cultural Wealth Model: Six
             Additional Forms of Capital   101

Foreword

STORY 1

From an early age, I was taught to cover up, to shield my Black body in uniforms. This covering up was intended to help me fit in—to assimilate into the predominantly White spaces I occupied as a Ghanaian immigrant. Covering up, in essence, hid my Black body and enabled me to feel less threatening to my White peers and teachers.

STORY 2

As the program director of the Student Affairs in Higher Education program at Miami University, I call candidates who come to campus to interview for admission to the program. I call to tell them whether the faculty is admitting them, waitlisting them, or denying them admission. When I call candidates to tell them we are not offering them admission, I like to provide them feedback about their interview in case it is helpful as they move forward. I dread these calls. I find myself struggling with being honest and telling people why we did not admit them. I find that I often tell them that they were strong candidates but just not a good fit for the program. And even as I interact with candidates, I find myself often saying that I hope they choose a program that they feel is a good fit for them. I usually say this and don't give it much thought.

Reading *Debunking the Myth of Job Fit in Higher Education and Student Affairs* has pushed me in a way I was not expecting. As the editors and contributors suggest, *fit* is a seemingly innocuous word, filled with little meaning. We use this word so many times throughout the day. And yet, it is the word that can leave an applicant feeling further oppressed, stunned, or shamed. As the two stories I shared illustrate, I have, on the one hand, tried desperately to fit in to White spaces—to make myself more palatable to White people. On the other hand, I illustrate my power to deny people admittance into certain spaces and the privilege I hold in making those determinations. As the contributors to this book portray, one can be in positions to make decisions about someone's fit, while simultaneously being positioned as the person not deemed fitting into a space. Holding these two positions in the same space is necessary as a way to make changes.

I applaud the contributors for taking on this topic and not letting "fit" remain so innocuous. This book works so well because of the combination of story-sharing from the contributors' own lives, as well as the practical tools for those making hiring decisions. Most importantly, the editors and contributors critique commonly held assumptions and language, language that we use because we are afraid to be honest with candidates about what we are seeking in a job or because we are unwilling to acknowledge our own stereotypes, assumptions, and safety.

Let me go with the last word in that string—*safety*. It is safer to work with people who share our identities, beliefs, and values. It is comfortable. It is safe to work with what we know. It is because of our safety that we use code words like *fit* to not reveal our hidden assumptions. And I have to include myself in this process. I have used *fit* because it is the safer word, rather than, for example, saying I am afraid to mess up and potentially misgender or mis-recognize someone who does not share my own identities and experiences, someone who intimidates me because of my own insecurities. And so, I say that person doesn't fit and move on.

What if we took the less safe route, as the contributors have done? What if we named our assumptions, beliefs, euphemisms, and code words and took time to unlearn internalized dominance? What if those of us with more power and who hold more dominant identities pushed our colleagues to challenge the language of fit? For far too long, we have relied on those with minoritized identities to come into our spaces and try to fit in to them. And then we balk when they challenge our norms and assumptions. The most significant feat of this book is that each chapter poses these kinds of questions for readers to consider. The questions, stories, and critical lens provoke unsettling feelings, which is a good thing.

I am left with three takeaways from this book. First is the importance of naming. When we use euphemisms like *fit*, we hide our true beliefs and assumptions. Naming has the power to make the hidden curriculum known, so that those unfamiliar with this curriculum can feel empowered to shape it. Second, history is important. The word *fit* did not just come out of nowhere. As the contributors illustrate, fit is tied to White supremacy, cisgenderism, and neoliberalism, and each time we use it, we collude in perpetuating systemic oppression. Third, stories matter. Each contributor is vulnerable in sharing their stories without knowing how readers will receive them. They share their stories so I, and others, can learn. My job, as someone who holds both minoritized and dominant identities, is to not just learn from their stories, but to actually engage in practices that dismantle oppression in places where I hold power (e.g., admitting masters and doctoral students to Miami's Student Affairs in Higher Education program).

We cannot keep using fit to describe other things we are refusing to name. To the editors and contributors, I hear you, and I appreciate you sharing your stories with readers and for working to dismantle the notion of fit.

Stephen John Quaye
Miami University
Oxford, Ohio
March 27, 2018

Acknowledgments

FROM BRIAN

Mahalo nui e Jace Kaholokula Saplan for being a centering force throughout the writing and editing process and for providing perspective in the times it was most needed. And for always listening. Thank you, Mom, for continuing to inspire me and for reminding me that we can change the world around us through words. And, finally, thanks to Kristin Zerbe, my high school English teacher, who encouraged me to explore the written word as a means for analyzing and understanding the world around me.

FROM VU

My deepest thanks go to robbie routenberg, who provided the encouragement I needed to get involved with the Commission for Social Justice Education. If not for robbie, I would not have connected with this wonderful group of professionals, found a home for myself within ACPA, and ultimately become involved with this book project. More importantly, robbie was one of the first people in my life to teach me to embrace my "weirdness" and that I can fit in and belong in the workplace even with all of my quirks.

FROM ELLIOTT

I would like to thank my former adviser and mentor Nancy J. Evans who provided me invaluable support and advice during my job search and subsequent PhD application process. As a queer man from the South who felt the tension between returning home to do the hard work and seeking a queer-affirming environment, she told me that "sometimes you go where you are needed, and sometimes you go where *you* need to be." Thank you for giving me the courage to accept my first job at the University of San Francisco! I would also like to thank Warren J. Blumenfeld for his mentorship as a seasoned queer scholar. His friendship, encouragement, and research mentorship have been life affirming. I would also like to thank Michelle Boettcher,

Natasha Croom, and Cameron Beatty, who encouraged me early on that I could one day become a professor. Lastly, I would like to thank my coeditors who have supported me through a job search, a PhD program application and interview process, and a subsequent move from California back to my birthplace in east Tennessee to pursue my dream of becoming a counseling psychologist.

FROM GABBY

Claire Robbins, thank you for being an incredible friend and mentor to me. If not for you and your encouragement of my academic writing, I would not be a part of this remarkable team of passionate scholars. To my mom, Andrea, and my brother, Patrick: Thank you for encouraging me to keep chasing my dreams and pushing my limits. To Rachael and Gabby: Thank you for being the sisters that I never had and for cheering me on every step of the way. Last, but certainly not least, I want to thank Brian, Vu, and Elliott. Thank you for welcoming me onto this team after you all had begun this amazing project. Thank you for pushing me to be a better professional and scholar. Most importantly, thank you all for your awesome friendship.

FROM ALL OF US

The contributors would like to collectively thank Paul Shang, whose invaluable advice and input were catalysts at various points throughout this project. Thanks also to Robert Palmer, Eboni Zamani-Gallaher, and Tricia Fechter Gates from ACPA for their support of this project throughout the publishing process.

Finally, special thanks to the dedicated activist-scholars who comprise the ACPA Commission for Social Justice Education (CSJE) for the origination of the idea for this book. Through them, the commission continues to grow and evolve to meet the needs of our members and to push the envelope of this profession. Without CSJE, as a community and as a home, this project would not be possible.

1

From Fit to Belonging

New Dialogues on the Student Affairs Job Search

Brian J. Reece, Vu T. Tran, Elliott N. DeVore, and Gabby Porcaro

> *"Fitting in is about assessing the situation and becoming who you need to be to be accepted. Belonging, on the other hand, doesn't require us to change who we are; it requires us to be who we are."*
>
> —Brené Brown, *The Gifts of Imperfection*

FIND YOUR FIT.

It seems to be a simple task. Just find a position that aligns with your skills and knowledge, an office that provides you with a supportive work environment, and an institution that agrees with your values and meets most of your individual needs.

> *Does it pay well enough? Check.*
> *Is the geographical location suitable? Check.*
> *Do the job functions match your skills and competencies? Check.*
> *Is there opportunity for professional growth? Check.*

So many of these factors seem obvious. They are often the ones that get pointed out when job seekers search for advice from seasoned professionals in the field (i.e., those currently in stable jobs). But what if our perceived fit is not shared by hiring managers? Tell us if you have heard this story before:

1

A student affairs professional is a finalist for a position. They complete the on-campus interview with flying colors, develop wonderful rapport with the students and staff at the institution, and feel quite optimistic about their odds for the position. Shortly after their on-campus interview, they receive the call that many folks in student affairs know all too well. It sounds something like this: "You were a very qualified candidate, and we really enjoyed interviewing with you. However, we are not able to offer you a position at this point. It really came down to a matter of *fit*."

No matter how many times we experience this kind of rejection, it never gets any easier. What adds salt to the wound, however, is the insertion of *fit* into the explanation. There is a certain vagueness to the term that causes all sorts of questions to seep into our minds: *Really? Fit? Are they just telling me that to let me down easy? Maybe they didn't like those shoes that I wore to the interview. I knew I should have dressed more conservatively!* These types of paranoid thoughts can surface when we are told that we didn't get a job because of fit. We sometimes begin to question our own professional merits and capacities. It can be difficult not to take the rejection personally while our self-confidence and self-efficacy become gradually degraded each time we are turned down for a job opportunity. At least if employers were honest and direct about their feedback, there would be more of a sense of finality, which would make things easier to accept.

Although the rhetoric of fit regularly appears in exchanges between employers and candidates, the usage of the term *fit* extends far beyond such scenarios. It is common for seasoned professionals to provide advice on job searching to graduate students by addressing dynamics of fit, almost as if it were part of the professional preparation curriculum. Even prior to applying to graduate programs, future student affairs professionals are already being conditioned to acknowledge fit as a part of the fabric of the profession. A well-meaning mentor might say, "Make sure you choose a program that's the right fit for you," while graduate assistantship interview days are often preempted with the idea that a primary goal of the process is to "match" candidates to employers to ensure a "good fit." By introducing this concept at the very beginning of the student affairs experience, the word *fit* is embroidered into the vernacular of aspiring student affairs professionals and the larger professional culture.

Like many compelling ideas, this critical examination of job fit in student affairs began rather innocuously and spontaneously. By critical, we refer to a perspective that considers systemic forms of oppression that reinforce inequality, ultimately working toward liberation for all. All four editors have been involved in different capacities with the American College Personnel Association (ACPA) Commission for Social Justice Education (CSJE), where credit for the origination of this book must be given its due. At the 2014 ACPA convention in Indianapolis, CSJE directorate body members sat in a meeting room and brainstormed about current issues in student affairs. One member brought up a recent negative experience they had with a job search process, and the conversation spiraled into a spontaneous dialogue where many others related and shared their own negative experiences. The energy from that conversation propelled the ideation of this book, which has transformed into the product that you see today.

Since that conversation, we have discovered that *fit* is a term used by just about everyone in higher education and student affairs throughout hiring, disciplinary, and even termination processes. At its best, fit is used in a benevolent fashion with positive intent from employers to find an ideal candidate to match a position based on technical qualifications. However, the lack of questioning of this concept from the profession is concerning. From search committees and hiring managers to supervisors and human resources (HR) professionals, fit remains an uninterrogated concept in job searching and hiring and therefore continues to be a mystery in terms of its application in practice. While fit has been explored in many ways in a variety of academic fields, it has rarely been analyzed through critical theoretical frameworks. The purpose of this book is to catalyze conversation about the use of job fit as an uncriticized tool for exclusion in student affairs by exploring the concept through multiple frameworks, lenses, and standpoints. In the process, we hope to validate the experiences of marginalized populations who feel the negative impact of fit throughout their careers.

APPLYING A CRITICAL LENS TO FIT

Job searching and placement has developed into its own unique entity within student affairs. Some large student affairs conferences host their own version of a job placement fair (e.g., The Placement Exchange, The Oshkosh Placement Exchange) where job seekers and employers attend with hopes of finding, respectively, jobs and employees to meet their needs. Professional search firms such as William Spelman are regularly called on to facilitate the search process for many senior level positions. Job descriptions are now becoming more sophisticated as tools that convey expectations and responsibilities. And in the middle of this growth, there is a noticeable diversification of the field regarding ability, age, class, ethnicity, gender, language, race, nationality, religion, sexuality, and other forms of identity.

A great deal of attention has been paid to the career development of higher education professionals. Most notably, Peter Magolda and Jill Ellen Carnaghi (2004; 2014) and the contributing authors in *Job One* and *Job One 2.0* provide excellent reflections and analyses regarding the job search, hiring, and orientation processes. Additionally, *Where You Work Matters: Student Affairs Administration at Different Types of Institutions* (Hirt, 2006) put forth various studies that explored the lives of student affairs practitioners across different institutional types. However, even with these impactful contributions, higher education literature is lacking in critical perspectives on job searches and hiring processes, including the ways in which individuals with salient marginalized identities navigate these terrains. The contributing authors of this book integrate concepts of critical theory with research and literature regarding job searches in higher education by highlighting problematic aspects of the rhetoric of fit embedded in higher education and student affairs culture. This book particularly focuses on the perspectives of job candidates seeking to meet their own needs in potential jobs and job settings.

To further emphasize the significance of this topic, matters of social justice have become a vital part of higher education discourse. As a profession, student affairs specifically strives for inclusion and acceptance of all people. Within the context of university life, student affairs professionals are often considered key advocates for inclusivity on college campuses. Multicultural competencies have been a mainstay within the profession since they were adopted from the field of counseling psychology in the 1990s (Pope, Reynolds, & Cheatham, 1997). ACPA and NASPA–Student Affairs Administrators in Higher Education (NASPA) recently revised their joint publication of the *Professional Competency Areas for Student Affairs Educators* (ACPA & NASPA, 2015), which includes "Social Justice and Inclusion" as one of its 10 core competencies. The outcomes in this area, such as understanding "how one is affected by and participates in maintaining systems of oppression, privilege, and power" (p. 30) and engaging "in hiring and promotion practices that are nondiscriminatory and work toward building inclusive teams" (p. 31), indicate that these practices have been and are an area of concern for the profession. Moreover, a brief look at scholarly student affairs journals indicates the values toward which many individuals in student affairs strive—and, at the same time, the amount of work yet to be done. The profession has made remarkable progress in the ways it serves students; however, there seems to be a disconnect between how we talk about inclusion of students and how that same value plays out in our treatment of one another as student affairs practitioners and scholars. Given the high anxiety created by job searches, we ask: To what extent is fit a rhetorical tool that limits historically marginalized people from job opportunities?

WHO THIS BOOK IS FOR AND HOW TO USE IT

It would be unrealistic to suggest that any book can be all things to all people. While we feel strongly that a critical lens of job fit is relevant to everyone who works in student affairs, the scope of our book is intended to offer attention to the experiences of *job seekers* who are looking to evaluate fit in their current and possible future positions, as well as *hiring managers* who face challenges in creating equitable hiring processes. Thus, the contributors will speak to specific issues, while acknowledging that there are numerous perspectives to keep in mind. A critical examination of job fit can be beneficial to job seekers, whether they are entry-level, mid-level, or senior-level. We acknowledge that job search processes may look very different based on a candidate's professional level, as many entry-level job seekers tend to gravitate toward larger search processes such as The Placement Exchange, whereas mid-level and senior-level positions may have more targeted approaches using professional networks and search firms. However, even though experienced professionals may be more familiar with dynamics of job fit, inherent systems of racism, classism, sexism, ageism, homophobia, and other oppressions cut across all job search processes, regardless of position level.

In addition to showing up in the job search and hiring processes, job fit is a dynamic that impacts individuals who are currently employed and experiencing challenges in their workplace. At first, most employers and employees have a certain amount of optimism about their new workplace relationship. However, various experiences on the job and interactions with others can serve as points of validation or disappointment about the anticipated job fit for an individual. Positive experiences can serve as confirmation about fit for the employee or employer. *I knew this would be a great place for me to work.* However, negative experiences can quickly sour a person's viewpoint of their office environment, institution, or job tasks. *I'm so tired of the student culture here.* Important to the context of this book is how broader forms of systemic oppression (e.g., homophobia, racism, classism, sexism, and cissexism) may contribute to and factor into these negative experiences, which are often intertwined with things such as changes in job responsibility, departmental structure, and budget allocations.

Challenging the norms and rhetoric about job fit in student affairs means that scholars and practitioners alike must be able to incorporate this topic explicitly into various aspects of the profession. Thus, the chapters selected for this book aim to help job seekers develop a greater awareness of their needs and priorities throughout the job search process while being conscious of how institutional and systemic forms of oppression may hinder their access to certain opportunities. Professionals who are currently in positions of uncertainty regarding their cultural and institutional fit can reflect upon the various questions and ideas that the contributing authors of this text provide. Faculty in student affairs preparation programs can incorporate this text into professional seminar courses that are intended to prepare students for job searches. Similarly, department and organization leaders can incorporate a critical lens of job fit into the professional development opportunities they offer to staff in addition to examining their own hiring processes.

SO WHAT IS FIT, ANYWAY?

As with any concept, there are many ways of viewing and understanding fit. Whether referred to as such or by another term, *fit* commonly appears in college student development, vocational psychology, and in popular and mainstream discussions in the context of career development. Certainly not unique to higher education, fit takes on many forms and shows up unexpectedly in a variety of processes. Is fit about matching skills to job requirements? Is it about getting along with coworkers, sustainable interest in a position or career trajectory, or alignment of personal and professional values? We argue that there is not one suitable definition of *fit*; rather, we maintain that the construct of fit is complex and multifaceted and that it would be a disservice to the spirit of this book to put forth a single definition even if it would be more convenient. Therefore, you will find that each author throughout this book has their own nuanced definition of *fit*.

Take notice of how often you use the word *fit* in your everyday life. Fit shows up when discussing how a puzzle piece physically fits or doesn't fit into a jigsaw puzzle. Or consider how fit shows up metaphorically when speaking about how to make a new program or initiative fit within the constraints of an institutional or departmental mission or even inside limited budgetary or personnel resources. Fit shows up when we are shopping for clothes and deciding whether they're appropriate for work or when we are trying on a pair of jeans we haven't worn in a while. In many ways, *fit* is a mundane word, one that seems to deserve little attention due to its ubiquitous nature in our lives. Even as we were selecting chapters of this volume, we attempted to avoid speaking the word *fit*, yet it became clear how difficult this would be right from the start. We were shocked at how impossible it was to talk about our decisions without using the word. Instead of giving up or giving in, however, this only reinforced how important it was for us to get at the core of this term.

Even a simple review of definitions confirms that *fit* is not easy to define. The *Oxford English Dictionary*, for example, contains 8 entries for the word *fit*, each containing multiple definitions. One entry, the first of 3 for fit as a verb, contains 25 different definitions of the word. Meanings range from the expected "to be suitable for" to the subtly unexpected "to fashion, modify, or arrange so as to conform or correspond to something else" (Fit, v.1, 2016). Even after reviewing the varied definitions and origins of *fit* at this basic level, we were left wondering what fit really means, particularly in the context of this book. In our own review of fit in student affairs literature and a diverse array of other disciplines, we noticed a similar pattern. *Fit* seems to be a widely used term to describe a variety of phenomena from how well two people get along or the similarities between employee strengths and employer needs to the strength of a cultural match or alignment of values. And while researchers tend to work toward clearer definitions of *fit* in their work, their definitions vary and even sometimes contradict one another. Practitioners, in contrast, seem to use fit more often without consciously invoking any definition at all. In other words, fit is often something unexplainable. It's just one of those things we somehow know—and expect others to understand. As the chapters that follow reveal and critique, leaving fit unexamined in this way can lead us to fall prey to the oppressive systems and structures that surround us.

WHY TALK ABOUT FIT?

Most researchers seeking to define *fit* assume that fit is something that can be examined logically. One of the most commonly used theories of job fit in career advising and counseling, for example, argues that when an individual's interests align with their work-related activities and environment, the result is a happy employee (Holland, 1959). While there is obviously merit—and certainly a great amount of research—in this line of thinking, we argue that accepting the use of fit as a tool in job searching and hiring can also lead job seekers and hiring authorities to make decisions without examining their biases. We further argue that job fit is more complicated than matching person and environment. Collins (1990) and Harding (1998), for example, discussed the role of standpoint and epistemology—how we know what we know—in understanding our experience of oppression. We each interpret and experience the job search through a multiplicity of identities, and we are each therefore affected differently by systems of privilege and oppression through this intersectionality (Crenshaw, 1991). For example, a job seeker who identifies as a Black woman may also identify as upper middle class, cisgender, and straight. While statistics about and resources for Black women on campus or in the local community may play a role in her decision to apply for or accept a particular job, cost of living or the (non)existence of university policies, local ordinances, and state laws protecting queer and transgender individuals from employment discrimination may not play as big of a role.

Because job searching and hiring are processes with many layers, components, and steps, uncovering how and why people take in and process information in order to make choices is critical to understanding the concept of fit. Otherwise, fit, when accepted without critical inquiry, is something that occurs naturally, something to be left alone. It is *just how things are*. If the values of an individual and those of the institution do not align, for example, that person will not want to work there and may not apply. If they do apply, they may not make it to the interview—or may not be offered the job. The job search and hiring processes, however, are not so straightforward or logical, particularly because each step of these processes requires making a series of conscious and unconscious decisions—to apply or not to apply, to hire or not to hire. What drives our intuition? What biases do we hold that influence our decisions? Who designed our hiring processes and how do they reflect or reject our values of equity and inclusion? For example, at some institutions, all hiring is done using a process by a centralized HR department and involves thorough training on affirmative action, unconscious bias, and fair hiring practices. This process may also be monitored and audited by that same centralized department. At other institutions, the hiring process is entirely up to the supervisor looking for an employee. Neither option is inherently wrong or bad, but when we leave these underlying processes unexamined, we ignore issues of equity and inclusion as well as the potentially detrimental impacts of fit throughout the job search and hiring processes.

WHERE DOES FIT SHOW UP?

We seek to bring the realities of unconscious bias in the workplace to light while answering the question of where and how fit shows up in student affairs. Rather than simply talking about it in the abstract, we felt it would be more beneficial to offer up our own examples. We know that fit can take many forms and that we offer only a tiny snapshot of the possible experiences with the many nuances of identity within job searches and work experiences. Elliott N. DeVore speaks to the anxiety of being authentically femme and flamboyant and not being "too much" at work; Gabby Porcaro to the tension between her identities and the pervasive culture of the institution that employed her; Brian J. Reece to the struggle between living values authentically and aligning with the held and enacted values of an institution; and Vu T. Tran to an ambiguous job rejection that was substantiated through the rhetoric of fit. As it stands within the existing structure of the student affairs job search process, we were each left to wonder what was really going on and why.

As you will see in later chapters, values systems, standards of dress and speech, and even casual invitations to a meeting over coffee are inherently affected by our lived experiences as people with multiple identities. Our authors demonstrate the intricate ways in which the interview process and experiences on the job are riddled with unstated norms and expectations that may prove difficult to navigate without the appropriate cultural insight (Margolis & Romero, 1998). As candidates, we ask ourselves countless questions throughout the job search process that illustrate this struggle: *What do I wear? What language do I use to describe my experience? Will I be "the only one"? Is this interview process truly set up to evaluate me as a candidate or are they testing my ability to "be friends"? Do my values align? Will they understand my personality?*

Such questions arise in our own day-to-day lives outside of work, representing how many of us feel in new social settings. Much like a first date, interpersonal dynamics are a critical component in any interview process. In such settings, we often watch for subtle cues to inform us of the way others are perceiving us. While those dynamics are important—that is, getting along with others in the workplace is important to some extent—at least equal attention should be paid to the candidate's skills and professional interests.

Additionally, when does judging others based on fit border on choosing people purely because they are personally compatible with potential colleagues? Research has shown that groups that are more diverse produce better outcomes (Johnson & Johnson, 2009; Kuk, Banning, & Amey, 2010), but as Rivera (2015) has pointed out, relying on personal fit can limit the growth of workplace diversity. Unfortunately, the practice of excluding others based on personal compatibility may allow more easily for cultural biases to influence hiring, onboarding, and the development of positive relationships at work.

We all face a never-ending tug-of-war between individuality and conformity at work. *Should I just be myself, or should I try to match what others are doing here on campus?* Elliott experienced this phenomenon firsthand:

> Perhaps because my personality tends to match others' stereotypes of gay men being flamboyant, feminine, and funny, my identity and personality have almost always been closely tied together. During my graduate program, a few of my colleagues would visibly roll their eyes when I asked how the topic at hand impacted queer students or when I shared how I was afraid that my queer identity might affect my job search. At times, I was asked how that was relevant to the discussion. While at two universities in different regions, I felt the need to act more "professionally" than others when at work to conform to a more "reserved" atmosphere. In actuality, acting more "professionally" and "reserved" meant feeling pressure to be less effeminate. This conscious restriction negatively impacted my creativity and emotional connection with others. I often felt that I could not talk about my passion for drag or queer literature and art without being "too much" or "always talking about gay stuff." If my interests were more "normative" and my sexuality, or more arguably my gender, not so "obvious," things may have been different.

Elliott's experience illuminates the detrimental impact restricting one's social identities has on overall well-being. Having direct experience with others critiquing his comments and behavior led to him feeling afraid that his actions and even his identity were not appropriate for the workplace. These feelings led him to be more self-conscious and suspicious in that environment. Unsurprisingly, when he began his first full-time job search, Elliott actively sought out a place where he did not have to restrict himself like he did in the past. When asked during interviews at a student affairs job placement program what he did outside of work for balance, for example, he intentionally mentioned wanting to become enmeshed in the drag and queer arts community to weed out institutions and locations that would or would not be accepting of this aspect of his identity.

Gabby experienced similar challenges while in her graduate program. However, Gabby handled this misalignment of values by developing professional relationships that provided the necessary security for her to persist in such an unfavorable environment:

> As a young cisgender woman, I found myself renegotiating my sexuality for the third time while in graduate school. Many students I advised and individuals I worked with spoke about the chilly environment for queer individuals at this institution, which made me feel isolated as I came to understand a developing aspect of my own identity. Additionally, my lower socioeconomic status made me feel incredibly isolated from my peers, as they had access to experiences and resources that I never imagined possible for myself. What made me feel safe persisting in graduate school were the positive relationships I formed with my direct supervisor, my faculty adviser, and my practicum mentor. My first year in graduate school was incredibly difficult. I felt unimaginably isolated as I worked to exist in an environment that did not embrace or uplift my most salient identities. I took these relationships for granted my first year because I did not realize how crucial individual support would be to my overall well-being. During my second year in graduate school, I was able to find support by relying on these three key relationships.

Individual relationships provided Gabby the space and safety she needed to navigate an environment that made her feel isolated. These relationships helped her understand how to survive within an institutional culture that didn't embrace her identities. Additionally, this experience caused Gabby to specifically seek institutions that provided support services for marginalized faculty and staff members. Some of the things Gabby looked for in her first professional position were free access to financial advisers, community building programs like "First Thursdays," and diverse representation on university staff councils or faculty/staff senates.

During the search process, one typically receives more bad news than good. The rhetoric of fit can sometimes creep its way into conversations between employers and job seekers, especially in the context of a rejection conversation. Vu recalled an experience he had with being turned down for a position that left him wondering exactly which aspect of fit led to this outcome:

> I applied for this one job that I felt really excited for. In my mind, I thought that I was more than qualified for the position and that I would really connect well with the people who worked in that office. However, I wasn't entirely confident about getting the job, because I knew some of the other people who applied and I knew that they were just as qualified. In some ways, I was prepared to receive bad news if it came to me. The interview went well, and I received some pretty good feedback. It took a few days for the employer to call back, and it turned out that they offered the position to another candidate. That wasn't all too surprising because I knew the other folks who applied. However, the rationale that was given to me was that even though I was very qualified, it all came down to a matter of *fit*.

To use the dating analogy here, this would be the equivalent of the employer saying, "It's not you, it's me." This was a case where the use of fit rhetoric could create paranoia for a job seeker. *What did the employer mean by* fit*? Did they not like my personality? Was it what I was wearing? The tone of my voice? Did it have anything to do with dynamics of gender, race, class, or other salient identities?* We acknowledge that not all uses of the word *fit* within the job search are coded discrimination. A candidate may, in fact, lack the expertise or skills that would aid an organization's move in a desired direction. However, when fit is provided as the reason for rejecting a candidate with little additional detail, the ambiguity can lead to all sorts of incorrect assumptions about what happened between the employer and the candidate. Moreover, many employers are hesitant to give additional detail, perhaps due to a fear of backlash or advice from well-meaning human resources professionals, further complicating the matter.

While personal compatibility is certainly one aspect of fit to show up in the search process, another is the alignment of values. For example, when a school asks you to speak about diversity or social justice, are they fishing for specific values or concepts? Is this a way to see "where you stand" and if you will mesh with the "average student"? Reflecting on the concept of values across different contexts, Brian shared a story that illustrated the point. As someone who has been involved in social justice education and activism for many years, his values related to social justice are very important to him and are integrated within his professional identity:

> I remember during my interview, my supervisor-to-be said that my institution was not always "good at social justice." He felt I should know this because my application materials and my interview responses had made it "clear" that this

was important to me. I thought this was an interesting thing to say during an interview, and I have thought about it many times since accepting the job offer. What is "being good at social justice" and how have these conflicting sets of values influenced my success and even happiness at my job?

Although our personal beliefs on gay rights, abortion, climate change, gun control, and other highly politicized issues are not necessarily directly related to our ability to perform our job functions, the extent to which our campuses support and/or challenge our beliefs can impact the way we experience that job. Student affairs practitioners' views on social justice education and conceptions of privilege and oppression are not isolated from the sociopolitical context in which they work. In other words, although it was seemingly unrelated to his job, Brian's boss may have been onto something by disclosing this context to him and, at the very least, preparing him just a little for what he was stepping into. However, are there any institutions that are always good at social justice? How might different candidates interpret and react to such a statement differently? For example, is "not being good at social justice" another way of saying "not welcoming to certain groups of people" or does it simply mean that social justice efforts are individually led and sporadic rather than ongoing and institutionalized? Regardless of the statement's intended meaning, potential employees will interpret this through their own lenses and visions for an ideal work environment. While some may hear it as a call to action, others may hear it as a warning.

Student affairs professionals encounter challenges related to fit through institutional culture and values that often cause feelings of identity conflict or dissonance about our personality and other characteristics that are a product of environmental socialization. We argue that each of these intrapersonal dynamics are inextricable from our identities and must be examined throughout the process. In the following chapters, you will find such complexities painted in detail through our authors' scholarly writing and personal narratives, and it is our hope that you will able to connect in a way that provides insight into their experiences and those of others.

OUTLINING THE BOOK

As we reviewed potential chapters to include in this book, we intentionally grounded ourselves in theory to guide our decision-making process. For such a complex topic as fit, choosing a single theoretical framework was too limiting. Abes's (2009) concept of theoretical borderlands (Anzaldua, 1987), or a bridging or blending of theoretical frameworks, provided insight into a potential solution for examining fit through multiple frameworks simultaneously. This concept allowed us to consider fit by examining it through our own theoretical borderlands, specifically, the ecological model (Bronfenbrenner, 1994), intersectionality (Crenshaw, 1991), and anti-oppressive pedagogical theory (Kumashiro, 2002). In doing so, we intentionally chose chapters that viewed fit from a variety of standpoints and identities at a range of levels of our social systems and that provided insight into how we could actively work against oppression rather than merely observing or critiquing it. In the chapters that follow, the contributing authors challenge the ambiguous notion of fit in student affairs and our reliance on this notion in our hiring practices.

In many ways, the broad array of perspectives put forth in this book formulates a theoretical bricolage. The contributors in the chapters that follow use frameworks and theoretical guidance of their own choice to argue their own definitions and critiques of *fit*. Moreover, these scholarly inquiries are infused with personal testimonials that are intended to help develop a more nuanced understanding of fit in student affairs. While the chapters selected from this book approach fit from a scholarly perspective, many of the authors have embedded their own personal stories to bring these perspectives to life by illustrating the concepts and themes explored throughout.

David Hòa Khoa Nguyễn and LaWanda W.M. Ward begin chapter 2 seeking to combat discrimination in student affairs hiring practices by interrogating existing case law pertaining to employment discrimination in higher education. Using critical frameworks, Nguyễn and Ward work to illuminate the significant burden of proof plaintiffs must showcase to prove that the notions of fit have been used against them in a discriminatory manner to suggest tangible changes hiring managers can make to address these concerns. In chapter 3, Léna Kavaliauskas Crain and Mathew J.L. Shepard analyze data from the National Study of the Student Affairs Job Search (NSSAJS), which identified fit as a significant criterion in the latter stages of decision-making in job search processes. Crain and Shepard use these data to provide recommendations for hiring officials to combat fit being used inequitably when making hiring decisions. These recommendations provide opportunities for hiring managers to remove the discriminatory tendencies present in various hiring teams.

Chapter 4 brings a shift in focus away from the hiring committees as Jessica Bennett, Van Bailey, Marshall Habermann-Guthrie, Luis Jimenez

Inoa, Meghan Gaffney Wells, and Akiko Yamaguchi work to understand the impacts of inequitable hiring practices on the job seeker. Throughout the chapter, Bennett and colleagues discuss the challenges student affairs professionals with multiple marginalized identities face when working to establish agency—the ability to make decisions for one's self in the workplace—while simultaneously battling the inequities found in institutions of higher education. Their work also explores the difficulties job seekers experience in developing their own narrative agency, or the ability to determine one's own fit through their own thoughts and feelings, throughout the hiring process. In chapter 5, Sonja Ardoin and becky martinez continue to explore how individuals experience marginalization throughout their job search, specifically along the lines of socioeconomic status and class identity. Individuals from working-class, blue collar, or poor backgrounds are regularly discriminated against in both the hiring process and the work environment because they often may not have the financial means to build professional networks like those of their peers with more wealth.

Predominantly White institutions (PWIs), or institutions that have a majority White student population, have long histories of racism that can require their employees of color to internally negotiate different aspects of their marginalized identities to find their fit. In chapter 6, Stacey D. Garrett and Natasha T. Turman discuss the experiences of Black women moving through a student affairs job search and the ways Black women are expected to suppress aspects of their selves in order to cater to the oppressive notions of fit that are often upheld by institutions. Next, Heather O. Browning and Patrice M. Palmer examine fit as a layered concept and explore the institutional perpetuation of coded language that has systematically excluded people of color and their ability to be their authentic selves in the workplace in chapter 7.

Genderism within higher education creates harmful norms and environments that prevent members of the trans or nonbinary communities from safely expressing their gender at work. In chapter 8, C.J. Venable, Kyle C. Inselman, and Nick Thuot use their individual experiences as well as a critical examination of institutional politics to discuss the pervasive cisnormativity that creates oppressive work environments for many members of these communities. While the harmful influence of cisnormativity prevents individuals from equitably or safely working at institutions of higher education, Kyle Ashlee examines the primacy of Whiteness in higher education throughout chapter 9. Ashlee asserts that higher education is a system that perpetuates White supremacy and causes Whiteness to be viewed as the norm in student affairs hiring practices. The book concludes in chapter 10 with thoughts from Walter P. Parrish III, who synthesizes the preceding chapters by stitching together the interconnected narratives and analyses found throughout the book. The chapter additionally places a charge to the field by urging a continuation of the conversation about fit and offering possible additional areas for exploration and continued critical discussion.

CONCLUSION

As you read the following chapters, we hope you will consider the problem of fit in its many facets. Remember that being difficult to define is not what makes *fit* problematic; in fact, it is the field's lack of exploration about the problematic aspects of fit that leaves us vulnerable to its impact. More importantly, the problem of fit seems to disproportionately affect each of us, which is to say that some of us may benefit from fit while others suffer. As editors, we chose chapters that challenge the typical understanding of fit and provide critical insight into the impact of fit in higher education and student affairs. We also acknowledge that challenging fit is not an easy task, so the personal testimonials you will find woven throughout the chapters in this book serve to ground the discussion in the experiences of professionals in our field. It is our hope that these narratives and personal expressions make real for you the problem of fit.

At the 2016 ACPA Annual Convention in Montreal, the editors of this volume presented a session introducing the topic of this book and opening our call for chapter proposals. We were overwhelmed by the response and moved by the stories shared with us both during and after that presentation. Although we certainly felt it before then, our sense of urgency grew even stronger as dozens of ACPA members divulged their experiences with job fit and, quite frankly, with discrimination in the hiring process. At the same time, members also shared stories of triumph and examples of positive experiences with job fit. While the chapters that follow will explore the problematic nature of job fit, fit in and of itself is not inherently problematic. Fit as a concept and tool is embedded within hierarchical systems of power, privilege, and oppression that, unquestioned, lead to its use in problematic ways. This book aims to reveal those problems in the context of hiring and job searching in higher education and student affairs. In doing so, we can open up a conversation about how to begin working toward change.

REFERENCES

Abes, E. S. (2009). Theoretical borderlands: Using multiple theoretical perspectives to challenge inequitable power structures in student development theory. *Journal of College Student Development, 50*(2), 141–156. doi:10.1353/csd.0.0059

American College Personnel Association, & National Association of Student Personnel Administrators. (2015). *Professional competency areas for student affairs educators.* Professional Competencies Task Force. Washington DC: Authors. Retrieved from https://www.naspa.org/images/uploads/main/ACPA_NASPA_ Professional_Competencies_FINAL.pdf

Anzaldua, G. (1987). *Borderlands/la frontera: The new mestiza.* San Francisco, CA: Aunt Lute Books.

Bronfenbrenner, U. (1994). Ecological models of human development. In P. Peterson, E. Baker, & B. McGaw (Eds.), *International encyclopedia of education* (Vol. 3, 2nd ed.; pp. 1643–1647). Oxford: Elsevier.

Brown, B. (2010). *The gifts of imperfection: Let go of who you think you're supposed to be and embrace who you are.* Center City, MN: Hazelden.

Collins, P. H. (1990). *Black feminist thought: Knowledge, consciousness, and the politics of empowerment.* New York, NY: Routledge.

Crenshaw, K. (1991). Mapping the margins: Intersectionality, identity politics, and violence against women of color. *Stanford Law Review, 43*(6), 1241–1299. doi:10.2307/1229039

Fit, *v.1* (2016). In *OED online.* Retrieved from http://www.oed.com/view/ Entry/70748

Harding, S. (1998). *Is science multicultural?* Bloomington, IN: Indiana University Press.

Hirt, J. B. (2006). *Where you work matters: Student affairs administration at different types of institutions.* Lanham, MD: University Press of America.

Holland, J. L. (1959). A theory of vocational choice. *Journal of Counseling Psychology, 6,* 35–45.

Johnson, D. W., & Johnson, F. P. (2009). *Joining together: Group theory and group skills* (10th ed.). Upper Saddle River, NJ: Pearson.

Kuk, L., Banning, J. H., & Amey, M. J. (2010). *Positioning student affairs for sustainable change: Achieving organizational effectiveness through multiple perspectives.* Sterling, VA: Stylus.

Kumashiro, K. (2002). *Troubling education: Queer activism and antioppressive pedagogy.* New York, NY: RoutledgeFalmer.

Magolda, P. M., & Carnaghi, J. E. (2004). *Job one: Experiences of new professionals in student affairs.* Dallas, TX: American College Personnel Association.

Magolda, P. M., & Carnaghi, J. E. (2014). *Job one 2.0: Understanding the next generation of student affairs professionals* (2nd ed.). Lanham, MD: University Press of America.

Margolis, E., & Romero, M. (1998). The department is very male, very White, very old, and very conservative: The functioning of the hidden curriculum in graduate sociology programs. *Harvard Educational Review, 68*(1), 1–33.

Pope, R. L., Reynolds, A. L., & Cheatham, H. E. (1997). American College Personnel Association strategic initiative on multiculturalism: A report and proposal. *Journal of College Student Development, 38*(1), 62–67.

Rivera, L. (2015, May 30). Guess who doesn't fit in at work. *The New York Times.* Retrieved from http://www.nytimes.com/2015/05/31/opinion/sunday/guess-who-doesnt-fit-in-at-work.html

CASE STUDIES

We end this introductory chapter and begin the rest of this book by presenting two case studies written by the editors, one from the perspective of a hiring committee and the other from the vantage point of a job seeker. These case studies, while fictional as presented here, are inspired by our real experiences with job searching, hiring, and finding and creating fit in and through our work in student affairs. Read through these case studies and think through the discussion questions before you read the rest of the chapters ahead. When you have finished the book, take some time to read through them once more. Consider how your perspective has changed and how you might approach each scenario differently now that you have considered the ideas laid out by the contributors. If you are a faculty member, consider using these case studies to drive discussion in your courses or with your mentees and advisees.

Case Study #1: The Hiring Committee

St. Margaret University is a private Christian university boasting a student population of roughly 5,000 undergraduates and 1,000 graduate students. The university prides itself on graduating students that are ready for their respective professions. One of the largest tools the university has is a talented career services staff, which is currently looking for an additional career adviser. While a religiously affiliated university, the student body is not entirely made up of Christian individuals.

There is a new vice president of student life at the university who has a goal of "increasing religious diversity on campus." The Career Services Center is the first department within student life to hire a staff member under this new senior administrator. The director of the department is feeling pressured to hire a staff member who is not Christian to help achieve the goal of "increasing diversity." Additionally, the director wants to remain in the new vice president's good favor, so there is a desire to continuously appease this new senior administrator. The director of the center has compiled a search committee that he believes will help achieve this goal of ultimately hiring a non-Christian career adviser.

The original applicant pool was not as religiously diverse as the search committee was hoping to see. The application required individuals to submit an essay that served as an affidavit of belief or an explanation of how they would support a largely Christian student body if they themselves were not a Christian. Only two applicants are not Christian. Of these two people, one has limited related experience and would typically not be considered for a phone interview. The other non-Christian candidate, who identifies as agnostic, is more qualified for the role than the first non-Christian applicant.

One of the search committee members, Janise, is the associate director for the department as well as the search committee chair, and she identifies as evangelical. Although it isn't talked about much, people know her from her work off-campus in a congregation that espouses controversial views about women, queer folks, and people of other religious backgrounds. Alan is a senior student employee at the career center who identifies as Jewish. Alan has struggled to feel supported on campus, particularly when it comes to missing class for religious holidays and feeling comfortable talking about his faith with friends, faculty, and staff. Alicia is a student leadership adviser who identifies as Protestant and has expressed concern over having "too many" non-Christian employees working at the institution. The last member of the committee is Warren, an active member of student government who has never discussed his religion with the other members of the committee.

Each search committee member is asked to identify 5 to 7 candidates out of a pool of 70 applications who they think should advance to the phone interview stage. The meeting at which the committee convenes to discuss their recommendations is the first time the group is together all at once. Janise starts off the meeting by sharing the director's wish that they diversify the center to keep in line with the vice president's goals. Janise states that she was recommending the committee advance the two non-Christian applicants to phone interviews to show the vice president they were actively working to achieve this goal.

Alicia speaks up first and states that she is not sure this is the wisest decision. Alicia has questions about the qualifications of both candidates. Additionally, Alicia states that she is not sure the candidates' values regarding specific health insurance expenditures would align with the Christian mission of the institution. Alan speaks next and states that he is also not sure that is the wisest decision. Alan shares that, at times, it can be difficult for non-Christian individuals to feel supported on campus, specifically surrounding non-Christian religious holidays. Alan's comments are short because he feels particularly vulnerable as the only known non-Christian student at the table.

Warren speaks next and, with great enthusiasm, agrees with the chair of the committee. Warren thinks that hiring a non-Christian staff member will make non-Christian students feel significantly more comfortable seeking guidance from Career Services. However, Warren does state that, as a member of student government, he values seeing faculty and staff members in attendance at university Christian services. He is worried that, if hired, a non-Christian person would not show the same commitment and would thus make the majority of the student body feel isolated from Career Services.

Conversation remains contentious throughout the deliberation process. Seven individuals are selected for phone interviews. Despite much debate, both non-Christian individuals are selected for phone interviews.

Discussion Questions

1. Is it ethical to hire new staff members when you are aware that there is a lack of community of support for that person?
2. How can calls to "diversify your staff" cause harm?

3. What could Janise have done differently in setting up the search committee to lead to the outcomes she was hoping for? How could she have set up or prepared for the first meeting differently?

4. How can you help candidates who don't fit the campus norm make an educated decision?

5. How does tokenization show up in hiring committees for entry-level positions?

6. What risks is Alan taking by sharing or not sharing his concerns?

7. What can the committee do to ensure all voices are heard?

8. What are the advantages and disadvantages of having a senior staff member serve as the search committee chair for a position in their own department?

9. What kind of training do search committees need to adequately address issues related to fit through critical lenses?

10. What dynamics are at play for Warren? What are some actions he could take?

Case Study #2: The Job Seeker

Alex is a graduate student in a student affairs master's program and is on the market for their first full-time job. They have a great deal of interest in working in a position that is focused on equity, diversity, and inclusion and have extensive knowledge and experience related to working with students of color, including their current assistantship in a multicultural center. In fact, issues of social justice were what originally drew Alex into the field of student affairs. As an undergraduate student, Alex was a facilitator for an intergroup dialogue class and regularly volunteered with their local chapter of Amnesty International. Alex is completing a master's thesis on the unionization of custodial staff in higher education institutions and hopes to pursue a doctoral degree in the future.

Alex was well prepared for the job search. They had a strong résumé that went through numerous revisions with a career counselor and other student affairs professionals, and they created several cover letter templates that they could draw on for various job opportunities that might open up. However, Alex was not entirely sure whom to ask to serve as job references. Alex had a strong, positive relationship with their previous practicum supervisor but has a very rocky relationship with their current assistantship supervisor. There always seemed to be something that felt "off" about their interactions, and Alex was hesitant to ask for the reference. Alex decided that they would not include their assistantship supervisor and would deal with the consequences as they come.

Alex was also prepared with a wardrobe of suits. One of the pieces of advice that Alex received from trusted mentors was to invest in professional apparel for the job search process. Alex did not have a lot of disposable income, so this was a bit of an issue. After some consternation, Alex decided to apply for a new credit card to purchase two new suits. While it created a bit of financial anxiety for Alex, it made them feel more confident entering the job search process.

While the job search began with much optimism, Alex soon encountered a grim reality that many had warned them about: The preponderance of available student affairs jobs are in residential life. Having already invested two years into a master's degree, Alex felt like they did not want to consider other options outside of the field, so they ended up expanding their search parameters to include hall director positions. Alex even decided to participate in a national job placement program, even though they initially did not want to do so. But Alex was feeling the pressure to secure a job, and because so many of Alex's peers were attending the job placement, Alex decided to go along with it.

Alex was very intimidated by the size of the job placement conference they attended and was worried that they would get lost in the sea of people. The number of job options was overwhelming and made it more difficult to discern what to look for! Knowing that their job search was focused on residence life because of the availability of positions, Alex focused on jobs that afforded the opportunity to do social justice education work and the ability to facilitate intergroup dialogue. A list of schools with a "good" social justice culture worked its way through the grapevine and quickly found themselves at the top of Alex's list. An alumnus of two public universities, Alex feels strongly about working for a large public university that serves as an access institution. The process was not as bad as Alex thought—they were excited to leave with an on-campus interview at Mountain State University.

On paper, the job offered much of what Alex was seeking, but the location was unfamiliar and gave reasons to reflect on personal needs both in and outside of work. The salary was lower than other positions, but the more rural location had a low cost of living. Alex thought this might provide the opportunity to pay off some student loans.

Once Alex returned home, they received an e-mail with more information about the on-campus interview. Mountain State offered to reimburse 50% of their flight up front, and 100% of the flight only if they accepted the position. Given that this was the only current offer Alex had on the table, Alex decided to add this airline ticket to their mounting credit card expenses. Given that the interview itself was scheduled for 2 weeks from the e-mail, it made flights that much more expensive.

The itinerary consisted of a full day of 60-minute interviews with different constituents, including student staff, peers, campus partners, and departmental leaders. There was also a presentation component, which asked candidates to explain their approach to issues of inclusion within campus communities. Alex was quite excited for this portion, since it gave them the opportunity to display a strength of theirs.

When Alex arrived on campus at Mountain State the evening before the interview, they were greeted by a host who picked them up and took them to a hotel near the institution. They were told that dinner was on their own, so they decided to take the opportunity to walk around and get a feel of the surrounding area. It was a much slower pace than what Alex was used to, since they grew up in an urban environment. It was also very racially homogenous—mostly individuals who appeared to be White along with businesses, restaurants, and markets that were culturally American. Disappointed, Alex decided to grab a quick burger and call it an evening.

The day of the on-campus interview itself was a blur. All the interviews were very formal and seemed to include the same types of questions. Alex felt like they had a hard time reading people's faces in all the interviews, since most people had their eyes focused on their interview notes. Then came the presentation, which Alex felt like they aced. They focused on current issues that students of color face at predominantly White institutions, and the audience seemed fairly receptive. One attendee even cited a recent bias incident that occurred on campus and shared that Alex would be a helpful resource.

Unfortunately, there were a few people who seemed a bit less interested in the presentation. The director of the department appeared to be glued to their laptop the entire presentation and abruptly stepped out halfway through. Additionally, Alex was disappointed that there were no individuals from the intercultural center in attendance, even though the presentation was made public. These observations stuck with Alex as they continued through their interview day, which ended with a wrap-up conversation with the associate director of the department.

A week after returning from the on-campus interview, Alex received a phone call from the search committee chair offering the position. The committee chair stated that Alex had three days to make a decision. This was difficult to hear because Alex was flying to another on-campus interview the next day and knew they might want more time to decide. So, Alex nervously asked for more time to decide; the chair said five days was the limit. Creating a list of pros and cons was the first thing on Alex's list so that they could review it with their mentor and friends. Although there were a lot of positives about the job, Alex was not sure what to ask about. Insurance options, institutional matching for retirement? What about that awkward conversation with the would-be supervisor?

Beyond the tangibles of the job, Alex had to figure out if living at Mountain State would be the best place for them personally. Alex knew they would be the "only one" which would be difficult, but it would also provide a lot to the students at the campus; Alex would fill a huge void for that community. Alex's mentor always said, "Sometimes you go where you're needed and sometimes you go where you need to be." Alex wondered where on that spectrum might this job be, and if they could be happy. Did those things matter more than securing a job to pay off debt? Could Alex find their own community outside of work? How much weight would each of these factors have? Should Alex take this job?

Discussion Questions

1. What are the key issues in this case?
2. What factors seem important for Alex to make their decision?
3. In which parts of the job search does Alex have agency?
4. What are some systemic factors that affect Alex's entire job search experience?
5. Who are some individuals that were (positively or negatively) influential in Alex's decision?
6. What are some things that Alex could have done differently?
7. What are some things that the institution could have done differently?
8. What role does life off campus play in the decision-making process?
9. What does Alex's feeling of disappointment while walking through the town speak to more broadly?
10. What does the apparent disinterest of some interview attendees say about what Alex's experience on that campus might be?
11. Does Alex have some allies or peers they can seek support from and identify with?

2

Innocent Until Proven Guilty

A Critical Interrogation of the Legal Aspects of Job Fit in Higher Education

David Hòa Khoa Nguyễn and LaWanda W.M. Ward

S TATUTORY, REGULATORY, AND CONSTITUTIONAL law heavily regulates employment discrimination law. Discrimination based on race, color, religion, national origin, sex, age, or disability is prohibited under federal law and the provisions of many state laws, most of which are applicable to both public and private institutions of higher education. Principal among the federal statutes that cover employment discrimination are Title VII of the Civil Rights Act of 1964 (42 U.S.C. § 2000e et seq.), Title IX of the Education Amendments of 1972 (20 U.S.C. § 1681 et seq.), section 504 of the Rehabilitation Act of 1973 (29 U.S.C. § 794 et seq.), the Americans with Disabilities Act of 1990 (42 U.S.C. § 12101 et seq.), the Equal Pay Act of 1963 (29 U.S.C. § 206[d] et seq.), the Age Discrimination in Employment Act of 1967 (29 U.S.C. § 621 et seq.),[1] Immigration Reform and Control Act of 1986 (8 U.S.C. § 1101 et seq.),[2] and the Genetic Information Non-discrimination Act of 2008 (42 U.S.C. § 2000ff et seq.). However, there are discrepancies between state and federal law and their protections for certain groups; for example, while some states and locales have laws and ordinances protecting against sexual orientation discrimination, there is not yet a federal law to afford such protection nationally. Several of these laws also prohibit retaliation against employees for the exercise of their rights as provided by these laws, which is also a form of discrimination. In addition, some state and federal courts have ruled that discrimination against transgender individuals qualifies as sex discrimination and a violation of the Civil Rights Act (*Smith v. City of Salem*, 2004).[3]

This chapter provides a foundation of employment discrimination law so that individuals who experience discrimination can determine and address the burden of proof applicable to cases of employment discrimination. For the purposes of this chapter, we concentrate on examining Title VII and issues of discrimination based on race, sex, color, religion, and national origin. The authors introduce a critical framework to examine an employment discrimination case involving a faculty member to provide practical strategies for prospective student affairs applicants to identify and document potential instances of discrimination. However, it is necessary to be realistic in knowing and understanding that the law has limitations because of its narrow interpretation and absence of legislation that promotes inclusivity. Therefore, the student affairs profession should continue leading by example as a societal institution that demonstrates how to address and eradicate employment discrimination.

JOB FIT AND HIGHER EDUCATION

Given the nature of the higher education profession, its social justice tenet, and the importance of being critical of educational and social contexts, many professionals may be challenged by their fit during the interview, hiring, and job performance stages. Carbado (2013) asserts there is a persistent invisibility of intersectionality that includes gender, race, and sexual orientation due to society and the courts using lenses that are colorblind and gender- and heteronormative. The normativity of the dominant culture's expectations of appearance and behavior of applicants can outweigh as well as conflict with institutions' promotion of diversity and inclusion. The lack of recognition of oppressive forms of normativity result in evaluations such as "female like a heterosexual White woman," "gay like a White heterosexual man," and "Black like a man" (Carbado, 2013, pp. 818–836). These comparisons are not illegal, yet they are damaging and serve as a key component in the maintenance of homogenous environments.

In 2006, the Council for the Advancement of Standards in Higher Education (CAS Standards, 2006) developed a set of characteristics to be embodied and implemented by all higher education practitioners.

The following are the main categories: (a) general knowledge and skills, (b) interactive competencies, and (c) self-mastery. Within each category there are several "professional competencies," including ones that pertain to personality and behavior. Additionally, in 2015, as a joint initiative, the American College Personnel Association (ACPA) and NASPA–Student Affairs Administrators in Higher Education (NASPA) assigned a task force with the responsibility to "establish a common set of professional competency areas for student affairs educators" (p. 4). Serving as guiding tenets, the ACPA/NASPA competencies include (a) personal and ethical foundations; (b) values, philosophy, and history; (c) assessment, evaluation, and research; (d) law, policy, and governance; (e) organizational and human resource; (f) leadership; (g) social justice and inclusion; (h) student learning and development; (i) technology; and (j) advising and supporting. As a profession, we expect student affairs professionals to develop and enhance these proficiencies throughout their service in the field.

Through a critical race theory (CRT) lens using the current federal law that one would invoke if they alleged a hiring discrimination claim, we discuss the challenges to success that exist for an applicant because of the status quo maintaining expectations that are encompassed in higher education discourse. Most, if not all, higher education institutions tout commitments to diversity and inclusion through various marketing outlets, yet the student enrollment, curriculum, professors, and staff continue to perpetuate Whiteness. This overwhelming Whiteness manifests as White supremacist practices that operate as the norm (Patton, 2015). McLaren (1997) defines *Whiteness* as a societal construct that emerged "at the nexus of capitalism, colonial rule, and the emergent relationships among dominant and subordinate groups. . . . Whiteness operates . . . as a universalizing authority . . . [that] appropriates the right to speak on behalf of everyone who is non-White while denying voice and agency" (p. 267). For this chapter the authors define *social justice* from a legal perspective in which the law contributes to the fair and equitable treatment of all people with regard for socially constructed identities that limit access to resources and full engagement in society.

One example of the intersection of social justice and fit follows when a public state college president commented on how well a new administrator was performing in their role but expressed concern that they were not "fitting in" within their department (Tierney, 1988). The president did not give substantive feedback with their comment, leaving the administrator to ponder what it meant to not "fit in." How do higher education and student affairs practitioners determine if they will fit in with a department and campus culture, especially if their skills, knowledge, and disposition match a job description and they can provide concise and measurable work experience examples that align with the 10 ACPA/NASPA competencies? Applicants may possess the educational background, relevant experiences, and proven skills for a position but their personality or fit is not always easily determined from their résumés or curriculum vitae. Title VII applied rigidly to a perceived wrongful employment action, such as hiring, firing, or demotion, makes it difficult to prove fit is a cloaked method for discrimination because courts are reluctant to allow the effects of historic and current systemic exclusionary behavior toward marginalized populations to serve as evidence. Therefore, a favorable ruling for the student affairs applicant or employee who files a lawsuit is unlikely.

Within the study of environments and human interactions there has been a focus on the positive and negative results of combining human characteristics and values inside various spaces (Lewin, 1935, 1952; Parsons, 1909). Specifically, "fit has been a central concept in organizational theory literature since the 1960s when person-environment fit models became prevalent" (Kezar, 2001, p. 86) by the works of numerous researchers. Fit is relevant within organizational research because prior studies have revealed that "individuals were most successful and satisfied when their skills, aptitude, values, and beliefs matched the organizations" (p. 87). In a student affairs context, the profession prides itself on being inclusive and welcoming of individuals who will add value to departmental missions because of their unique perspectives and experiences. The importance of interrogating how and in what ways fit becomes a proxy for discrimination in higher education and student affairs is needed to ensure inclusive-centered approaches are utilized and not ones that "collude to maintain disparities and reinforce social inequity" (Chambers, 2017, p. 10).

Two key criticisms have emerged regarding the concept of organizational fit (Kezar, 2001). First, historically marginalized people are challenged with how to best present themselves to be viewed as the right fit for positions (Carbado & Gulati, 2000). Second, the likelihood of assimilation increases because of the expectation to meet some unspoken criteria that may not align with one's own unique expression and values (Kezar, 2001). Hence, institutions of higher education hiring participants should make every effort to be cognizant of the environment that exists and interrogate what message it embodies and communicates to those seeking employment. This critical assessment of fit is warranted because it may be difficult for marginalized people in society to present themselves in an authentic way that will be considered the right fit for an organization. There are different ways one can articulate or perceive job "fit," and the recognition of this should heighten the sense of awareness for decision makers. Work environments that are encumbered with a "culture of hegemonic collegiality" that is "a set of norms that demand that subordinated groups conform their behavior and interactions to the expectations of the group in power in order to 'get along'" (Cho, 2006, p. 812), can be stressful and result in premature departures.

CRITICAL RACE THEORY

CRT is a legal-based theoretical framework that emerged in the mid-1970s as a challenge to mainstream notions of race, racism, and racial power in American society. Jones (2009) states it "is an exciting, revolutionary intellectual movement that puts race at the center of critical analysis. Race has no necessary epistemological valence, we are told, but depends on the context and organization of its production for its political effects" (p. 17). CRT probes the legal system and questions established and accepted foundational doctrines such as equality theory, legal reasoning, and neutrality in constitutional law (Delgado & Stefancic, 2001).

CRT has expanded beyond the legal field and emerged in various disciplines, such as sociology, political science, and education. Ladson-Billings and Tate (1995) charted a CRT for education that theorized education as rife with racialized and racist cultural constructs and demarcations. Since their seminal writing, many education scholars have used CRT in the K–12 and higher education settings to "raise questions, engage in conscientious dialogue, and produce research in which CRT would serve as a tool and framework to unsettle racelessness in education" (Patton, 2015, p. 2). To be more inclusive in higher education, analytical tools that question and name the operation of Whiteness are necessary to address covert and coded racism.

Through a critical lens guided by CRT, we provide examples of challenges in higher education for individuals who are nonmajority members of society.

EMPLOYMENT DISCRIMINATION LAW

History of Title VII

Title VII of the Civil Rights Act of 1964 is the most comprehensive federal statute and prohibits discrimination in employment based on race, sex, religion, and national origin. The law prohibits discrimination in individual employment decisions as well as employer policies or patterns of conduct that discriminate broadly against members of protected groups. As a result, it is unlawful to discriminate against any employee or applicant for employment in regard to hiring, termination, promotion, compensation, job training, or any other term, condition, or privilege of employment. This extends to employment decisions based on stereotypes and assumptions about the abilities, traits, or performance of individuals. Discrimination based on an immutable characteristic associated with race, such as skin color, hair texture, or certain facial features, violates Title VII, even though not all members of the race share the same characteristic (Gross, 1998; Kahn, 2005).

Both intentional discrimination and neutral job policies that disproportionately exclude minorities and that are not job related are prohibited.[4] For example, equal employment opportunity cannot be denied because of marriage to or association with an individual of a different race; membership in or association with ethnic-based organizations or groups; or attendance or participation in school or places of worship generally associated with certain minority groups. Title VII was amended in 1978 to include pregnancy-based discrimination in its prohibition of gender-based employment discrimination. The Pregnancy Discrimination Act of 1978 provides that "women affected by pregnancy, childbirth, or related medical conditions shall be treated the same for all employment-related purposes . . . as other persons not so affected but similar in their ability or inability to work" (42 U.S.C. Sec. 2000e[k]). Related medical conditions include lactation, breastfeeding, and abortions (42 U.S.C. Sec. 2000e[k]). This is important to note, as any discrimination against women for these related medical conditions would be a violation of Title VII for any institution that receives federal funding, public or private. Similarly, the Family and Medical Leave Act of 2006 outlines similar requirements for pregnancy leave and pregnancy-related conditions to ensure that women are not discriminated against for their leave (29 U.S.C. §§ 2601-2654).

With the Lilly Ledbetter Fair Pay Act of 2009, Congress added language to Title VII that prohibits unlawful employment practice with respect to discrimination in compensation. This includes protections for individuals subject to discriminatory compensation decisions or practices, or those negatively affected by the application of a compensation decision. Discriminatory compensation decisions or practices include those related to time wages, benefits, or other paid compensations (42 U.S.C. § 2000e-5[e][3][A]).

Title VII also prohibits discrimination on the basis of conditions that predominantly affect protected groups, which are the various classifications mentioned in our explanation of Title VII, such as race, gender, disability, age, and so on, unless the practice is job-related and consistent with business necessity, termed a *bona fide occupational qualification* (BFOQ). BFOQs may apply to situations involving religion or sex (Lilly Ledbetter Fair Pay Act, 2009). The protected characteristics of race and national origin are excluded as a BFOQ for college and university positions (Kaplin & Lee, 1995). For example, while a private, religious institution may discriminate and interview and hire only those candidates that ascribe to the institution's religious teachings, the institution may not discriminate against the candidate's race or national origin. The candidate's understanding of the institution's religious mission is paramount in their work, but their race or national origin is not critical to the delivery of the mission.

The Role of the Equal Employment Opportunity Commission

If an individual has experienced discrimination based on the various protected classes mentioned, the individual may file a complaint. The Equal Employment Opportunity Commission (EEOC) enforces Title VII. It may receive, investigate, and resolve complaints of unlawful employment discrimination. It may also initiate lawsuits against violators or issue right-to-sue letters to complainants. For an individual to succeed, Title VII gives employees two possible causes of action. Under a theory of *disparate impact*, plaintiffs allege that an employer's seemingly neutral policies have a discriminatory effect on a protected group, and the employer cannot justify the policies by business necessity. Under a theory of *disparate treatment*, plaintiffs allege that an employer intentionally discriminated against a member or members of a protected group and a shifting burden of proof applies to the determination of liability. Disparate treatment is more common in postsecondary education. It can manifest when an individual is denied a job, promotion, or tenure or claims to be treated less favorably than their colleagues because of their race, sex, national origin, or religion and is subjected to a detrimental working condition (*Lynn v. Regents of the University of California*, 1981).

Figures 2.1 and 2.2 help potential complainants understand the complaint process when first filing a claim with the EEOC. All employment discrimination laws that are enforced by the EEOC, except for the Equal Pay Act, require complaints to be filed with the EEOC before civil lawsuits may be commenced against the alleged discriminator.

It is critical to note that a complainant must file a complaint with the EEOC within 180 days from the incident.

Figure 2.1. EEOC charge-filing process.

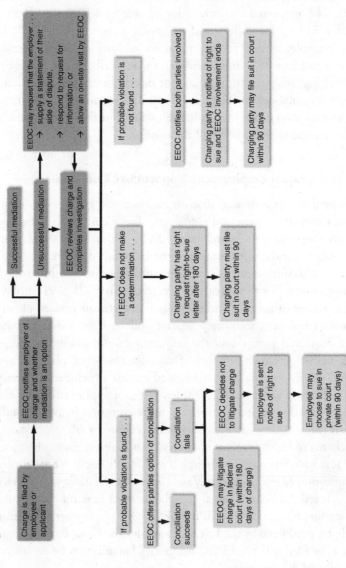

Note: Graphic by A. King-Kostelac. Information adapted from the U.S. Equal Employment Opportunity Commission. (n.d.-a). Retrieved from www.eeoc.gov/index.html

Figure 2.2. Filing employment discrimination charges with the EEOC.

Filing Methods	Filing Process
By Telephone • Charges cannot be filed by phone. A call can be used to initiate the process and to receive additional information about where and how to file.	**Before Filing** Complete the Online Assessment Questionnaire via the EEOC Assessment System to determine if the EEOC is the right place to file the charge.
Online • EEOC Public Portal can be used to file a charge after completing the Online Assessment and completing an interview with an EEOC official. • If there are 60 days or fewer to file the charge, the EEOC's site can provide information on how to file the charge quickly.	**Time Line for Filing** → All discrimination charges must be filed **180 calendar days from incident.** → If there is a state or local law governing the alleged violation, the deadline is extended to **300 calendar days.** **Note:** Unless the allegation involves ongoing harassment, deadlines apply to **each individual instance**, not to the most recent incident.
In Person • Charges can be filed at an EEOC office or at a state or local Fair Employment Practice Agency (FEPA) • Location, hours, and appointment information should be confirmed prior to visiting an office for either agency. • All necessary documentation must be brought to appointment. • Dual filing: Charge can be filed through a FEPA and the EEOC simultaneously by visiting an office of either agency.	**Necessary Documentation** • Contact information (name, address, e-mail, and telephone number) for complainant and employer to be charged • Number of employees employed by the organization subject to the charge • Description of the actions believed to be discriminatory (firing, demotion, harassment, etc.) • When the discriminatory action(s) took place • Description of why complainant believes they were subject to discrimination: race, ethnicity, national origin, color, religion, sex, gender identity, sexual orientation, pregnancy, disability, age, genetic information, retaliation **Note:** The EEOC Online Assessment Questionnaire will help to determine the exact documents required for each specific charge.
By Mail • Appropriate documentation can be mailed along with a signed letter. **If the letter is not signed, the charge cannot be investigated.** • Letter and documentation is reviewed and complainant is contacted if more information is needed.	

Note: Federal employees and applicants for federal jobs have a different complaint process. Graphic by A. King-Kostelac. Information adapted from the U.S. Equal Employment Opportunity Commission. (n.d.-b). *How to File a Charge of Employment Discrimination*. Retrieved from www.eeoc.gov/employees/howtofile.cfm

A Case Example in the Higher Education Context

Carbado and Gulati (2000) argued there are three problems with anti-discrimination law in proving discrimination in the workplace. We adopt their challenges to assert how employers can cloak discriminatory practices by higher education institutions in their hiring practices under the guise of fit. The first challenge is that courts do not give credence to applicants who are members of marginalized populations and how their positionality subjects them to stereotypes and misconceptions regardless of the applicant's credentials. Because evidence, direct or circumstantial, is expected to support claims of discrimination, it is challenging to establish fault with an individual or the organization (Carbado & Gulati, 2000), especially because institutions will rely on their nondiscriminatory policies.

The second challenge is producing evidence to support the claim. Institutions of higher education have established policies and programs that present a persona of inclusive and nondiscriminating environments. Since an applicant will have only limited interactions with the institution during the interview process, it would be difficult to show how a person was not hired unless someone says or does something that is deemed discriminatory.

The third and final challenge surrounds the question that must be answered for all discriminatory claims: "Was there intentional discrimination based on the plaintiff's membership in a protected class, such as race, gender, or disability?" (Carbado & Gulati, 2000, p. 1297). As long as an employer can show nondiscriminatory reasons—e.g., "We did not hire X because their answers did not reflect an understanding of our department's goals, it's not because they are [blank]"—this is difficult to prove. Unless there is evidence that the university's hiring officials said or did something discriminatory, fit will be couched in nondiscriminatory language despite the candidate knowing what they experienced. "In most cases, plaintiffs have to rely on circumstantial evidence of intentional discrimination" (Carbado & Gulati, 2000, p. 1297). Circumstantial evidence would need to illustrate the alleged discrimination similarly to the assertion made by the discriminated applicant. For example, an individual denied a student affairs position might find forth evidence of a pattern of not hiring individuals with certain characteristics or hiring ones with homogenous traits to be useful. To illustrate the application of Title VII in the higher education context, we have selected a faculty example to analyze through a CRT framework. Many of the lawsuits filed in higher education in the area of employment law involve faculty denied tenure. Hence, the following case addresses a faculty concern with relevant application to student affairs professionals.

Girma v. Skidmore College (2001)

In September 1999, Paul B. Girma, a Black male of Ethiopian national origin, filed a race, national origin, and age discrimination lawsuit in a New York federal district court against Skidmore College, a private liberal arts institution located in Saratoga Springs, New York. Skidmore hired Girma, who possessed a doctorate in finance, on a three-year renewable contract to teach courses in the business department. At the time of Girma's lawsuit, he asserted in his complaint that, in addition to what he viewed as incidents with racially discriminatory overtones, there had been no Black tenured professors at Skidmore since its inception (*Girma v. Skidmore College*, 2001, p. 340). The racial overtones are known as racial microaggressions, or "brief, commonplace, and subtle indignities (whether verbal, behavioral, or environmental) that communicate negative or denigrating messages to people of color" (Constantine, Smith, Redington, & Owens, 2008, p. 349). Unspoken and differing standards of evaluation of Whites and their non-White peers have been documented. Institutions of higher education have historically been and currently comprise predominantly White faculty members. Courts have transitioned from finding merit with how structural and innocuous policies result in racial inequality to requiring evidence of intentional racial discrimination (Harris, 2014). The result of such legal decisions is that "the reach of anti-discrimination measures and permissible remediation have been restricted rather than expanded" (Harris, 2014, p. 103). Because law tends to be steeped in the notion of formal equality in which all people come into courts as equals, courts execute decisions that reflect a color-blind and gender-normative analysis. The plaintiff has to prove the nondiscriminatory intended practice has a harmful effect. Therefore, Eurocentric practices and expectations are placed on faculty of color (Patton, 2015). Without legal protection unless behavior is deemed blatantly discriminatory, faculty of color, especially on predominantly White campuses and on the tenure track, are subject to unchecked discriminatory practices and a thriving system of racial inequities (Louis, Rawls, Jackson-Smith, Chambers, Phillips, & Louis, 2016).

While teaching, scholarship, and service were key components for reappointment, student evaluations were heavily relied on in the decision. Girma's evaluations in his first year were numerically below the score needed for reappointment so he was encouraged to improve them. Students' comments reflected a frustration with Girma's pedagogical approach, "citing his inability to support the students' needs and respond adequately to their questions during classes" (*Girma v. Skidmore College*, 2001, p. 332). Research has shown that Black faculty members experience challenges and critiques of their credentials by both White colleagues and students (Flowers, Wilson, González, & Banks, 2008; Pittman, 2012). Relevant to Girma's experience, student evaluations of faculty of color have been examined and found to be lower than their White professors (Huston, 2006; Littleford, Ong,

Tseng, Milliken, & Humy, 2010; Littleford, Perry, Wallace, Moore, & Perry-Burney, 2010). Based on the court's narrow perspective of Girma's claims, the student evaluations research may not have been analyzed as providing legitimate support for him.

Girma provided two examples, which the court did not view as rising to the level of racial or national origin discrimination. The first, regarding the way in which Girma was hired, reflected an interest convergence theory. Interest convergence is a CRT tenet describing when people of color are provided an opportunity of advancement only when it benefits the dominant group (Delgado & Stefancic, 2001). A former White female professor testified that she had recommended Girma for consideration, but it was not until a selected candidate declined the offer that he was hired. The White female professor alleged that the White male chair, Roy Rotheim, told her the department had to hire someone or the faculty line would be taken away and the White female dean "was not likely to refuse to hire a minority candidate" (*Girma v. Skidmore College*, 2001, p. 336). The court responded to the first contention by stating the following:

> Even assuming this occurred, it indicates that race played a role in Girma's initial hiring, not in the decision whether to offer him a second three-year contract. While these circumstances may have some value in developing a circumstantial case of discrimination (as may other circumstances mentioned here), they are hardly a smoking gun. (*Girma v. Skidmore College*, 2001, p. 336)

The court's refusal to view the tokenistic agenda of the chair is problematic. Also problematic is evidence having to be synonymous with a "smoking gun" analogy, meaning that "policy documents or evidence of statements or actions by decision makers exist that may be viewed as directly reflecting the alleged discriminatory attitude" (*Girma v. Skidmore College*, 2001, p. 335). A disparate impact analysis was absent from the court's perspective on how Girma was hired. Dismissing the ways in which dominant groups use *diversity* as a way to meet departmental expectations, as opposed to genuine efforts to diversify faculty, stymies efforts to "restructure higher education and create a socially just society" (Chambers, 2017, p. 1).

The second assertion made by Girma involved a meeting with the department chair during his second year to discuss his student evaluations and their impact on his reappointment. This meeting took place in the campus student cafeteria over coffee, which offended Girma and caused him to feel embarrassed due to the lack of privacy of the setting. The verbatim conversation was not provided to the court. However, Girma viewed this incident as a deliberate act by the chair that "breached the confidentiality of personnel evaluations . . . to provoke a reaction from [him] in a public forum" and believed "Professor Rotheim would not have similarly embarrassed Caucasian professors" (*Girma v. Skidmore College*, 2001, p. 336). The court once again showed a lack of cultural awareness by not taking into consideration how a person of color perceived the setting in which this important meeting took place. The court was dismissive of accusations about racist behavior exhibited by the chair because the court did not assess the way in which the meeting took place as discriminatory. It responded:

> There is no evidence indicating that anyone other than Girma and Rotheim heard the content of the conversation, nor is there any indication that the content of the conversation or its setting supports an inference that Rotheim harbored any racial or ethnic animus against Plaintiff (or anyone else). Despite Plaintiff's subjective beliefs about this encounter, it is not evidence of direct discrimination. (*Girma v. Skidmore College*, 2001, pp. 336–337)

Additionally, the court referenced another case involving a Black female professor who was denied promotion to full professor after two failed attempts. The court in *Bickerstaff v. Vassar College* (1999) established that "feelings and perceptions of being discriminated against are not evidence of discrimination" (p. 456). The court's lack of recognition of the importance of a chair's role in the tenure-track faculty journey, microaggressions, and the lack of support that can take an emotional toll on faculty of color are all results of systemic racism's impact on the tenure process. Until courts acknowledge the fact that systemic racism and exclusionary practices cloak the tenure process, faculty of color will continue to face challenges in the court of law especially if they do not have direct evidence of the discrimination. From the "facts" presented in the district court's opinion, Girma lacked support from the decision-making members of his process ranging from his all-White colleagues and department chair to the dean and the college president. Allies do not have to be and should not be only from one's ethnic or racial group, because cultural awareness and competence are valuable to everyone involved in the tenure process. "Changes in the university ecology cannot occur by itself; the support of administrators at all levels, faculty peers, faculty development offices, department chairs, deans and provosts are essential" (Louis et al., 2016, p. 470). Ultimately, the court ruled in favor of Skidmore College:

> Despite the fact that the Court must draw all reasonable inferences in his favor, Plaintiff has offered nothing from which a reasonable trier of fact could conclude, using the employer's criteria, that he was qualified to continue holding the position or that the criteria was not applied uniformly. Consequently, there is no support for the position that the stated basis for the College's determination was a pretext for discrimination. (*Girma v. Skidmore College*, 2001, pp. 344–345)

STUDENT AFFAIRS PROFESSIONALS AND LAWSUITS

Lawsuits involving student affairs professionals have not received the attention of the courts in the same manner as faculty. The use of CRT to analyze Girma's situation offered one perspective of challenges in employment law. Other critical frameworks such as critical feminist, critical queer, LatCrit, and TribalCrit can be employed to expose and analyze the ways in which societal norms oppress and marginalize individuals. Critical theories that address power and inequity allow student affairs professionals to gain a useful understanding of the challenges that are associated with proving discriminatory practices by drawing parallels with Girma's case. Consider the situation of an individual with marginalized identities who is hired into an entry or mid-level student affairs position. The person is cognizant that they will be the only person of their race, nationality, gender, religion, sexual identity, sexual orientation, or intersecting identities in their new office. During the interview process, the person may have perceived their future colleagues to be individuals who were self-aware and conscious of language and behavior that could be problematic for students and their peers. However, when the person attends their first staff meeting, they are surprised by comments that are made by not only peers but also their supervisor. As a result, in the new person feels isolated and offended. Seeking advice and overall support, the new person consults with a mentor at another institution about what to do. The mentor reminds the new person that fit can be viewed as an innocuous employment tool yet serve as a cover for discrimination. The advice that the mentor provides is a way to be proactive in the matter. Depending on one's comfort level, they could name the behavior and request a specific change in behavior by their colleagues.

Organizational change could manifest in various ways, including a one-on-one with the supervisor or the colleagues. If an environmental issue were perceived, discussing with a supervisor the opportunity to bring a trained professional to conduct a workshop would be useful in "unlearning" normative behavior and discourse. One must decide to the extent they desire to challenge people and environments in which fit is utilized to maintain spaces of exclusion and intolerance.

If hired, a student affairs professional can reasonably expect to receive constructive and substantive feedback at various intervals regarding their job performance. Student affairs professionals have the support of the ACPA/NASPA competencies as a way to guide a conversation about ensuring each staff member works in places that exemplify professional ethics even if the law does not provide the same protection.

PRACTICAL STRATEGIES

When going through the interview, hiring, and/or promotion process, higher education and student affairs professionals should keep the following strategies in mind to ensure that intentional and unintentional discrimination does not occur as both a job seeker and a search committee member. Many institutions are now using affirmative action advocates who provide an outside perspective during the search process. There is an inherent culture in any department or unit that may influence the interpretation of a candidate's fit without fully vetting their skills and qualifications to fulfill the position description. The following suggestions offer several practical strategies, in no particular order, that may be helpful to job seekers and search committee members.

Student affairs professionals must recognize how their own biases can influence decision-making in hiring practices. Self-awareness can influence how culture is shaped and maintained in the work environment. If an institution is seeking to determine how welcoming or uninviting its campus culture is, an assessment of the climate is warranted (Harper & Hurtado, 2007). Student affairs professional can influence and shape campus culture.

A case study can serve as an example. Kye is a multiracial transgender male going through portions of the gender confirmation process. He applied for an assistant director position at a public institution in an office consisting of White, heterosexual, and cisgender females and males. During Kye's lunch for his campus visit, one of his potential future colleagues asked, "How does your family feel about your decision to physically transition?" Kye was taken aback, chose not to answer, and changed the subject. After the campus visit, the staff discussed applicants for final consideration. Several staff members, including the staff member who posed the question, stated Kye was qualified but he did not seem like the right fit for the office. If you are the office director, how do you engage your staff in a conversation about fit? A staff conversation that ideally probed for specific examples of how Kye would not add value to the team is warranted. Most importantly, the director could facilitate a dialogue that includes a call for self-reflection on perspectives and biases that maintain inequities and perpetuate hegemonic notions of fit that contribute to exclusive environments.

Social justice competency is necessary for leadership to engage staff in these types of conversations. Staff members should also "do the work" to not only participate in conversations but also suggest behavioral changes for self and peers. "Social justice is both a process and a goal" (Chambers, 2017, p. 10); therefore, continually reading and discussing scholarship that highlights hegemonic forms of normativity, such as hetero- and cisnormativity, enhances the likelihood of unlearning biases. Additionally, student affairs professionals should make a consistent commitment to be transformation agents who are equipped with knowledge and solutions by attending conferences that offer a variety of workshops and presentations that focus on ways to serve diverse student populations as well as contributing to personal and professional development.

Behavior-based questions should be used by both the applicant and the hiring committee to probe the ambiguity behind job fit. Hypotheticals and detailed questions that will inform all parties how social justice is incorporated into everyday decision-making and interactions in a department and institution should be used. While this will allow the search committee to gauge the applicant's fit to the department's values, it will also help the applicant understand the department's level of commitment to social justice. Applicants can ask, "On a daily basis, what efforts are made by staff to demonstrate an understanding of systemic racism in higher education and to implement behavior that addresses it?" Applicants can also ask more probing questions, such as: "How does this department/unit define *social justice*? What professional development opportunities are available that enhance knowledge about inclusion and equity? If I were to speak with the undergraduate student workers and graduate assistants who work in this area, would they be able to articulate specific social justice programs or initiatives that are sponsored or supported by this office?" Depending on the responses to these questions, all parties can learn more about philosophies and perspectives.

Job descriptions should be written with as much specificity as possible to inform potential candidates more about the climate and culture of the overall institution and of the specific department. While employers want to present their institutions as "best places" to work, they should be honest with themselves and with their candidates about what newcomers can expect out of the job, institution, and locale. If employers are honest about their climate and working conditions, job seekers are more likely able to have an accurate read of the fit and will most likely remain in the position longer than if they misread their expectations of the climate. Honesty should address the challenges of programming, limited resource allocations, and any other known factors that could require individuals to be creative in their solution-focused thought process. However, honesty would require employers to have introspection of their culture and working environment, which is a limitation. Those units that can build an organizational and working culture that reflects this type of honest reflection of their own reality are more likely to be able to communicate this culture to their candidates. Frequent workshops focused on reducing bias can promote an inclusive environment. It could also provide a platform for colleagues to discuss issues and reduce human resources complaints and staff turnover. Employers who are intentional in their use of language and interview protocols that promote inclusivity are more likely viewed as ideal "fits" for job seekers.

It is necessary to be realistic in knowing and understanding that the law has limitations because of its narrow interpretation and absence of legislation that promotes inclusivity. These two challenges slow progress for marginalized applicants. For example, Congress has not enacted federal laws that recognize the mistreatment of gender-variant individuals. The Employment Non-Discrimination Act (ENDA), which would "prohibit workplace discrimination based on sexual orientation or gender identity" (ENDA, 2009), is a much-needed law. However, in its current proposed format, religious entities, including religiously affiliated higher education institutions, would be exempt from complying with it. "The narrow protections afforded currently under Title VII establish the need for ENDA if there is to be any meaningful federal prohibition of workplace discrimination and harassment based on sexual orientation and gender identity" (Reeves & Decker, 2011, p. 78). However, institutions have been proactive to implement protective policies that address discrimination of any form, whether or not local, state, or federal law mandates enforcement.

Institutions and departments should begin leveraging the benefits of implementing initiatives focused on recruiting faculty and staff of diverse backgrounds. With this commitment, institutions and departments can address their own unconscious biases that become an issue of fit during the hiring process. Some institutions have hired specialized recruiters to help units and departments create advertisements that attract a diverse pool and address any vagueness that can become issues during the search, interview, and hiring process. In addition, to address the implicit bias as mentioned previously, some institutions have created positions of *search advocate* who go through training to understand implicit bias, the legal environment, and recruiting and screening strategies. These search advocates are other faculty or staff of the institution. While most if not all institutions have an "outside" member on search committees, most of these outside members do not have such specialized training to address these issues.

CONCLUSION

"Antidiscrimination law is about freedom from legal constrictions, but it is limited in its ability to empower anyone to do anything as it does not take into account the reality of social inequity" (Chambers, 2017, p. 276). Hence, student affairs departments and units should be intentional and ground their hiring practices in inclusion and not homogeneity. Social justice and multi-culturalism "involve student affairs administrators who have a sense of their own agency and social responsibility that includes others, their community, and the larger global context" (ACPA & NASPA, 2015, p. 28). While the hegemonic perception of the student affairs field is one of multicultural-ism, which may erroneously encourage us to seek out, hire, and work with others whose values align with our own, this format pressures applicants to conform to a persona that is inauthentic. Therefore, our profession must internally assess how to resist expectations and behaviors that cause aliena-tion. An unbiased examination of a candidate's fit to successfully accomplish the required job tasks begins with determining what *fit* already means to a unit. While many times fit serves as a mask for employment discrimination of one or more of protected and unprotected classes, we hope the strategies and information we have presented will help job seekers and search commit-tee members avoid violating the law. We also hope the strategies we discussed will help all individuals involved in job searching and hiring to cease and discontinue hegemonically normative methods that are exclusionary. A successful search yields the candidate who best serves students and works in an inclusive environment. Fit is best left for shoes.

NOTES

1. 29 U.S.C. § 621 et seq. The Age Discrimination in Employment Act of 1967 (ADEA) prohibits age-based discrimination in employment for persons 40 years of age or older. The law prohibits age discrimination in hiring, discharge, pay, promotions, and other terms and conditions of employment. As part of the Fair Labor Standards Act, its application is to institutions with 20 or more employees and which affect interstate commerce. The standards for coverage parallel those of Title VII.

2. Along with Title VII, the Immigration Reform and Control Act of 1986 prohibits discrimination against aliens.

3. The Equal Employment Opportunity Commission (EEOC) made a historic decision in *Macy v. Holder*, Appeal No. 0120120821 (2012), by stating that transgender discrimination is gender discrimination and therefore protected under Title VII.

4. See, e.g., *Hazelwood Sch. Dist. v. United States*, 433 U.S. 299 (1977) (examining intentional discrimination); *Dothard v. Rawlinson*, 433 U.S. 321 (1977) (examining unintentional discrimination).

REFERENCES

ACPA: College Student Educators International & NASPA–Student Affairs Administrators in Higher Education. (2015). *ACPA/NASPA professional competency areas for student affairs practitioners*. Washington DC: Authors.

Age Discrimination in Employment Act of 1967, 29 U.S.C. § 621 (1967).

Americans with Disabilities Act of 1990, 42 U.S.C. § 12101 (1990).

Bickerstaff v. Vassar College, 196 F. 3d 435 (1999).

Bickerstaff v. Vassar College, 992 F. Supp. 372 (S.D.N.Y. 1998).

Carbado, D. W. (2013). Colorblind intersectionality. *Signs: Journal of Women in Culture and Society, 38*(4), 811–845.

Carbado, D. W., & Gulati, M. (2000). Working identity. *Cornell Law Review, 85*(5), 1259–1308.

Chambers, R. C. (2017). *Law and social justice in higher education*. New York, NY: Routledge.

Council for the Advancement of Standards (2006). CAS statement of shared ethical principles. In Council for the Advancement of Higher Education (Ed.), *CAS professional standards for higher education* (6th Ed.). Washington, DC: Author.

Cho, S. (2006). *"Unwise," "untimely," and "extreme": Redefining collegial culture in the workplace and revaluing the role of social change.* (Doctoral Dissertation). Retrieved from https://lawreview.law.ucdavis.edu/issues/39/3/race-sex-working-identities/DavisVol39No3_CHO.pdf

Civil Rights Act of 1964, 42 U.S.C. § 2000e (1964).

Constantine, M. G., Smith, L., Redington, R. M., & Owens, D. (2008). Racial microaggressions against Black counseling and counseling psychology faculty: A central challenge in the multicultural counseling movement. *Journal of Counseling and Development, 86*(3), 348–355.

Delgado, R., & Stefancic. J. (2001). *Critical race theory: An introduction.* New York, NY: New York University Press.

Educational Amendments of 1972, 20 U.S.C. § 1681 (1972).

Employment Non-Discrimination Act, H.R. 3017, 111th Congress, Section 4(a) (1), (e) (2009).

Equal Pay Act of 1963, 29 U.S.C. § 206(d) (1963).

Family and Medical Leave Act of 2006, 29 U.S.C. §§ 2601–2654 (2006).

Flowers, N., Wilson, S. A., González, E., & Banks, J. (2008). The study of faculty of color experiences at IUPUI. Paper completed for Center for Urban and Multicultural Education (CUME), School of Education, Indiana University – Purdue University Indianapolis.

Genetic Information Nondiscrimination Act of 2008, 42 U.S.C. § 2000ff (2008).

Girma v. Skidmore College, 180 F. Supp. 2d 326 (N.D.N.Y 2001).

Gross, A. (1998). Litigating Whiteness: Trials of racial determination in the nineteenth century South. *Yale Law Journal 108*(1), 109–188.

Harper, S. R. & Hurtado, S. (2007). Nine themes in campus racial climates and implications for institutional transformation. *New Directions for Student Services, 120,* 7–24.

Harris, C. I. (2014). Limiting equality: The divergence and convergence of Title VII and equal protection. *The University of Chicago Legal Forum, 1,* 95–144.

Huston, T. (2006). Race and gender bias in higher education: Could faculty course evaluations impede further progress toward parity? *Seattle Journal of Social Justice, 4*(2), 591–611.

Immigration Reform and Control Act of 1986, 8 U.S.C. § 1101 (1986).

Jones, R. A. (2009). Philosophical methodologies of critical race theory. *Georgetown Law Journal & Modern Critical Race Perspective, 1,* (17), 17–39.

Kahn, J. (2005). Controlling identity. *Plessy,* privacy, and racial defamation. *DePaul Law Review, 54*(3), 755–781.

Kaplin, W. A., & Lee, B. A. (1995). *The law of higher education* (3rd ed.). San Francisco, CA: Jossey-Bass.

Kezar, A. (2001). Investigating organizational fit in a participatory leadership environment. *Journal of Higher Education Policy and Management, 23*(1), 85–101.

Ladson-Billings, G., & Tate, W. F. (1995). Toward a critical race theory of education. *Teachers College Record, 97*(1), 47–68.

Lewin, K. (1952). *Field theory in social science: Selected theoretical papers.* London, UK: Tavistock.

Lewin, K. K. (1935). *A dynamic theory of personality.* New York, NY: McGraw-Hill.

Lilly Ledbetter Fair Pay Act of 2009, 42 U.S.C. § 2000e-5(e)(3)(A) (2009).

Littleford, L. N., Ong, K. S., Tseng, A. Milliken, J. C., & Humy, S. L. (2010). Perceptions of European American and African American instructors teaching race-focused courses. *Journal of Diversity in Higher Education, 3*(4), 230–244.

Littleford, L. N., Perry, A. R., Wallace, S. L., Moore, S. E., & Perry-Burney, G. D. (2010). Understanding student evaluations: A Black faculty perspective. *Reflections, 20*(1), 29–35.

Louis, D. A., Rawls, G. J., Jackson-Smith, D., Chambers, G. A., Phillips, L. A., & Louis, S. L. (2016). Listening to our voices: Experiences of Black faculty at predominantly White research universities with microaggression. *Journal of Black Studies, 47*(5), 454–474.

Lynn v. Regents of the University of California, 656 F.2d. 1337 (9th Cir. 1981).

McLaren, P. (1997). Unthinking Whiteness, rethinking democracy: Critical citizenship in gringolandia. In P. Mclaren (Ed)., *Revolutionary multiculturalism: Pedagogies of dissent for the new millennium* (pp. 236–293). Oxford, UK: Westview.

Parsons, F. (1909). *Choosing a vocation.* Boston, MA: Houghton, Mifflin.

Patton, L. D. (2015). Disrupting postsecondary prose: Toward a critical race theory of higher education. *Urban Education,* 1–28.

Pittman, C. T. (2012). Racial microaggressions: The narratives of African American faculty at a predominantly White university. *Journal of Negro Education, 81*(1), 82–92.

Pregnancy Discrimination Act of 1978, 42 U.S.C. § 2000e(k) (1978).

Reeves, J. E., & Decker, L. D. (2011). Before ENDA: Sexual orientation and gender identity protections in the workplace under federal law. *Law & Sexuality, 20,* 61–78.

Rehabilitation Act of 1973, 29 U.S.C. § 794(1973).

Smith v. City of Salem, 378 F.3d. 566 (6th Cir. 2004).

Tierney, W. G. (1988). Organizational culture in higher education: Defining the essentials. *The Journal of Higher Education, 59*(1), 2–21.

U.S. Equal Employment Opportunity Commission. (n.d.-a). Retrieved from http://www.eeoc.gov/index.html

U.S. Equal Employment Opportunity Commission. (n.d.-b). *How to file a charge of employment discrimination.* Retrieved from http://www.eeoc.gov/employees/howtofi le.cfm

3

Employer Definitions of and Reflections on *Fit* in Hiring Processes

Léna Kavaliauskas Crain and Mathew J.L. Shepard

I N STUDENT AFFAIRS AND higher education, community members frequently share stories of their experiences as job candidates and, far less frequently, as prospective employers. Discussions and processes that shape hiring decisions tend to happen discreetly, sheltered by layers of coded language and bureaucratic complexity. Perhaps the decision makers were within the same small group, the hiring committee was quietly tapped without strategy, or decisions were made in disordered haste while students' needs piled and persisted with urgency. We purport to be human-centered and communicative in student affairs, but our humanity and communication seem to lapse in our approach to human resources. We shrug our shoulders and say things like, "Well, you know how hiring committees are." The trouble is that, until recently, we didn't know much. When the National Study of the Student Affairs Job Search (NSSAJS) expanded its studies to explore employers' actions and experiences in 2013, the team sought to illuminate the behaviors and structures that exist inconspicuously. Reviewing the experiences of employers in their own words provides employers and candidates with insight into hiring methods that unfold regularly. One thing is certain: The concept of fit in the job search was notable in their stories.

This chapter will discuss the definition and role of *fit* in the hiring process according to student affairs hiring officials (employers) themselves and explore them through a critical theories framework. Participants in this study were 10 hiring officials who interviewed with the researcher every other week for the duration of each official's hiring process. Our study was rooted in the critical constructivist idea that, because individuals make meaning based on their own understanding and experiences, cultures and environments can be reformed by community attention (Taylor, 1996). As such, we sought employers' experiences with and reflections on their hiring time lines, criteria for candidates, and how hiring committees made decisions throughout their processes. Fit was identified by many participating employers as one of the significant late-stage criteria for candidates' success. Each employer in the study defined *fit* differently; employers' ideas of fit included a candidate's professional qualifications, alignment with organizational cultures, possession of desirable personality or demographic traits, and interpersonal connections with campus community members. The study yielded three themes: fit as ambiguous, fit as connected, and fit as comprehensive. Employers' definitions signify space for job candidates to be authentic and seen in the hiring process, but for some employers, fit seems to be an ambiguous criterion used to justify social barriers in the hiring process. Using data from the NSSAJS (Kavaliauskas Crain, 2016), this chapter will provide empirical information on a topic that is often approached solely with anecdotes. This chapter will provide narrative excerpts from hiring officials, analysis of themes related to the definition and importance of *fit* in the hiring process, and recommendations for employers when considering fit in inclusive, equitable hiring processes.

BACKGROUND AND RESEARCH

Although ample resources exist about job search processes outside higher education, literature related to the job search in higher education and student affairs is relatively limited. Outside of the field, resources range from advisory and anecdotal to empirical studies of corporate hiring practices and candidate criteria. Within the field, Sandeen and Barr (2006) expressed that job search practices frequently articulated outside of higher education might not pertain to the student affairs job search. The limited transferability of the corporate job search literature might relate to the highly nuanced nature of job searching in higher education and student affairs. Institutions of higher education vary greatly by type (e.g., size, public or private, virtual or brick-and-mortar, and focal academic programs). Similarly, even within a type, institutions vary greatly in their organizational structure (Keeling, Underhile, & Wall, 2007).

In the context of student affairs, the functional areas represented and structured within the spheres of student affairs, enrollment management, and academic affairs differ among institutions, including affiliated auxiliary units.
This inconsistency makes the expectations, organization, and even the ability
to identify position listings highly variable from institution to institution.
Next, the cycle of the academic calendar and specific needs of each functional
area create hiring seasons that range across several months by functional area
(Kavaliauskas Crain, 2016). Additionally, job seekers conduct simultane-
ous searches in multiple functional areas, making it necessary for candidates
to navigate the nuances of each. Placement exchanges, such as those conducted at American College Personnel Association's (ACPA) Career Central,
NASPA–Student Affairs Administrators in Higher Education's (NASPA),
The Placement Exchange, and regional functional area conferences provide
additional nuances. Finally, student affairs personnel enter the field from
innumerably varied pathways, including through graduate preparation programs in higher education and programs and careers outside of higher education. This variability makes it challenging to explore, let alone understand,
patterns in hiring behaviors and processes.

In addition to the limited study of job search processes in student affairs
and the numerous distinctions of the field, there is also a historic dearth of
studies related to fit in the job search. Anecdotally, student affairs personnel know that professionals and employers consider fit as a criterion for job
selection and longevity. However, until recently, the profession lacked robust
empirical support for how employers define and apply *fit* in hiring processes.
This absence of information contributes to the inequities created and perpetuated by hiring processes. As such, this chapter seeks to identify and address
such inequities through use of critical theories and employers' reflections on
fit. This chapter is an empirical study of hiring officials' definitions of *fit* and
the significance of fit in the hiring process, including how these concepts
connect to social justice and implications for employers and candidates.

Critical Theories as a Framework for Fit

Originating from German philosophers in the early twentieth century, critical theory aims to illuminate the ways in which people are oppressed with
the goal of eliminating all social injustices (Bohman, 2016). Critical theory
"provides the descriptive and normative bases for social inquiry aimed at
decreasing domination and increasing freedom in all their forms" (para. 1).
Providing a philosophical and practical underpinning for the liberation of

specific identity groups, narrower subsets of critical theory developed specific to these social movements (Bohman, 2016). These subsets of critical theory recognize the centrality of identity as it intersects with oppressive structures and include critical race theory (CRT), LatCrit, feminist theory, and queer theory, among others (Delgado Bernal, 2002). Critical theorists seek to challenge dominant ideologies and commit to dismantling oppressive systems and practices for social justice (Delgado Bernal, 2002). Furthermore,

> a critical theory is adequate only if it meets three criteria: it must be explanatory, practical, and normative, all at the same time. That is, it must explain what is wrong with the current social reality, identify the actors to change it, and provide both clear norms for criticism and achievable practical goals for social transformation. (Bohman, 2016, para. 3)

A central tenet of critical theories describes systemic oppression as prevalent and permanent in United States society (Bell, 1992). As colleges and universities in the United States as a whole have a storied history of racial discrimination, gender exclusion, and hostility toward LGBTQ inclusion, critical theory suggests that today's institutions of higher education continue to perpetuate oppressive systems through the exclusion of nondominant identities (DeCuir & Dixson, 2004). CRT describes Whiteness as a form of property (Bell, 1992; Harris, 1995) thus highlighting how oppressive structures reward dominant cultures and apply deficit models to non-White—and arguably non-male, non-heteronormative—ways of thinking and knowledge. Because colleges and universities were created by and built for people with dominant identities, knowledge, competencies, relationships, and experiences, those outside of the dominant paradigm are viewed as less prestigious and their people and cultures as less desirable (Yosso, 2005). These deficit models contribute to modern educational segregation in elite programs by excluding nondominant ways of thinking and personalities while including and rewarding those who subscribe to the dominant paradigm (Ladson-Billings & Tate, 1995). Therefore, critical theories offer stark critiques of institutions making incremental changes toward equality as they fail to dismantle social inequities while serving to the tolerances of those who hold power (DeCuir & Dixson, 2004).

This study employs critical theory as its theoretical framework. In using critical theory as a framework, this study and chapter are attuned to the ways that social identities, including race, ethnicity, gender, sexuality, religion, and ability, intersect with power and social forces to result in privilege and oppression in the job search. DeCuir and Dixson (2004) advocate for the use of critical theories in education research in order to

> unmask the persistent and oppressive nature of the normativity of Whiteness, the co-option and distortion of oppositional discourses, and the ways in which policies that are offered as remedies to underachievement and educational disparity may not be in the best interests of marginalized groups, but rather serve the elite. (p. 30)

In this chapter, we argue that institutions of higher education use the notion of fit in job hiring processes as a tool to perpetuate privilege and oppression. By examining the ways that fit is described by employers and utilized in their hiring practices through a critical lens, we hope to contribute to dismantling conscious and subconscious oppressive hiring practices and, furthermore, use employment and platforms in higher education to expose and address social inequalities.

Research Design

Because the hiring process serves as both the context and the phenomenon for NSSAJS studies, case study is a way to explore a "phenomenon within its real-life context, especially when the boundaries between the phenomenon and context are not clearly evident" (Yin, 2003, p. 13). This is especially true for the ways the deep-seated role of fit in hiring processes may shape candidates' and employers' experiences. Next, case study allows for gathering data from multiple perspectives and sources, which encourages richness and depth of information to build understanding of a phenomenon (Stake, 2006; Yin, 2003). Case studies allow for participants' narratives to be heard while allowing for patterns and themes to emerge to shed light on the case (Creswell, 2013; Yin, 2009). The NSSAJS studies, and this chapter, seek to operationalize the patterns shared by employers to contribute to transparency and equity in the job search.

Ultimately, we hope to bring attention to hiring processes in the field of student affairs so that we can change them, creating more transparent and equitable hiring mechanisms. Critical constructivists hold that communities can change culture and environment through concerted action (Taylor, 1996). Understanding the perspectives of employers, which have historically been inadvertently and intentionally concealed, gives us the foundation through which to change the culture and environment of hiring processes in student affairs. This theoretical background and the richness of collective case study methods were used to understand fit from the perspective of 10 hiring officials during their student affairs hiring processes. Seeking to understand the notion of fit and its potential as an oppressive mechanism in the hiring process, we designed research questions to examine the definitions and applications of *fit* used by employers. Specifically, we wondered:

- How did employers define *fit* during their hiring processes?
- How did employers recognize fit in candidates?
- How might the concept of fit relate to oppression or liberation in the hiring process?

Examination of employers' definitions of *fit* and how they assessed fit in candidates might allow us to make connections between intentionally or unintentionally exclusive behaviors in the hiring process. Additionally, we aspired to transform employers' insights into tools that they and candidates can use to better administer and navigate the process and to recommend emancipatory steps in hiring for candidates, advisers, and employers.

Participants and Procedures

Data for this chapter came from the NSSAJS, which examines variables and narratives related to candidates' and employers' search processes (Kavaliauskas Crain, 2016). In 2013, we conducted a study of employers' hiring practices and interviewed 10 hiring officials at U.S. institutions of higher education for the duration of each official's hiring process. Institutions represented included nine 4-year institutions and one 2-year institution; 6 public and 4 private institutions; and a mix of small private and large research-intensive institutions. Hiring officials were assigned pseudonyms to protect their personal identities and experiences.

Each hiring official was conducting a search for one or more entry-level positions in student affairs. Entry-level positions were identified based on the academic and experiential requirements for the position: bachelor's or master's degree and two or fewer years of experience required. The positions reported to the functional areas of academic advising, career services, multicultural programs, new student programs, residence life, and wellness programs.

Hiring officials each completed an intake interview and participated in subsequent biweekly interviews for the duration of their hiring processes. Based on the hiring time lines of each participant, individuals completed between 4 and 9 interviews. All hiring processes and interviews took place between February 2013 and August 2013. Interviews used a semistructured interview protocol, which included questions about employers' hiring time lines, hiring practices, and how employers identified and recognized criteria in candidates. All 10 of the hiring officials spoke about fit and evaluating candidates.

Limitations

The hiring officials who participated in this study represent a variety of institutions and functional areas in higher education. However, recognizing that only 10 hiring officials participated, their reflections may not represent their larger search committees or institutional perspectives. Also, information about the hiring officials' social identities was not collected formally, though some participants did disclose their identities and, occasionally, how their identities shaped their hiring perspectives and experiences.

Additionally, because employers shared their reflections in the general context of their hiring processes, the definitions and applications of *fit* they described did not specifically relate to the oppressive or emancipatory potential of fit in the hiring process. As a result, their reflections might lack deep insight related to equity and inclusion in hiring. On the other hand, not discussing the social justice applications of fit and the hiring process might have elicited more authentic responses, that is, narratives that truly encapsulated the role of fit in each hiring process.

Data Analysis

Each interview was transcribed, and transcripts were initially reviewed using microanalysis—manual line-by-line examination (Yin, 2009). The present study relied on portions of the interview in which hiring officials spoke specifically about fit and hiring criteria. After identifying passages from the transcripts that were relevant to this study of fit, open and axial coding were employed to yield themes by employer and across employers, consistent with collective case study analysis (Yin, 2009). The data revealed three themes related to employers' definitions and applications of *fit* in hiring processes: fit as ambiguous, fit as connected, and fit as comprehensive.

FIT IS AMBIGUOUS, CONNECTED, AND COMPREHENSIVE

Employers' varied descriptions of fit give testament to the ambiguity and subjectivity of fit as a criterion in the hiring process. Though each employer defined *fit* slightly differently, three themes emerged: fit as ambiguous, connected, and comprehensive. Within these themes, employers indicated that their definitions of *fit* are ambiguous, evolving, and broad. Hiring committees also seemed to formalize fit to different extents in hiring processes. Each section includes excerpts from and interpretations of employers' narratives.

Fit Is Ambiguous: "We Know It When We See It"

Several employers spoke about fit as vague and unclear. For many of these employers, it seemed that the ambiguity of fit was filled in intuitively, shaped by individuals' perspectives on candidates and hiring needs. Intuitive decision-making was reflected in employer Raquel's definition, as she described fit as a "know it when we see it, kind of thing." For some employers, *fit* seemed difficult to define, and others never discussed or defined *fit* as a hiring committee. Others described *fit* as highly connected to personal perspective, and as a result, as a composite definition built by hiring decision makers.

According to some employers, the definition of *fit* inevitably varies from person to person, for example, within a hiring committee. Kaia expressed this as "the personal opinion factor," which she described as individual lenses used to clarify criteria related to experience and skills. Similarly, Jacob described that the definition of *fit* depended on who was making the hiring decision, and suggested that the composition of the hiring committee shaped a collective definition of *fit*. He shared,

> I think every person on the hiring team has a different idea of what fit looks like. That's why we are considerate about having a diverse committee. . . . The committee reflects the diversity of campus and perspectives of departments that work with the position, so everyone has a slightly different idea of what is the best fit.

Jacob's and Kaia's reflections share the concept of fit as ambiguous and individualized, as well as their understanding of how various perspectives came together to present a group idea of fit. Kaia described, "Fit is not something we ever talked about as a committee. I think everyone understands it

is important. Everyone understands that it is the personal opinion factor."
Though Jacob spoke specifically about how diversity on the hiring committee meant diversity of perspectives, including that of fit, Kaia recognized the
importance of individual perspectives and shared that the convergence of
perspectives happened informally.

To some employers, the ambiguity of fit seemed to allow the concept
to evolve, even to complement more formal parts of the hiring process.
Randolph was one employer who described how the definition of *fit* evolved
for his hiring committee based on which stage they were in the process.
In his experience, because hiring committee members possessed evolving
knowledge about candidates, and had distinctive criteria at different stages
of the process, the definition of *fit* shifted to suit the occasion. Randolph
expressed,

> Fit for us meant different things at different points in the process. When we
> were reviewing applications, you can only tell so much about a person, so fit
> was more about "Did they fit with the job description?" as far as qualifica-
> tions. As we got further, I guess in that sense, when [the search committee]
> said fit, it was a good way to weed out the weirdos who snuck through the
> process and weren't a good fit personality-wise.

Christopher shared that his committee had used formal tools to evaluate
candidates, but that fit added an informal, ambiguous layer to the formal
scoring:

> We used score sheets for the phone interviews and individual reviewers, but
> fit isn't something that you can quantify. It is the gut-level feeling that sup-
> plements the score sheets. It probably influences the scores, too, because if
> someone is a good fit, they tend to do better overall.

To Randolph and his committee, it seemed that the initial definition of
fit related to competence. However, his later description seemed similar to
Christopher's, which related to fit with the institution and fit of personality.

Fit Is Connected: "Could I See Myself Hanging Out With Them?"

Many employers described fit as the connection among candidates and
institutional values; personalities; and members of the campus community,
including students, faculty, and staff. Within this meaning, *fit* seemed to

be defined as relational, where connection was with members of the campus community; personality and values-based, where fit was connection to qualities and interests shared with candidates; and institutional, where fit was determined based on connections to students and the community. Employers who described fit as connection emphasized the importance of candidates sharing interests and values with members of the campus community who participated in or shared input into the hiring decision. Nico described this as a "relatable interest" and shared advice that she had once been given as a candidate. Now, as an employer, she noted that fit in this sense meant, "Could I see myself hanging out with them? Someone told me to always have a relatable interest, like baking, because people automatically connect to how they would benefit." Teyana described relatable interests as "personal fit" but shared with similar importance for decision makers to "see yourself . . . with them." She shared, "Maybe you see yourself being friends with them, maybe that person said they have kids or are a great cook, and you see that personal fit coming into the workplace." This definition of *fit*, which is relational in nature, was solidified by employers for the connection of candidates to hiring authorities.

Fit Is Comprehensive: "The Total Package"

Finally, employers spoke about fit as a comprehensive description and evaluation of candidates. The all-encompassing perspective seemed to include candidates' alignment with criteria that were and were not included in the job posting and formal tools used to assess candidates' viability. The theme of fit as comprehensive included employers who described fit as competence-based, expressed as alignment with the job description, as well as qualities that were articulated as components outside of the position description.

To several employers, fit seemed to be a descriptor used for candidates who met multiple criteria that had been formalized throughout the hiring process. Candidates who conveyed skills important to the job description, for example, or who had been evaluated highly by various stakeholders and at different parts of the hiring process, showed fit in a complete manner. Naomi talked about fit as checking boxes, filling multiple skills-based criteria for a position. Describing her evaluation of fit as based in tasks and transferable skills, she said candidates who could do each part of a position were a better fit than those who did not possess or articulate experiences that related to the position's requirements. Christopher described this as, "If someone is a good fit, they tend to do better overall." Similarly, hiring official Jordan spoke about fit at the end of her hiring process, when she reflected on fit as totality in a candidate:

> The candidate we went with, she was a great fit, the total package. She had great experiences, she had worked in a similar department and university, she got along well with the hiring committee and students, and everyone who met her and interviewed her had really positive things to say.

In this case, the successful candidate's fit was determined by experience, transferable skills and institutional backgrounds, comfort with communication and relationship building, and overall positive evaluations. This type of fit seemed to be more competence-based, though Jordan's description indicates that personality and relational fit were also influential to the comprehensive definition.

Fit also seemed to reflect criteria that were not formalized in the job description, including community values and personality. One employer, Nico, explained what they described as "transparency" in the hiring process, such that candidates would also sense fit as congruence of values between them and the campus community, as well as the degree to which they could adapt as a member of the community. Specifically, Nico said,

> I hope that we're transparent about our values and community from the start, and certainly in the campus visits, so our candidates have a sense of whether they can see themselves in this community. Sometimes, the campus visit will tell us that it's not a good match, but usually I'm sure of the fit before they get here.

Lastly, one employer described fit as a comprehensive "tie-breaker," useful for when more formal assessment of candidates resulted in similarly qualified finalists. Teyana looked back on previous experiences with hiring committees and said fit had been the deciding factor. She said, "I've been on other searches in past years when, maybe it's a tie between two candidates, they're both qualified and did great in the interview process, and fit can be the tie-breaker."

INTERPRETING DEFINITIONS OF *FIT*

The perspectives employers shared provide insight into normally privileged information. From their candid reflections on hiring processes and the role of fit in selecting candidates, we can identify broad, evolving ways that fit interfaces with employers' decisions. Fit is ambiguous, ranging from a single, relational connection to a comprehensive view of qualifications and values alignment. Though no two employers shared identical definitions of *fit*, it appears that there are patterns in the ways that fit is used in hiring decisions. More specifically, it appears that there is great room for bias in the definitions of *fit* offered by employers, especially among those who interpreted fit as ambiguous or as having a connection. Randolph, for example, described an evolving definition of *fit*, and his later description of fit to "weed out the weirdos" seemed to relate to an attempt to rationalize match between a person and the institutional or departmental culture at best, and the ability to rationalize personal preferences and biases at worst.

Individuals with shared backgrounds, understanding, and even experiences with marginalization tend to seek one another out (Tatum, 1997). As such, what employers described as "connection" might unconsciously be selection of candidates with shared social identities or experiences. Bourdieu (1984) described that social class is solidified among members by a shared lifestyle and interests. In choosing candidates employers can see "hanging out with them," hiring officials may be selecting those who share similar levels of economic privilege and social capital. Roberts (2016) discussed the importance of leisure activities in culture and noted that culture is shaped through shared leisure interests. This affirms the possibility that employers who define *fit* through shared interests may be more likely to hire candidates from similar cultural backgrounds.

As Yosso (2005) argued, marginalized cultures have been labeled as culturally deficient because the dominant culture's capital is more valuable than knowledge of cultures outside the dominant paradigm. A historic look at class differences through a Bourdieuian lens shows that high levels of capital are equated to high levels of prestige (Barratt, 2011). Wearing the right clothing, acting the right way, and speaking with the appropriate vernacular all create a sense of prestige that revolves around identities as capital. As critical theories suggest, acquisition of prestigious capital can be exchanged for a place among the higher social strata as a form of property. Furthermore, Jacob used the phrase "what fit looks like," which could suggest an inherent connection to candidates' identities.

Recommendations for Praxis

Employers described fit as a significant late-stage criterion for candidates' success. While several employers acknowledged that fit was on the minds of those who participated in the hiring process throughout its duration, early portions of hiring processes seemed much more quantifiable than late-stage, including final decision-making. Interpreting employers' narratives creates implications for practice for employers (hiring officials and search committees), advisers (graduate preparation faculty and job search advisers), and candidates.

Hiring Officials and Search Committee Members.

Based on the perspectives of these 10 hiring officials, there is potential to formalize the role of *fit* in hiring processes, and in doing so, change the potentially exclusionary use of the term. Davis and Harrison (2013) urged educators to critically act to embrace what they called "disruptive performances" (p. 197), actions to counter systems of oppression that have become normed in praxis. Such normed, oppressive systems include behaviors and practices in the hiring process perpetuated by the ambiguous wielding of fit as a search criterion. As such, we recommend that hiring officials and search committee members (a) better define what fit means to the search, as well as when it matters in the hiring process, and quantify fit in the hiring process; (b) build well-trained hiring committees that include demographic and stakeholder diversity; and (c) employ democratic constituent decision-making for balance in hiring.

1. Define and Quantify Fit

Though variably defined, *fit* emerged as an important criterion to employers during their hiring processes, especially in late-stage decision-making. However, employers also agreed that fit is ambiguous, subjective, and ever-evolving. This ambiguity can dangerously masquerade as exclusivity, used to ignore or reject difference and perpetuate employment inequities. As such, hiring officials and search committee members should leave no place for uncertainty of fit as a tool for oppression in hiring. To address this, employers should work to strictly define what *fit* means to the search for a specific role. Descriptors, definitions, and rubrics, including the language that accompanies this chapter, help to quantify and embed fit in other more structured parts of the hiring process. This connects to Christopher's observation of the connection between intuitive fit opinions and candidates' formal scores, while providing a balance for the ways that vague, informal notions of fit might bias hiring processes.

2. Build and Train Diverse Hiring Committees

Employers described two trends related to hiring committees: composition and training. Jacob suggested that having a committee that represented campus demographics and opinions was a way to promote an inclusive idea of fit. On a hiring committee that reflects the diversity of campus and departmental viewpoints, where "everyone has a slightly different idea" of fit, it is possible that the varied perspectives of fit are similarly inclusive of diverse candidates. Hiring committees should include demographic and stakeholder diversity, as varied perspectives may balance advocacy for varied identities. However, because institutions of higher education are a part of and perpetuate societal oppression, individuals should be trained prior to participating on hiring committees to recognize their personal and institutional preconceptions and preferences, as well as how one's lenses and experiences can influence hiring decisions, especially as fit is concerned. For example, a hiring committee at a predominantly White institution that reflects the proportional diversity of the campus may still devalue the competencies and experiences of candidates with marginalized identities, as these shared identities would likely still be in the minority on the committee. It is also possible that even if marginalized identities were overrepresented on hiring committees, oppressive "norms" might lead to the devaluation of their opinions. In either case, thoughtful selection and training for search committees, coupled with tools to improve equity, provide a foundation for hiring decision makers to combat conscious and subconscious biases in hiring processes.

3. Employ Democratic Decision-Making in Hiring

Once hiring committees have achieved representative diversity and have been adequately trained, committees should employ democratic decision-making to balance perspectives on candidates and create a more equitable hiring process. This recommendation creates a checks-and-balances component to the first two recommendations for hiring committees and mitigates the risk of a single decision maker's definition (or lack thereof) of *fit* dictating the hiring outcome. Even after defining *fit* and employing diverse, well-trained committees, inherent biases make it difficult to completely shed behaviors that have become normed in hiring practices, especially given the vague and pervasive role of fit in hiring processes. Including many voices in the hiring process and making shared decisions is one way to offset potential individual biases, especially when coupled with other recommendations.

Graduate Preparation Personnel, Advisers to Candidates, and Candidates

Job search preparation is an important part of professional socialization, including through graduate preparation programs. There are ample avenues through which to introduce job search strategies into graduate preparation. Many graduate programs now include job search information in capstone coursework, workshops, and advising meetings, for example, and these discussions may also include conversations about fit. In doing so, advisers and faculty who discuss the job search in formal and informational ways should include information about fit that considers the critical implications discussed in this chapter and volume. As the hiring officials interviewed in this study describe, fit seems to be an important, albeit ambiguous and all-encompassing, mutual matching process. Faculty should explain ways for students to ascertain institutional and departmental values, for example, by reviewing outward-facing resources such as websites and publications, as well as annual reports and climate studies. As candidates advance in hiring processes, there are additional indicators of culture and fit. The questions that prospective employers ask during the search process are a reflection of values, desires, and focal points. Similarly, the absence of questions, including those related to equity, diversity, and inclusion, may also be telling. The composition of the hiring committee, campus hosts, and larger community may tell a story about which identities are dominant, welcomed, and valued. Gut feelings—of connection, of comfort, of belonging—also matter. To prepare candidates for the role of fit in the job search, advisers should discuss the importance of fit, as well as the descriptions outlined previously for how employers might determine fit.

It is also important for candidates to be prepared to interpret when fit might be used as a tool for exclusion or inclusion. This might have ugly implications. Candidates may feel the need to hide or suppress aspects of their identity and personality throughout the job search process, an act termed by Yoshino (2006) as *covering*, in the hopes that doing so could help them navigate the ambiguous, oppressive potential of fit. Alternately, candidates can use this understanding of employers' perspectives to assess whether employers and institutions align with their values and meet their needs. The NSSAJS found that approximately 75% of candidates accepted their first offers of employment, and women accepted initial offers at a disproportionately high rate (Kavaliauskas Crain, 2014; Kavaliauskas Crain, 2016). This information might suggest that individuals make compromises when evaluating prospective employers and could be better equipped to approach job searches authentically, discerning fit through their own lenses and redistributing power in the job search for candidates.

CONCLUSION

The study that informed this chapter provided one of the few currently available insights into employers' hiring perspectives and practices in student affairs. Perhaps this will inspire deeper discussion of hiring behaviors, especially fit, among candidates, employers, and other community members. As a direct examination of a generally closed process, there are perspectives on hiring that seem somewhat raw and unrefined. Unfortunately, employers who described ambiguous or evolving definitions of *fit* might have indicated fit as a euphemism for exclusion. This indicates that, in the process of adopting fit as a means of promoting adherence to institutional or organizational missions, it has inadvertently evolved into a tool for systematic exclusion by potentially reinforcing the deficit models used to devalue competencies, experiences, and relationships of marginalized individuals.

The good news is that employers, candidates, and advisers can use this data to redesign search processes and engagement with hiring. We can use our new insight into employers' inconsistent and varied approaches to call for clarity and hiring processes that align with the values of our professions. On one side, fit can be used to promote homogeneity and perpetuate inequities in the hiring process and in campus workplaces. On the other, especially when clearly and specifically defined and measured, *fit* may also be used to *address* inequities and promote equitable searches. By understanding employers' definitions, interpretations, and applications of *fit* throughout the hiring process, candidates, advisers, and employers can take steps toward more equitable hiring practices to further move institutions of higher education toward social justice.

REFERENCES

Barratt, W. (2011). *Social class on campus: Theories and manifestations*. Sterling, VA: Stylus.

Bell, D. A. (1992). *Faces at the bottom of the well: The permanence of racism*. New York, NY: Basic Books.

Bohman, J. (2016). Critical theory. In E. N. Zalta (Ed.), *The Stanford encyclopedia of philosophy* (Fall 2016 ed.). Retrieved from https://plato.stanford.edu/archives/fall2016/entries/critical-theory/

Bourdieu, P. (1984). *Distinction*. London, UK: Routledge.

Creswell, J. W. (2013). *Qualitative inquiry and research design: Choosing among five approaches*. Thousand Oaks, CA: SAGE.

Davis, T., & Harrison, L. M. (2013). *Advancing social justice: Tools, pedagogies, and strategies to transform your campus*. San Francisco, CA: Jossey-Bass.

Delgado Bernal, D. (2002). Critical race theory, Latino critical theory, and critical raced-gendered epistemologies: Recognizing students of color as holders and creators of knowledge. *Qualitative Inquiry, 8*(1), 105–126.

DeCuir, J. T., & Dixson, A. D. (2004). "So when it comes out, they aren't that surprised that it is there": Using critical race theory as a tool of analysis of race and racism in education. *Educational Researcher, 33*(5), 26–31.

Harris, C. (1995). Whiteness as property. In K. Crenshaw, N. Gotanda, G. Peller, & K. Thomas (Eds.), *Critical race theory: The key writings that formed the movement* (pp. 276–291). New York, NY: New Press.

Kavaliauskas Crain, L. (2014). Lessons from higher education administrative professionals' job search. *Women in Higher Education, 23*, 18–19.

Kavaliauskas Crain, L. (March 2016). *The entry-level student affairs job search: Recommendations for candidates and employers*. Presented at ACPA: College Student Educators International, Montréal, Québec, Canada.

Keeling, R. P., Underhile, R., & Wall, A. F. (2007). Horizontal and vertical structures: The dynamics of organization in higher education. *Liberal Education, 93*(4), 22–31.

Ladson-Billings, G., & Tate, W. (1995). Toward a critical race theory of education. *Teachers College Record, 97*(1), 47–68.

Roberts, K. (2016). *The business of leisure: Tourism, sport, events, and other leisure industries*. London, UK: Palgrave.

Sandeen, A., & Barr, M. J. (2006). *Critical issues for student affairs: Challenges and opportunities*. San Francisco, CA: Jossey-Bass.

Stake, R. E. (2006). *Multiple case study analysis*. New York, NY: The Guilford Press.

Tatum, B. D. (1997). *Why are all the Black kids sitting together in the cafeteria? And other conversations about race*. New York, NY: Basic Books.

Taylor, P. C. (1996). Mythmaking and mythbreaking in the mathematics classroom. *Educational Studies in Mathematics, 31*(1/2), 151–173.

Yin, R. K. (2003). *Applications of case study research* (2nd ed.). Thousand Oaks: SAGE.

Yin, R. K. (2009). *Case study research: Design and methods*. Thousand Oaks, CA: SAGE.

Yoshino, K. (2006). *Covering: The hidden assault on our civil rights.* New York, NY: Random House.

Yosso, T. J. (2005). Whose culture has capital? A critical race theory discussion of community cultural wealth. *Race Ethnicity & Education, 8*(1), 69–91. doi:10.1080/1361332052000341006

4

Holograms, Misfits, and Authentic Selves

Fit as Narrative Agency Through Inequality Regimes

Jessica Bennett, Travis T. York, Van Bailey, Marshall Habermann-Guthrie, Luis Jimenez Inoa, Meghan Gaffney Wells, and Akiko Yamaguchi

YOU MAY REMEMBER *JEM and the Holograms* (Bacal, Bacal, Griffin, & Loesch, 1985), a cartoon that aired on television between 1985 and 1988 and was remade into a feature film in 2015. Hardworking but imperfect Jerrica Benton, after pressing her earring, transformed into the "truly outrageous" diva with pink hair, Jem, with the help of Synergy, a holographic computer. Jerrica's real life, and her life as Jem, were in constant negotiation as she sought to find love, success, and happiness. Also complicating Jerrica's world were the Misfits, who sought to upstage and disrupt Jem's performances.

Jerrica's dilemma speaks to some of the challenging dynamics one can encounter when navigating fit within student affairs. We like to think that being hardworking, smart, and capable are enough to be successful. However, we are often asked to be "truly outrageous," like Jem, enacting a hologram to cover our true selves to fit into a predetermined mold of how to be successful, how to be professional, or how to just get by. There are also times when the needs of our students, or ourselves, demand that we upset, disrupt, or challenge the status quo, effectively turning us into Misfits.

This chapter explores the challenges of student affairs professionals by highlighting the ways in which student affairs professionals are often caught, frustrated, and challenged in our efforts to fit in our departments, divisions, institutions, and the profession. We begin by exploring the basic challenge of understanding fit and what it means for us, the power dynamics within institutions that make finding fit so difficult, and how we make sense of those processes through narrative. Finally, we explore how student affairs professionals might navigate our institutions with a sense of agency, making intentional choices out of the options available to us.

To ground this exploration of fit in student affairs, we explore the commonalities and differences in our own narratives and attempt to identify lessons learned from our own stories. By connecting the developed theoretical frame to our individual and collective stories, we hope to provide insight into how universities can provide specific opportunities for growing, for thriving, for resistance, and for disappointment. With a diversity of gender, race, class, and sexuality identities represented among our ranks, we also hope to interrogate some of the failures of the student affairs profession to embody the ideals of social justice it espouses for its professional corps. This chapter aims to highlight the limitations of these promises for a profession embedded in what Coser (1974) called "greedy institutions," organizations that demand high commitments from their members. We also seek to identify ways in which practitioners and institutions can counteract or mitigate these challenges.

WHAT ROLE DOES FIT PLAY IN STUDENT AFFAIRS?

In all areas of university[1] hiring, fit is a key determinant in how hiring officials, search committees, and job-seeking student affairs professionals make decisions. When graduating master's degree students enter the job market, they are often reminded that the search should be a mutual process where they interview the institutions just as the institutions interview them. When search committees evaluate a pool of equally qualified candidates for a position, the deciding factor often comes down to perceptions of candidate fit with institutional, divisional, or departmental culture. Most of what we know and understand about fit in the scholarly literature has been developed from the point of view of universities (or other organizations) and not from potential or actual hires in student affairs (Billsberry, Ambrosini, Moss-Jones, & Marsh, 2005; Kristof-Brown & Billsberry, 2013).

To complicate matters further, traditional views of fit are conceived of as single-point-in-time determinations—you fit or you don't, you are hired or you're not. Conversely, we suggest that fit is an ongoing process of sensemaking, positioning, and self-narrative (Shipp & Jansen, 2011). Sensemaking refers to the process of making order of our experiences (Weick, Sutcliffe, & Obstfeld, 2005). Multiple identities define our positioning, giving us particular viewpoints on the world, *and* situating us in particular locations within power structures, giving us access to more or less power to navigate the world (Crenshaw, 1991). Jones and McEwen's (2000) model of multiple dimensions of identity, revised and extended with the addition of Abes, emphasized that the saliency of a particular identity dimension, or combination of dimensions, changes based upon the given context, environment, and time within which individuals find themselves (Abes, Jones, & McEwan, 2007). Abes, Jones, and McEwan argued these intersections within power structures pair with the developmental complexity of our meaning-making process to create a filter through which we are able to strain external forces and value structures. This process results in our sensemaking.

The stories we tell about ourselves—our self-narratives—are a product of our positionality and the resulting sensemaking we do about our experiences. Fit is the evolving outcome of this storytelling in work situations. Once we get past that initial intuitive sense of "this place might work for me," or anticipated fit, student affairs professionals engage in a complex navigation of the culture, structure, and values of departments, student affairs divisions, university environments, and professional norms in which we extend and iterate our ongoing conceptions of fit.

A narrative theory of fit suggests that we make sense of our experiences *in medias res*, or in the middle of things (Shipp & Jansen, 2011). By considering what has happened before, what is happening now, and what we think will happen in the future, we make sense of our position in the institution through our stories about our experiences. Who we are; what our outlook on life is; our stance as an activist, pragmatist, or party-line person; the environments in which we have been educated and mentored; and the importance we place on each of these dynamics (Shipp & Jansen, 2011) will influence these stories. Moreover, we continually negotiate the priority we place on these sometimes conflicting, sometimes mutually reinforcing aspects of our worldview and environment. When our sensemaking reveals a lack of fit, a choice is presented on how to proceed: deny, avoid, or change.

It is this choice, or crossroads, that is the seat of fit as narrative agency. The stories we tell ourselves about and through our experiences expose the dynamics inherent in our working lives. Two of us may have experienced the same graduate level course, were in the same staff meeting, had the same mentors, or worked in the same division, but how we move through those experiences will be determined by our worldview, sense of agency, and our social location among the inequality regimes at work in our institution. *Agency* is the feeling we have that we can effect change in our work lives; it is bound by a sense of power, will, and desire (O'Meara & Campbell, 2011). How much agency we can bring to our situation may play a role in whether we feel we fit and what kinds of changes we can make to our expectations or environment to make that fit better (Johnson, Tain, Chang, & Kawamoto, 2013).

In terms of fit, these agentic choices may result in fitting or misfitting, and the choice to misfit may be the only way we can be authentic to ourselves or to the student communities for whom we advocate. Other times, our choice to fit will feel unreal, like a hologram, when we present the version of ourselves that is expected or demanded by the situation to survive for another day. Still, at other times, fitting is being completely ourselves and having that self be honored and met with appreciation and gratitude. Fitting is finding a story we can (mostly) live with to account for ourselves and will be the story of our experiences as misfits, holograms, and authentic selves.

The University as an Organization Embedded With Inequality Regimes

Our experiences with fit and the narratives we produce about ourselves within our professional lives will be the function of how we navigate the organizational terrain of our universities. While the local specifics of how organizations operate vary widely, we argue that all organizations have gender, class, race, and sexual identity assumptions and privileges baked into how they operate (Alvesson, 2002; Smith, 2005). These dynamics are not functions of these institutions alone, but are enacted at the local, departmental, divisional, institutional, and professional levels (Jansen & Kristof-Brown, 2006). These nested subcultures greatly affect the experience of each professional and may produce location-specific experiences.

We have used as a starting point Acker's (1990, 2006, 2012) theories proposing how organizations are embedded with inequality regimes. Inequality regimes are invisible systems and structures comprising practices, beliefs, and values that prioritize and reward particular ways of being (Acker, 2012). Acker's (1990) theory of the gendered organization suggests that all work organizations have practices, cultures, and values that presume (a) an unfettered commitment to work; (b) a lack of embodiedness in that work commitment; and (c) a series of arrangements that reinforce those practices, cultures, and values to deeply embed them in how the organization operates. The result is a conceptualized ideal worker who performs according to a perfect script and embodies the hologrammed existence demanded by the organization. It is in the better interest of work organizations to ignore outside-of-work obligations, previous life experiences, and experiences that relate to the social inequalities of the world, and to expect only productive, committed workers.

These demands are how universities enact their role as greedy institutions, demanding total commitment to the purposes and goals of organizations (Coser, 1974). Navigating this greediness becomes even trickier with education institutions; their ostensible "good" motives and goals of educating global citizens, creating new knowledge, and engaging their communities often elicit narratives that being of service to these goals is sufficient reward for the totality of commitment. Analyzing how these institutions might be exploitative can make one susceptible to allegations of being motivated by the wrong things or not prioritizing the needs of students or others who are served.

Acker (2006, 2012) expanded her initial concept of the gendered organization to the broader term *inequality regimes*, which accounts for a wider set of practices that mark Whiteness, ability, maleness, straightness, middle-age, and other dynamics as hallmarks of ideal workers. Inequality regimes function by guiding how people are hired, by structuring how labor is divided among employees and how wages are distributed, by informal interactions between individuals at work, and by how supervision is enacted. Inequality regimes will vary in their visibility and legitimacy in the work environment (Acker, 2006). Inequality regimes will privilege those who have been deemed most like the ideal, who have been deeply enculturated into those practices, or who are willing to project the right hologram.

Following are some examples of how these inequality regimes might work in student affairs. Hiring in student affairs often uses daylong on-campus interviews that privilege those who are extraverted and energized by interactions with new people, rather than those who are more introverted and need reflection and quiet time. In terms of how labor is organized, in many campus unions the professional staff in leadership tend to be White, while custodial staff and staff working in programs specifically serving underrepresented populations tend to be people of color. Informal interactions also serve to enforce inequality regimes, such as a department director asking a new hire who identifies as lesbian if she has a husband or failing to incorporate language reflective of culture-based fraternities and sororities into discussions of recruitment and intake. Finally, supervisors may presume that single employees are more available for late night or weekend responsibilities than their partnered or parenting counterparts, unevenly distributing work among peers. These are just a handful of examples of how inequality regimes may function to deny individual characteristics, preferences, or needs and to reinforce the modes of ideal work in the student affairs profession.

Methods

We came together as colleagues who have served in student affairs roles at various institutional types and career stages to write scholarly personal narratives (Nash & Bradley, 2011). *Student affairs professionals*, as defined here, encompasses those who do direct student services work, educate student affairs professionals, and advocate for student affairs professionals on a broader stage. Scholarly personal narratives allowed each of us to let our experiences speak to the scholarly topic at hand—that of fit as narrative agency through institutional inequality regimes. A scholarly personal narrative approach does not seek to provide definitive evidence, but rather offers testimony of personal experience that resonates with readers and helps them to engage in their own process of self-discovery (Nash & Bradley, 2011). In the process of creating the scholarly personal narratives, the practitioner-scholars have engaged in their own process of deep reflection on, and analysis of, their experiences in the profession, offering insights into what those experiences have meant. By connecting our personal stories to the theoretical frame, we hope that the stories we tell about ourselves serve to help others understand how, when, and why we fit—or experience misfit—and how the understanding of fit as narrative agency advanced in this chapter may inform one's own knowledge of self and institution.

The first author contacted current and former student affairs professionals with whom she had professional or personal relationships to serve as coauthors of and contributors to this chapter. While a diversity of multiple identities was sought in recruiting coauthors (Abes, Jones, & McEwen, 2007), we cannot claim to be representative of the field as whole. Instead, we believe our individual experiences, backgrounds, and viewpoints, intersecting in our unique satellite of identities, can offer multiple views and experiences with fit. The filters we applied in constructing our fit narratives and expressing our identity commitments were revealing. For some of us, our desire to work as an ally, advocate, or educator around issues of justice was prominent in our narratives; for others of us, despite a strong emphasis of these roles in our professional lives, these commitments featured less prominently in the narratives themselves. Not surprisingly, the coauthors of color centered these desires and activisms more centrally than the White coauthors.

Table 4.1 summarizes key pieces of information about our identities (self-identified and defined) for reference. These self-identifications offer some insights into the awareness and ownership of roles as allies and advocates each of us hold, as well as the communities with which we identify. All coauthors have master's degrees; two have doctorates and two are doctoral candidates. An unexpected commonality between most participants was their status as first-generation college students, with all but one participant being among the first in their family to attend a four-year institution. All of us have worked in residence life as undergraduate resident assistants, graduate professionals, or as full-time professionals.

Although we have all signed our names to this chapter, we also chose to use pseudonyms in the analysis of our narratives for a few reasons. First, some of us are sharing stories about our current roles or experiences that were difficult to reveal. Second, the work of analysis, critique, and commentary was made slightly easier through approaching these stories as coming from others, not ourselves. Given the existing relationships among the authors, which were multiple, the pseudonyms allowed us to consider the content of the narratives and mitigated any preexisting conceptions we had of each other. Third, our efforts to be honest about our institutional experiences were enhanced by having the lines between our experiences and our résumés slightly obscured.

Each practitioner-scholar composed a narrative of their fit journey through student affairs. They were also asked to address three prompts in their narratives:

1. Please speak to which aspects of your identities have felt most salient to you in your journey.
2. Please share your student affairs origins stories. What drew you to work in student affairs?
3. How have your experiences with supervision (as supervisor or supervisee) affected your understanding of your fit?

The first author used narrative analysis techniques to draw connections between and across our scholarly personal narratives (Kim, 2016). Each

TABLE 4.1

Self-Reported Characteristics of Coauthors

Pseudonym	Gender Identity	Racial Identity	Class Identity	Sexual Identity	Educational Attainment	First Generation	Additional Identities*
Akari	Female	Asian	Middle	Straight	Master's	No	First Generation U.S. Resident; Experience living abroad
Beau	Man	White and Native American	Raised Low to Middle; Currently Upper Middle	Gay	Doctorate	Yes	Christian
Gene	Transmasculine, nonbinary	Black	Lower Middle	Queer	Doctorate	Yes	Depression, Anxiety, PTSD
Gigi	Cis female	White	Middle	Straight	Master's	Yes	Anxiety
James	Cis male	White	Raised Poor-Working Class; Currently Middle	Straight	Master's	Yes	N/A
Liz	Woman	White	Middle	Straight	Doctoral Candidate	Yes	Anxiety; Single; Feminist
Tito	Male	Black-Latino	Middle Class	Hetero	Doctoral Candidate	Yes	Father, Husband, Grandfather, Allied Womanist

*Each author was asked to identify any identities they felt were important in their journey and experiences in addition to the categories listed.

author's narrative was analyzed to identify key experiences and reflections that shaped their sense of fit. Attention to language, metaphor, and thematic content informed the analysis (Kim, 2016), with specific attention paid to key concepts from the theoretical frame: the role of past, present, and anticipated future events; an expectation of utter commitment to the work; a lack of space for embodiedness or physical reality; and experiences with inequality regimes of class, race, gender and ability manifested through hiring practices, division of labor, wage setting, informal interactions, and supervision. Thematic analysis of this kind draws connections between multiple narratives and the extant literature as well as dominant narratives featured in the media or literature (Riessman, 2008), or, in our case, within student affairs. All authors were then invited to comment, react, and offer suggestions on the analysis, connections drawn, and conclusions provided.

NARRATING OUR FIT

We have shared our stories by addressing the key elements found in our narratives from the theoretical frame: expectations about the ideal worker, experiences with hiring practices and job searches, and experiences with supervision. We further break down these elements of our narratives into examples of us enacting holograms, engaging in misfit behavior, or living as our authentic selves. As anticipated, no single narrative landed squarely in just one of these categories. Parsing inequality regimes in this way, as authentic selves, holograms, or misfits, has also allowed us to address how inequality regimes may have served us, as well as harmed or restricted us. We conclude with a section on stray observations; these experiences and insights did not fall neatly inside the package of the theoretical frame but are still essential for understanding who we are and what we have learned about fit through this process.

Expectations of the Ideal

Across our narratives, there were several permutations of running up against standards of the ideal way to do the work or be a student affairs professional. Some of these encounters were positive, some were negative, and some were a source of continual challenge.

Authentic Selves

For most of us, our entry into the field of student affairs was driven by dual needs: a need for home (literally or metaphorically) and some initial experience of acceptance for who we were. This came about through mentors identifying the positive contributions we made to our campus communities or postgraduation reflections on the activities that had most fulfilled, challenged, or excited us during our undergraduate years.

James entered his undergraduate institution with little money, no safety net, and a strong work ethic. He held multiple jobs, stretched single meal card swipes into multiple meals, donated plasma, and thought he was simply living the "poor college student" life. A job in residence life provided him housing and a paycheck and allowed him to graduate college debt-free. After graduating and working in manual labor and other low-skill jobs, James realized that his work as a resident assistant had been not just financially stable but also fulfilling. Gene was a homeless college student who found their way into campus engagement for similar reasons—they needed a place to live and a way to pay their bills. A mentor encouraged Gene to pursue graduate education; this mentor admired their passion and commitment to others with marginalized identities and thought they could make a difference.

Tito sought professional work in residence life because it seemed like a good way to provide for his young family while also being affirmed by a Black woman mentor and supervisor. For Liz, early struggles to find a place at her undergraduate campus led her to be involved in Greek life. Like James, she did not consider student affairs to be a career option until after graduation, when a sales job working with undergraduate students highlighted what she liked (helping students) and what she did not like (working on commission). Akari was involved as a resident assistant as an undergraduate and saw a natural alignment between her skills and the traits needed in the field. Gigi felt valued and appreciated in her undergraduate community through her involvement and engagement in student affairs–supported activities and took an entry-level position in residence life a year after completing her bachelor's degree.

Each of us entered this field because we felt recognized, confident, qualified, excited, and intrigued by the possibilities offered through this profession. The acceptance and values that were communicated to us as undergraduate students formed the foundations for what we expected the field to be and, for some us, have served as a source of conflict as we have navigated our careers. Beau's narrative expressed this tension most clearly. Beau realized in the fall of his senior year that he could parlay his work as a resident assistant into a career and was offered a position at his faith-based alma mater upon graduation. The tight integration of student services into academic affairs meant that the curricular and cocurricular portions of the campus experience were deeply intertwined. Both the academic and social aspects of campus life at his college were grounded in the faith traditions of the sponsoring denomination. As he wrote:

> [Institution] provided my foundational experience of student affairs. It is the institution I attended for my undergraduate degree and where I became a resident assistant. It is the institution that offered me a full-time residence director position on the day of my graduation. A position I accepted and worked in for three years while I got my master's in higher education and began teaching as an adjunct. Though my view of student affairs has greatly diversified since my time at [Institution], my experiences there and development as a person are inextricably linked to my experiences of fit and misfit throughout my career.

He goes on to explain how his feelings of fit and misfit have been a constant tension between the academic and the practical, the scholar and the practitioner. Being formed in his alma mater's image of an ideal professional, one who integrates the curricular and the cocurricular with faith, his path to finding another role that fully accepts him and mirrors his ideal has been long and winding.

Holograms

Many of us experienced situations in which we were asked, explicitly or implicitly, to be something other than what we are. The institutions in which we have worked are complex places with competing agendas. For a variety of reasons, we felt required to project an image of meeting the expectations of the role of a student affairs professional in ways that hid essential parts of ourselves.

For Akari, her first post-master's degree position was an opportunity to challenge herself. She moved across the country from an urban to a more rural setting and, upon arriving at the campus for her residential life position, realized that her racial identity became the first thing that people noticed about her. The lack of other people with Asian identities serving in administrator roles on the campus gave her no natural allies or role models. Her self-esteem and confidence began to erode as she struggled to manage microaggressions both on campus and off.

I needed to learn how to deal with these moments of discomfort in a way that was firm and productive, and I didn't later regret what I said or didn't say in response to difficult moments. Through many hours of internal dialogue, I realized that I can allow my self-doubt to take over or I can develop resilience to the negativity that occupied my mind. I reminded myself that I would gain more from this experience by looking for ways I fit in rather than looking for ways that I don't. What qualities do I possess, how do I authentically present them, and what long-lasting contributions can I make to my community? I honed in on my ability to be adaptable without compromising parts of my identity and values.

Akari had to reprioritize her identity commitments, natural sources of strength, and solidarity to fit the model of a confident, at-ease professional demanded by her environment. Akari's decision to focus on points of connection between herself and others illustrated an active choice to tighten the filter described by Abes and colleagues (2007) to limit some external forces from her environment. Akari's ability to shift from being defined by her identities (i.e., a socialized mind) to considering herself as an individual with multiple identities (i.e., a self-authored mind) that she could actively prioritize allowed her to construct a hologram which was helpful to her professionally and healthier to her personally given the agentic nature of her choice (Kegan & Lahey, 2001).

It may seem strange to call this a moment of hologram projection, but it shows that we are often forced to fake it until we make it in challenging environments. While Akari feels she gained strength from this realignment of her point of view, she had also not been prepared for these possibilities because she had been shaped, like Beau, in a particular environment. She was used to working and living in a diverse region that afforded her some invisibility and in which microaggressions[2] did not feel so personal. She did not feel able to express these concerns publicly to garner support from her colleagues but instead had to engage in an internal realignment to project a hologram of professionalism.

Beau completed his undergraduate and graduate education at a small, private faith-based college. His first professional role was also at this institution. As already discussed, his vision and ideal of an integrated curricular and cocurricular experience was based on his positive experiences there. However, this sense of rightness was challenged as he worked to reconcile his strong faith identity with his identity as a gay man:

> I was unwilling to leave the church or forsake my faith life and after years of trying to change my identity, I realized this was not possible. By the time I was in my master's, I began to question the mutual exclusion of my faith and sexual identities from scriptural, philosophic, and identity-formation angles. My exposure to student development theory certainly aided my progression from self-hatred to self-understanding and love. . . . Once I had decided I was ready to come out personally, I felt the need to hold off until I completed an upcoming career transition knowing that I would have lost my job otherwise.

Although much of Beau's challenges with reconciling these competing commitments were internally driven, he was also working and learning in an environment that reinforced a mutually exclusive view of faith and his sexuality. Even when he was at a place of internal acceptance, he had to maintain the hologram that he was straight to keep his job and remain financially secure. While Beau felt intense emotional stress from being in the closet after reconciling his sexuality, his ability to maintain the hologram was aided both by a decision to depart from his current institution and a growing awareness that he wasn't a "gay Christian" but rather that he was an individual with these, and other, identities.

Both Liz and Gene wrote about their struggles with acceptance of their mental health struggles in the field of student affairs. Gene, a transmasculine man, wrote about how some of these pressures came to a head while they were in graduate school, leading to a suicide attempt. In addition, Gene's struggles with depression have been tied, in some ways, to struggles for acceptance as a nonbinary queer person by family and other significant others. Gene also struggles with the linkages others might make between these identities:

> There is always tension between my mental health and my identity as trans*. Trans bodies are constantly under scrutiny, especially by those involved in the medical industrial complex. One of my biggest fears is that someone will link my mental health with my trans identity. Meaning, they might see my transness as a symptom of my mental health and not as an intersectional identity. Having to navigate the academy has meant having to negotiate silence when it comes to my mental health.

Gene's hesitation to share their experiences with colleagues within the field is understandable. It is far easier to project a hologram of perfect mental health than to risk being seen as irreparably damaged by misinformed others. Gene's narrative around this, in particular, highlights that those who hold the least understood or supported positionalities have the most to lose by rejecting the ideal (D'Augelli, 1994). Holograms become essential to their navigation of hostile environments.

For Liz, a lifelong struggle with anxiety and depression has always served as a source of shame. Entering a doctoral program and managing a student affairs assistantship exacerbated both her anxiety and depression. Fear of looking incompetent led her to hide these elements of who she is:

> The shame surrounding these parts of who I am features large when I have days when I cannot get out of bed. I use coded language to discuss feeling badly—stomachaches, migraines, etc.—because I don't know how to tell a supervisor that I won't be there due to overwhelming sadness. It has been in working with students who struggle similarly that I have developed a different approach. I want to model an openness with them that allows them to share their own struggles because I understand.

Liz has developed trusting relationships with particular supervisors where she can explain her "codes" to them, so that she can be honest later about how she was struggling. Despite the narratives about responding to the mental health issues among college students, neither Gene nor Liz have felt there was space for them to be open with these struggles within the student affairs profession. The shame, stigma, and lack of understanding in our culture around mental health means that many students and student affairs professionals feel they must project a hologram to cover this part of themselves to be perceived as successful.

Misfits

There were few misfits on the general expectations of the work described in the professionals' narratives. In part, as has been highlighted, we entered this profession with high hopes and strong faith in the goals and purposes of the field. However, two of us are currently taking a break from student affairs and higher education. Liz left the field to explore other public-sector work through a full-time internship within the federal government while she is finishing her doctorate. Another contributor, Gigi, left the field and is still unsure if she will return. Gigi wrote:

I took my final role because I thought it was a high-functioning community where I could be a student affairs generalist. I thought I could create new programming, focus on one functional area, and still have a life outside of work. . . . Less than two years later, I met with my boss, expressing that I felt close to a breakdown after a series of crises left me working every day for two months. I was told that as a salaried employee, I needed to work until the work was done. The truth is the work will never be done in such a complex environment. As the stress at work built up from role to role, I had lost the ability to be resilient, and I was diagnosed with anxiety. Shortly thereafter, I submitted my notice.

Gigi made the choice to remove herself from the profession to protect her well-being, regain her sense of self-respect, and refocus on her priorities. While her entire career was not filled with these exact kinds of incidents, the bad outweighed the good. The ethics of professionalism, theory- and research-grounded practice, and self-care that she was encouraged to cultivate and consider during her graduate training were rarely enacted at the universities at which she worked. The difference between the espoused values of the field and her lived experiences proved too much to bear.

James, while working at a private liberal arts college with a wealthy student population, struggled with reconciling feeling connected to devoted and wonderful coworkers and the casual acceptance and indulgence of a harmful student culture at the institution. James felt a constant tension, unidentified at the time, with a student body that was predominantly very wealthy. The students at this college preferred an aesthetic culture that borrowed markers from the working class (beat-up cars, cheap beer, "work" clothes) while simultaneously verbally reminding staff of the tuition they paid. This borrowing of identity markers that James authentically held made him feel invisible and disconnected. When he attempted to hold them accountable in terms of the student conduct code or speak his concerns to fellow staff, he was often shut down because the student affairs culture was permissive and catered to the students' view of themselves.

My inability to reconcile how professional, creative, intelligent colleagues could surround me and yet still feel so out of place in my work tormented me. In the time since, I've come to understand myself better and, in turn, why I felt thwarted in my work, depressed in my personal life, and why I eventually left the position as a matter of emotional survival with little personal savings, no concrete job prospects, and no future plan.

James, like Gigi, had to quit a position because he was not capable of managing these discrepancies long term. He realized after leaving the role that he needed to work with students who had backgrounds more similar to his and that this would create a feeling of home.

We all encountered struggles with aspects of the ideal. When we are made invisible because who we are cannot be tolerated in a particular professional context, we are denying opportunities for authentic engagement with others and for role modeling to students and other professionals how to navigate these challenges. Beau, Gene, and Liz reveal that despite the professional rhetoric of the field, many student affairs professionals feel they must hide parts of who they are to successfully navigate their professional spaces.

When the espoused ideal of values of the field are expressed and felt by us, we are our most capable. These include items such as social justice and inclusion, student development and learning, leadership, and ethical foundations (ACPA & NASPA, 2015). For most of us, we experienced the enactment of these values during our lives as undergraduate students. These experiences formed the foundation of our psychological contracts, or sense of mutual obligations, with the field, which were broken at times (O'Meara, Bennett, & Niehaus, 2016). In other words, the implicit expectation that those ideals would also shape how we would be treated as professionals in the field loomed large for us, and when we were not treated in that way, there was a sense of disappointment, disengagement, and broken trust with the profession. Many of us asked variations of the question: Why do we articulate a set of values for our work with students that do not translate to our work with each other? As Gene expressed, "If we truly want to foster a sense of belonging on our campuses, we must genuinely meet people where they are at. This mantra is not just for our students. Belonging does not stop on the student level."

Being Hired and Accepting the Job

The conversation about fit most strongly features in discussion of student affairs careers as professionals enter the job market. Student affairs master's programs often spend a lot of time reminding graduating students that they are looking for the right fit, that they are interviewing the campuses just as much as they are being interviewed (Renn & Hodges, 2007). Most of us entered the profession prior to the Great Recession of 2008, so these narratives of choice did not sound as ridiculous as they might now to those who are facing a tight job market and feel pressure to accept any institution that might be willing to have them. We share here our experiences of both being selected for and not selected for a job.

Authentic Selves

For Tito, finding the right position for most of his career was about being seen by, and recognizing a version of himself in, potential supervisors. These gatekeepers worked their internal systems to open the door for him. He writes that his wife "had grown accustomed to the pattern of securing the next position. I would go to a conference, I would interview and I would come back gushing about someone I had met and how I wanted to work for them." For each of his previous positions, he saw a potential mentor in one of his colleagues or supervisors who exemplified skills he hoped to improve on. For Tito, fit was often about the interpersonal, not the institutional.

Liz was choosing between two similar positions for her first job, both in residence life at small, private, highly selective, residential, liberal arts colleges in the same region of the same state. She felt strong fit with colleagues at one and students at the other. She bet on the students and found herself in a community where "I felt like I could be authentically myself—and that was met with an equal recognition from my friends and colleagues." Her long-lasting connection with colleagues and former students at this institution have reaffirmed her sense of fit, even as she has moved into other roles.

After resigning from a position that was both sublime and surreal, James relocated to the West Coast. His partner had secured a full-time student affairs position in her home state, but James did not have any strong job prospects. After 18 months of searching, he had 2 back-to-back on-campus interviews at the same campus for different positions. He had completed his second on-campus interview on the second day and was walking through the student center when he ran into Jack, the supervisor for the first position he had interviewed with the prior day. Wearing the same, and only, suit he owned, James recalled how awkward he felt during the interaction. Much to his delight, however,

> Jack called that afternoon to offer me the job. He later confided in me that he figured I must have had another interview on campus and rushed back to push through the hiring approval before he "lost me." After my long, arduous search and all the self-doubt, Jack sharing this with me helped me restore my faith in myself. I felt valued for my abilities and my identity and began the longest and most satisfying tenure of my academic career.

James' experience of being affirmed by a future supervisor who ignored the obvious awkwardness of the situation was restorative. Working with students in a federal TRIO program, James' background as a low-income, first-generation student had finally been seen as an asset. Owning only one suit and wearing it two days in a row was not a liability, it was an affirmation of the commonalities he might have with his students and the understanding he could bring to the position. His authentic self was valued.

Holograms

The hiring process for most jobs is a projection of a hologram. Candidates refine cover letters and résumés attempting to project the attributes, values, and experiences they perceive universities most want to see. As mentioned, James was on the student affairs job market for 18 months before being hired. During that time, he worked lower-skill jobs to maintain an income during his 2-career hiring process. He regularly felt the need to strip responsibilities and complex language from his résumé to be considered for entry-level jobs in the field. James had to project a hologram that assured potential employers that he was genuinely interested in entry-level roles.

Gigi experienced a different kind of hologram: By narrowing the focus of her search to certain characteristics, she stepped into several roles where the cultures challenged her values as a professional. At one institution, there was no value placed on professional development and therefore no expectation for staff to evolve with the changing best practices of the field. At another, students were not sufficiently engaged in their own learning. Gigi regretted the questions she did not ask. Both she and the institution projected holograms, creating a severe lack of fit that could not be overcome by hard work, a positive attitude, or better communication.

Tito has been asked to project a different kind of hologram. He recently applied for a higher-level position at his institution. As an internal candidate who had lovingly given of himself to the campus for many years, he had been assured and affirmed by members of the campus community that he was the obvious successor to his retiring supervisor. Yet an external candidate was selected. In his narrative, he shifts into the third person as he recounts this experience, noting that the shift is in part because he is still narrating and sensemaking this part of his journey:

> Tito did not get the position and this wounded Tito. His labor became invisible. The positive feelings Tito had about [Institution], about working

and serving at [Institution], were now filled with shame. . . . [Institution] was a more complicated space for Tito now. The fit no longer felt exact. Tito was still well compensated. The benefits (particularly for his kids' tuition) were phenomenal. Beyond that, though, Tito found it necessary to ask himself what was important about the work that he was doing there and how he was doing it. Could he still be the best version of himself personally and professionally?

Tito is still struggling with the result of this hiring choice. For the sake of staff unity and his own sense of professionalism, he has had to work well with his new boss. He has had to remain positive for others, even when he has not felt positive for himself. He has had to project the hologram of "okay-ness" for it to maybe, eventually, become okay.

Misfits

Given the nature of the hiring processes, misfitting is often signaled by not being hired into a position. Beau, who holds a doctorate and has been a faculty member in a student affairs graduate program, experienced this messaging throughout his attempts to navigate and find a "good-fit" faculty position.

> I received feedback from hiring committees where I've applied for clinical professorships articulating a specific desire for hybrid faculty that work and teach in student affairs, saying, "With your publication record and research agenda, the committee felt we should bring you in as a traditional tenure-track faculty member." . . . Other hiring committees have argued that there were concerns regarding my enthusiasm for getting involved "beyond the department"—in other words, articulating a desire for collaborative work within student affairs.

These conflicting messages made securing the right kind of faculty job almost impossible for Beau. It also raises questions about why these dual commitments—to both engagement with practitioners and engagement with scholarship—appear to be so untenable for faculty roles in student affairs. Beau resolved this conflict, somewhat unexpectedly, by finding a position outside a single institution and within the world of higher education associations where he could engage both commitments.

The role of the hiring process is designed to allow employers to make a fit determination; however, individual managers and search committees often reinforce inequality regimes across the profession by creating untenable standards. This reinforcement can happen in a number of ways, including lack of transparency to prospective candidates regarding the challenges and dynamics of a particular position or perpetuating myths about how a candidate and their work will be evaluated. Further, even those standards that seem objective, such as years of prior experience or availability to work certain schedules, may be grounded in the experiences of privileged powerholders and reinforce the concepts of the ideal worker. Common pieces of wisdom abound in the student affairs professional community that reinforce inequality regimes in our profession, such as: Stay too long in one position, and you may be considered problematic or unambitious; supervisors always need prior supervisory experience; residence life skills are transferrable to all other areas of student affairs, except when they aren't. Student affairs professionals who are fortunate enough to make choices about where they work need realistic information to guide those choices. Similarly, the institutions that hire them should seek people who are ready and willing to take on the specific challenges present at their universities.

Supervision in Student Affairs

The final common element across our narratives was the role of supervision in our experiences. We have all been supervised, and many of us have been supervisors. While there are pervasive cultures and knowledge associated with the field of student affairs, supervisors can create strong local subcultures that can build on the best of what a university has to offer, counteract the worst of those cultures, or promulgate those structures and practices. Our stories with supervision reflect the importance of such roles, including supervisors' competency and mind-set in creating a welcoming and flexible culture.

Authentic Selves

We felt most powerful and supported in our work in student affairs when our supervisory relationships allowed us to engage as our complete, authentic selves. When we knew our supervisors had our backs or our teams understood our vision, we felt able to take on any task. For example, Gigi had wonderfully supportive supervisors in her early career roles, which allowed her to thrive:

> I know that my ideal work environment provides autonomy and support. The best position I had cultivated both. There, I was trusted and I flourished. When crisis occurred, I leaned on my training and made decisions others supported. I saw theory to practice in my daily work and managed a large staff and complex residential area with confidence and risk-taking.

A robust professional development model, a thriving cohort of supportive professionals, and a deep bench of senior staff who could mentor and encourage her development supported Gigi's experience in this position. These experiences were cultivated by the institution in a way that allowed her to thrive and took advantage of her developed talents.

Tito took advantage of the unconventional approach to student affairs at his university to engage in nontraditional approaches to recruiting and mentoring his staff. He upended the "usual" interview dynamic by having candidates interview him. He gives prospective staff a postinterview assignment to reflect on and assess their perceived fit at the institution and in the prospective role. Tito then uses that assessment to inform the selection of new hires. These early forays into upending the usual hiring process have allowed him to more clearly demonstrate the cultural expectations of his supervisory approach during the search process for new staff. He defines his approach to his work as enacting "love," and he seeks other colleagues who are willing and able to enact this approach:

> I appreciated the vast grey areas and the necessity to engage in the conversation and understand context when making decisions. However, what I quickly fell in love with was my capacity to bend an institution to be more accommodating and equitable in its practices towards historically marginalized students (those that looked like me). This upped the ante on intentionality and on the need to recruit a team that can do the "work." The "work" here is not defined by administrative prowess but by the capacity and willingness to invest emotionally and cognitively.

Here Tito describes how he seeks to increase his own sense of fit within the academy by paving a path for student groups he identifies with (historically marginalized students) within his work and professional approach. He achieves this by hiring staff who share his investments, amplifying his worldview to ensure that every student served by his department is getting a bit of the "love" he is trying to enact.

Similarly, Gene has also taken to heart their experiences with supervision to create a distinctive supervisory style:

> I knew I could not change the culture of [my institution] but I could set departmental standards that were countercultural. One of those standards was a dress code that met the socioeconomic class and positionality of the staffer. . . . When making requirements of my staff, I asked, "Is this accessible?" I did not make assumptions of what my staff could afford or deemed as professional or not professional.

Gene grounded an ethical practice of care for their employees that provided space for them to enact their own versions of professionalism, while simultaneously communicating expectations in supportive ways. As someone whose professional appearance was questioned by their own supervisor, through the "gift" of a new workbag and commentary on their appearance as "urban" and "aggressive," Gene sought to shield their staff from the scrutiny of their superiors. This went beyond setting standards to helping staff identify appropriate work wear at thrift stores and providing clothing to staff when possible. Gene knew that to support staff who were doing the difficult work of supporting marginalized communities, the staff themselves needed to feel valued and accepted for who they were.

Holograms

For many of us, one supervisor might have stood out as offering particularly good or bad conditions for us to thrive. Sometimes, though, the relationship becomes premised on an early hologram that can be difficult to leave behind. Liz's academic adviser had supervised her as a doctoral student for five years. When she began her program, she wanted to be faculty. At many points, she questioned whether academe was the career path for her:

> This truth is difficult to speak aloud in environments where those who desire to be faculty receive more attention, investment, and development from the faculty. It is also a difficult truth when you realize that you are being trained to do one thing: become a faculty member. How do you prepare yourself to do something else? At what point have you invested too much in getting a doctorate to turn back?

Liz has created a desirable hologram of a doctoral student who wants to be a faculty member. She has, at times, so fully enacted the hologram that others challenge her when she expresses doubt about her future. While her faculty adviser has been truly supportive of her unformed and changing plans, Liz continues to agonize over the decision and its meaning for her future. Liz can see the hologram, and recognizes it for what it is, yet continues to question—even in her new full-time position—if she has achieved authentic self.

Misfits

Some supervisors create hostile conditions that demand misfits. We have elaborated how Gene turned a negative experience with a supervisor into a positive culture with their staff. Gene eventually moved on to another university when it regularly became clear that there was little support for their presence on campus. Even earlier in the chapter, we illustrated how Gigi's supervisor poorly responded when she shared that she was drained, exhausted, and needed support.

Supervision is an important part of the experience in any job and is an essential competency in student affairs (Tull, 2006). Gene puts it perfectly when they state in their narrative, "People do not leave jobs, they leave managers." Managers who create a hostile, nonsupportive, nondevelopmental environment will quickly lose staff to other positions, institutions, or fields of work. Given the challenges of the work of student affairs, being able to show an authentic self to a supervisor is a gift; it allows an individual to grow, to fail, to express hurt over experiences, and to regularly reflect on their work. Supervisors get to create the environment that allows a fluidity for more people to fit.

Stray Observations

There were key pieces of our experiences on which comment is warranted. First, while Gigi has currently ended her career in student affairs, she remains optimistic about the promise of how she may find fit in other environments—even potential university environments. Sometimes distance is needed to come back refreshed, centered, and self-aware enough to enact our best selves. Her voice offers a weight to this chapter because her departure from the field indicated a failure of the structures and practices where she has worked—not of her. We would guess that she is not the only person whose spirit has been broken by intractability, lack of caring supervision, and an unrelenting pace of work.

Second, Gene's narrative offers insights into the tension between the espoused values of the field and the lived experience of student affairs professionals. Despite narratives in the field of unflagging support and unconditional acceptance of diverse people, Gene's experiences have indicated that their colleagues within student affairs often engage in actions and behaviors that deviate from their espoused values. Gene has had to find community outside of student affairs in spaces like the Brown Boi Project and bklyn boihood. These have allowed Gene to be held in all their complexities and has kept them connected to community educated organizers who hold their shared commitments. These external spaces have only asked of Gene to be themself. What might a student affairs profession that truly embodies those ideals look like?

Third, this chapter did not have room to delve much into the outside-of-work lives of the contributors and the lessons we might learn from them. Tito's growing family is an important part of what keeps him tethered to love, community, and commitment and emphasizes the role of external support networks in our professional lives. Gigi's recognition of her need for balance to be a committed professional is a call for managers to create flexible work environments that give employees space and time to engage in self-care. Liz's reflections on how the forms of work in which she has engaged have exacerbated her anxiety and depression are an important reminder of the self-awareness we would do well to cultivate. Beau's choice to come out at the time and place of his choosing affirms that we get to decide when we reveal our innermost selves to others. Akari's life in a thriving metropolitan area provides her the energy and anonymity to engage at work and emphasizes that location matters. James's attempts to plant deep roots in a community far from his family is a testament to the idea of making a home where you choose.

Fourth, we wanted to include a note about a commonality that emerged through this process. As a group of individuals who are (mostly) first-generation students, our engagement in this field has been grounded in a desire to make space for those like us, to pay back the spaces and individuals who helped us to be successful in college. York (2016) found that low-income and first-generation participants who engaged in actions to improve spaces for others with whom they identified felt more connected to both their home communities and their institutions. For some of us, student affairs was our first exposure to a profession and concepts of professionalism. Our efforts in student affairs to serve those like ourselves provide opportunities to engage in our professional communities without leaving behind the communities we came from. This lens on our work is important, and we do not take for granted the opportunities afforded us in attending and working in university spaces.

CLOSING THOUGHTS AND CALL TO ACTION

For many of us, the effort of writing the narrative was the first time we put into words the story of how we got to where we are and what has been meaningful to us in our journey through the student affairs profession. It is easy to think of fit as a one-time experience, something to think about only when we are job searching. Instead, we have found that our experience with fit varies across our experiences and changes as the institution reveals more of itself to us. Sometimes, we are surprised by how much a position can teach us about ourselves and connect us with something we have known all along but never put into words. Other times, institutional actors reveal the real priorities of the organization, and we are shocked that we fell for a false narrative or were blinded by a fancy name.

From our narratives, we see the ways universities allow practices to exist that deny the complexity of who we are. Whether those are struggles with mental health, with extreme class differences between students and the staff who serve them, with faith structures that tell us we are an abomination, or fearful comments that our background as a New York City kid has made us too rough for these rarefied halls, institutions, and the people who embody them, reveal their values as they attempt to make us invisible, secondary, or unloved. We are not naïve enough to think that behind these ivy-covered hallowed halls there exists an oasis from the struggles of the world. We do take issue, however, with the disparity between the espoused values of the field and the practices of so many professionals and scholars that indicates a lack of even trying to understand the multiplicity of identities that might coexist in the field. What would happen if we took seriously the notion of meeting people where they are? Could we create organizations that push back, just a little, on the harshness of the world? Could we create spaces for students that provide a learning environment that both challenges and supports their full selves? One that doesn't coddle, but that develops their skills, abilities, and cognition to equip them to be change agents who create a more just and equitable society?

As a community of professionals, it would behoove us to actively and strategically deconstruct these inequality regimes. Especially for those student affairs professionals who more easily conform to the demands of these regimes, it is important to take stock of when we are projecting a hologram and to ask ourselves what is at stake if we fail to project this image. There may be strides to be gained if those of us who have more latitude to break the unwritten rules of inequality regimes do so a little more often to provide cover for those who must break them.

Efforts to deconstruct these inequality regimes are often met with opposition and can feel risky or dangerous. We notice that within our narratives, masculine-identified participants often had more position-based power (as supervisors and directors), despite the women coauthors having similar tenure in the field, which allowed them to engage in more directive efforts to shape the field and push against existing power regimes. What is unclear is whether this observation is connected to gender, position, some interaction of the two, or is merely coincidental. We are not suggesting that others of us do not push back or that any one way of doing so is more effective, but there are some forms of change efforts that might be more legible. Our ability to make our change efforts legible to others is often predicated on a combination of positional power as well as the regimes we are working to deconstruct.

Because creating change in these systems requires personal, positional, and professional efforts, we recommend the following four activities to improve our field:

1. Individuals should identify ways in which they benefit from inequality regimes at their institutions and take steps to push against them when their power and positionality allow them the latitude to do so. They should also take steps to amplify and recognize the efforts of others that may not be as visible, but that still help to push change.
2. Departmental supervisors should integrate regular (at least once a year) opportunities for student affairs professionals (at all levels) to critically explore power structures within their department, institution, community, and the wider field.
3. Institutional leaders must commit to campus climate studies (at least every three years) that take seriously the lived experiences of students, faculty, and staff to inform decision-making.
4. Professional associations should consider the ways in which they can provide cover to historically underrepresented individuals in the field by highlighting inequities and power dynamics and publicly committing in word and action to their rectification.

While these recommendations cannot in and of themselves end inequality regimes, they can help to develop a praxis of reflection, critique, and change that infuses the profession.

In thinking about fit theoretically, we emphasized the role of agency in navigating these regimes; an individual praxis of fit is the result of the choices made available by the inequality regimes in which we operate. By engaging the language of holograms, misfits, and authentic selves, we have highlighted how these regimes may work and may not work for us and the paths they offer as we move through the world. The range of choices available to each of us have varied because of what we bring to the profession in terms of our bodies, our histories, our preferences, and our resilience at the times choices were to be made. The profession's praxis of fit widens or constrains the range of choices available to its members, and we suggest that the profession must focus on widening the range for all its members.

NOTES

1. For the purposes of this chapter, we use the term *university* to encompass the broad range of institutional types at which student affairs professionals work.

2. *Microaggressions* "are the verbal, behavioral, and environmental indignities, whether intentional or unintentional, that communicate hostile, derogatory, or negative racial slights and insults to the target person or group" (Sue, Capodilupo, Torino, Bucceri, Holder, Nadal, & Esquilin, 2007, p. 273).

REFERENCES

Abes, E. S., Jones, S. R., & McEwen, M. K. (2007). Reconceptualizing the model of multiple dimensions of identity: The role of meaning-making capacity in the construction of multiple identities. *Journal of College Student Development*, 48(1), 1–22. doi:10.1353/csd.2007.0000

Acker, J. (1990). Hierarchies, jobs, bodies: A theory of gendered organizations. *Gender & Society*, 4(2), 139–158. doi:10.1177/089124390004002002

Acker, J. (2006). Inequality regimes: Gender, class, and race in organizations. *Gender & Society*, 20(4), 441–464. doi:10.1177/0891243206289499

Acker, J. (2012). Gendered organizations and intersectionality: Problems and possibilities. *Equality, Diversity and Inclusion: An International Journal*, 31(3), 214–224.

Alvesson, M. (2002). *Understanding organizational culture*. Thousand Oaks, CA: SAGE.

American College Personnel Association, & National Association of Student Personnel Administrators. (2015). *Professional competency areas for student affairs educators*. Professional Competencies Task Force. Washington DC: Authors. Retrieved from https://www.naspa.org/images/uploads/main/ACPA_NASPA_Professional_Competencies_FINAL.pdf

Bacal, J., Bacal, J., Griffin, T., & Loesch, M. (Producer)s. (1985). *Jem and the holograms* [Television series]. Los Angeles, CA: Hasbro, Toei Animation, Sunbow Productions & Marvel Productions.

Billsberry, J., Ambrosini, V., Moss-Jones, J., & Marsh, P. (2005). Some suggestions for mapping organizational members' sense of fit. *Journal of Business and Psychology, 19*(4), 555–570.

Coser, L. A. (1974). *Greedy institutions: Patterns of undivided commitment*. New York, NY: Free Press.

Crenshaw, K. (1991). Mapping the margins: Intersectionality, identity politics, and violence against women of color. *Stanford Law Review, 43*, 1241–1299.

D'Augelli, A. R. (1994). Identity development and sexual orientation: Toward a model of lesbian, gay, and bisexual development. In E. J. Trickett, R. J. Watts, & D. Birman (Eds.), *Human diversity: Perspectives on people in context* (pp. 312–333). San Francisco, CA: Jossey-Bass.

Jansen, K. J., & Kristof-Brown, A. (2006). Toward a multidimensional theory of person-environment fit. *Journal of Managerial Issues, 18*(2), 193–212.

Johnson, R. E., Tain, M. U., Chang, C. C., & Kawamoto, C. K. (2013). A self-regulation approach to person-environment fit. In A. L. Kristof-Brown & J. Billsberry (Eds.), *Organizational fit: Key issues and new directions* (pp. 74–98). New York, NY: Wiley-Blackwell.

Jones, S. R., & McEwen, M. K. (2000). A conceptual model of multiple dimensions of identity. *Journal of College Student Development, 41*(4), 405–414.

Kegan, R., & Lahey, L. L. (2001). *How the way we talk can change the way we work: Seven languages for transformation*. San Francisco, CA: Jossey-Bass.

Kim, J. (2016). *Understanding narrative inquiry: The crafting and analysis of stories as research*. Washington DC: SAGE.

Kristof-Brown, A. L., & Billsberry, J. (2013). Fit for the future. In A. L. Kristof-Brown & J. Billsberry (Eds.), *Organizational fit: Key issues and new directions* (pp. 1–18). New York, NY: Wiley-Blackwell.

Nash, R. J., & Bradley, D. L. (2011). *Me-search and re-search: A guide for writing scholarly personal narrative manuscripts*. Charlotte, NC: Information Age Publishing, Inc.

O'Meara, K., Bennett, J. C., & Niehaus, E. (2016). Left unsaid: The role of psychological contracts in faculty departure. *Review of Higher Education, 39*(2), 269–297.

O'Meara, K., & Campbell, C. M. (2011). Faculty sense of agency in decisions about work and family. *The Review of Higher Education, 34*(3), 447–476. doi:10.1353/rhe.2011.0000

Renn, K. A., Hodges, J. P. (2007). The first year on the job: Experiences of new professionals in student affairs. *NASPA Journal, 44*(2), 367–391.

Riessman, C. K. (2008). *Narrative methods for the human sciences.* Thousand Oaks, CA: SAGE.

Shipp, A. J., & Jansen, K. J. (2011). Reinterpreting time in fit theory: Crafting and recrafting narratives of fit *in medias res. Academy of Management Review, 36*(1), 76–101.

Smith, D. E. (2005). *Institutional ethnography: A sociology for people.* New York, NY: AltaMira Press.

Sue, D. W., Capodilupo, C. M., Torino, G. C., Bucceri, J. M., Holder, A., Nadal, K. L., & Esquilin, M. (2007). Racial microaggressions in everyday life: Implications for clinical practice. *American Psychologist, 62*(4), 271–286.

Tull, A. (2006). Synergistic supervision, job satisfaction, and intention to turnover of new professionals in student affairs. *Journal of College Student Development, 47*(4), 465–480.

Weick, K. E., Sutcliffe, K. M., & Obstfeld, D. (2005). Organizing and the process of sensemaking. *Organization Science, 16*(4), 409–421. doi:10.1287/orsc.1050.0133

York, T. T. (2016). Exploring service-learning outcomes and experiences for low-income, first-generation college students: A mixed-methods approach. *International Journal of Research on Service-Learning and Community Engagement, 4*(1), 309–342.

5

No, I Can't Meet You for an $8 Coffee

How Class Shows Up in Workspaces

Sonja Ardoin and becky martinez

C*LASS IDENTITY* CARRIES a complexity of obscure definitions, fluidity, a sense of taboo, and intersection with other identities. While class is often considered to be solely economic capital—including income and wealth-based assets (e.g., land, home, car)—it is much broader than socio-economic status; involves other forms of capital, such as social capital and cultural capital; and encompasses nuances of the way one experiences daily life, including workspaces. Lubrano (2004) describes class as a "script, map, and guide. It tells us how to talk, how to dress, how to hold ourselves, how to eat, and how to socialize. . . . In short, class is nearly everything about you" (p. 5). Class is replicated through forms of capital; it is fluid and, thus, is constantly being created and recreated (Bourdieu, 1986; Yosso, 2005). In the context of higher education, academic capital is also pervasive (Barratt, 2011) and can be observed from college gear to type of degree. Moreover, although class and education can be connected and are often mistakenly interchanged, education is only one aspect that constructs class and class identity.

Higher education professionals from working class, blue collar, and poor backgrounds experience challenges in the job search and fit processes. These individuals are often expected to leave behind the class in which they were raised, known as *class of origin*, upon entering higher education (hooks, 2000); yet, they often find themselves in a place of "class straddling" where they can "pass" for middle class and are assumed to have "made it," while still experiencing and managing academia through a working-class lens (Hurst, 2007). Yeskel (2014) describes this concept of straddling as "having a foot in two different class realities or being bicultural with respect to class" (p. 3). There is a recognition of existing in distinct class worlds and having to navigate within and between them.

Issues of economic, cultural, social, navigational, academic, and linguistic capital (Yosso, 2005) can arise in every aspect of the job search and beyond—from "professional" dress to office potlucks. And while diversity is a stated value on college campuses, the complex factors of class result in challenging and limited conversations about this dimension of identity (Barratt, 2011). This chapter will explore how higher education's expectations and standards of social mobility and professionalism lead to the devaluing and exclusion of people from working-class or blue-collar backgrounds in the field, many times unconsciously and yet often damaging. This chapter will also suggest ways to view the class capital of poor and working-class individuals as assets and support those from working-class or blue-collar backgrounds to more effectively engage class in creating an inclusive work space.

AUTHOR POSITIONALITY

The topic of class, and subsequently class identity, is a labor of love for both Ardoin and martinez. It is also a very personal, almost sacred, subject matter for them as they engage class both cognitively and emotionally. Ardoin calls a rural, working-class Louisiana community home, despite her current address in a large northeastern city. Both sets of her grandparents were farmers and her parents held a variety of blue-collar jobs throughout their lives. Ardoin is a proud first-generation college student and holds that identity in combination with her newer place in the world as a faculty member with a PhD. She now identifies as a class straddler, owning that, while her income is middle class, many of her other forms of capital range from working class to upper class. Ardoin has experienced and witnessed the impact of class identity in higher education as a student, administrator, and faculty member and chooses to research, write, and present on social class in order to, hopefully, raise further class consciousness in the academy and work toward class equity in education.

martinez comes from a working-class background and more specifically identifies as a farmer at heart. She was raised in a working-class, pseudo-rural town in southern California, which has impacted her current frame, thoughts, and feelings about class and her class identity. As a first-generation college student and first-generation white-collar professional, martinez has found herself in unfamiliar, sometimes unwelcoming spaces having to navigate within and between two distinct class contexts. It was her consciousness of this juncture that prompted her to delve into class and class identity personally and intellectually, eventually leading to her interest and work with class. martinez recognizes the systemic structures intrinsic in academia that create in and out groups, and the need to interrupt and shift the dynamics of class inequity. She and Ardoin offer this piece to center class from the lens of those from poor, blue-collar, or working-class backgrounds as a means to increase understanding of the ways class, and its byproduct of classism, exist in higher education and to offer ways to be mindful of and interact with class through an inclusive framework.

DEFINING *SOCIAL CLASS*

Social class is about more than what individuals do for a living or the economic capital they possess. There are many components of class identity that are invisible. Class extends to include one's belief of "who they are, where they see themselves within their broader community, how they relate to others in society, and how others relate to them" (Svoboda, 2012, p. 37). Although typically presented as dichotomous (i.e., class of origin and current class), an individual's class identity actually comprises the following components: (a) class of origin, (b) current, felt class, and (c) attributed class (Barratt, 2011). *Class of origin* is the class identity into which an individual is born; it is about how one grew up and to what and whom they had access. *Current, felt class* is how one defines their class identity in the present moment. *Attributed class* is the assumptions others make about our class identity. Barratt (2011) summarizes this "tripartite" class identity as "where we came from, what we think of ourselves, and what others think of us" (p. 7).

If one or more of the three components is not in alignment, the individual will have to make choices about how to manage the complexity of their class identity. Hurst (2007; 2010) offers three portrayals of how poor or working-class individuals may choose to reconcile any misalignments: loyalists, renegades, and double agents. *Loyalists* are those who "redefine and commit themselves to the working class. In many ways, their working-class identities become strengthened" (Hurst, 2007, p. 83) through the dissonance they experience in educational institutions. Conversely, *renegades* "embrace assimilation" to the middle class and "transform their class identities . . . by adopting middle-class norms and behaviors" (p. 83). Finally, *double agents* manage their identity as true class straddlers; they pick and choose from aspects of the poor and working-class identity along with pieces from the middle-class identity, varying their choices based on context and community (Hurst, 2010). For example, Rosenblum (2014) describes how she functioned as a double agent:

> I could pretend up to a point but could never feel at ease. . . . Who I was changed according to who was seeing me and what context they knew me in. . . . It took me many years to find a place where all my mixed-up pieces fit. . . . . I am still learning to stop pretending; every year I feel a little bit bolder about just being who I really am. (pp. 194–196)

Because of the multifaceted and often invisible nature of class identity, one of the challenging tasks of discussing class is agreeing on definitions associated with such a complex identity. The concept of class identity is often framed through the work of Pierre Bourdieu (1986), who deconstructed class into economic capital, social capital, and cultural capital. Bourdieu (1986) viewed class through a societal hierarchy, where value was placed on the normative behavior, language, and networks of White middle and upper classes. He believed that poor and working-class individuals, and their broader communities, would have to learn these ways of being—termed *habitus*—to be respected and valued in society.

Additionally, Yeskel and Leondar-Wright's (1997) work on class and classism offers operational definitions of *poor* and *working class* to support this framework. They define *working class* as "the stratum of families whose income depends on hourly wages for labor" (p. 238) and *poor* as "the stratum of families with incomes insufficient to meet basic human needs" (p. 238). However, even these broad definitions focus mostly on income, or economic capital, which limits the ability to fully grasp the wholeness of class identity. While Bourdieu's (1986) concepts are highly utilized and Yeskel and Leondar-Wright's (1997) definitions offer a starting place, these concepts and definitions are also criticized for viewing poor and working-class communities through a deficit lens, similar to many other definitions of *class*. Therefore, when the terms *poor* or *working class* are used in this chapter, we are broadening the terms to their wholeness, including not only socioeconomic status or economic capital but also other forms of capital. As such, critical theory scholars studying class, including the two of us, use Yosso's (2005) community cultural wealth model to reframe class into a value-added or asset perspective.

Critical Framework: Yosso's Community Cultural Wealth Model

Yosso's (2005) community cultural wealth model focuses on "the array of cultural knowledge, skills, abilities, and contacts possessed by socially marginalized groups that often go unrecognized and unacknowledged" (p. 69). The model expands Bourdieu's (1986) concept of cultural capital into the following forms of capital: (a) aspirational, (b) familial, (c) social, (d) navigational, (e) resistant, and (f) linguistic capital (Yosso, 2005). Definitions for each form of capital are provided in Table 5.1.

While the model was originally created for racial and ethnic identities, Yosso's (2005) model has since been applied to social class as a way to consider capitals brought into spaces by poor and working-class individuals from an asset-based perspective. Bourdieu's deficit-based model implies that people need to be indoctrinated into middle- and upper-class ways of being to be successful—in the case of this chapter—in student affairs; conversely, Yosso's asset-based perspective illuminates that people offer a lot just by being who they are. If institutions of higher education, and those who hire for positions within them, can shift their views from the deficit model

TABLE 5.1
Yosso's (2005) Community Cultural Wealth
Model: Six Additional Forms of Capital

Form of Capital	Definition
Aspirational Capital	One's future focus and resiliency
Familial Capital	Connections to one's family and community through kinship and culture
Social Capital	One's network of resources and the use of those resources to assist others
Navigational Capital	"Acknowledges individual agency within institutional constraints" (Yosso, 2005, p. 80)
Resistant Capital	The recognition of inequity and the drive to challenge it
Linguistic Capital	The ability to communicate in more than one language or dialect

of Bourdieu to the asset-based perspective of Yosso, then higher education may begin to see greater value in the perspectives, skill sets, and experiences of poor and working-class professionals. This shift in perspective could create a new lens from which hiring managers and committees see poor and working-class professionals as fits for their positions and a way to increase diversity on campus. It could also aid poor and working-class professionals in finding fit, as well as a sense of wholeness, in the field of higher education.

CLASS AND HIGHER EDUCATION

Education can be experienced as a "harsh version of basic training . . . about class, class conflict, and differing class values," which can result in "class shame and embarrassment" (Collins, Ladd, Seider, & Yeskel, 2014, p. 56), particularly in academia. Higher education often sorts people and opportunities based on class identity, creating barriers with the use of academic jargon, acronyms, and structures that denote in-groups (middle and upper classes) and out-groups (poor and working classes); operational hiring practices that often benefit affluent White men; and socializing formats that favor middle- and upper-class norms. Jargon, such as *hegemony*, *leverage*, and *praxis*, is rooted in the academic and linguistic capital of the middle and upper classes and can ostracize poor and working-class professionals whose academic and linguistic capitals may favor "blue collar" terminology. People may shy away from contributing their perspective if they feel they cannot express themselves, or be received, when using their own language preferences. As for structures, the implicit meaning of professionalism—including language, attire, and behavioral expectations; the various forms and levels of professorship; and navigating a benefits package and retirement plan—clearly separate those who understand such professional structures and those who are disoriented by them. In 2012, the American Council on Education published that approximately 64% of college presidents were White men, presumably upper class given the capital involved with such positions. Because presidents set the foundation for organizational culture, this speaks to the norming and valuing of White, male, middle- to upper-class identities and experiences in the academy (American Council on Education, 2012; Rios, 2015).

In higher education, people from poor and working-class backgrounds often have "feelings of alienation, . . . anger, shame, sorrow, and intimidation" (Hurst, 2007, p. 82) that can lead to imposter syndrome for students, staff, and faculty alike. Begert (2005) writes, "I still feel a certain discomfort in both academic and blue-collar situations. I never feel I have the full birth-right of my peers who were born in academic or upper-middle-class house-holds. . . . [In short, I experience] imposter syndrome" (p. 171). Because class identity has many invisible aspects, poor and working-class individuals in academia frequently believe they are the only ones with their experience who are navigating an environment with a new language and codes of behav-ior (Hurst, 2007). Even when poor and working-class professionals have the self-assurance to discuss class identity, it can "be perceived as whining, as having a chip on the shoulder, or as claiming victimhood" (Arner, 2016, p. 57). Poor and working-class professionals make many sacrifices and expe-rience much guilt in order to join the academy, although this is often not recognized by their colleagues (Warnock, 2016).

When poor and working-class individuals experience differences between their background/home environment and their higher education environ-ment, they often find themselves in a position of "straddling," or living between two very different worlds and having to learn how to operate in each (Collins, 2014; Lubrano, 2004). This can be particularly emphasized for those working at four-year institutions. Hurst (2007) argues that poor and working-class people are faced with a choice to be loyal to their roots or to embrace the bourgeois or middle-class mentality of the academy:

> Working-class people are under great pressure to assimilate in order to suc-ceed, that this assimilation in practice means conforming to certain bourgeois cultural norms, behaviors, and expectations, as well as "leaving behind" those who do not share these norms, behaviors, and expectations. (p. 99)

A similar message is touted by hooks (2000): "There was no place in aca-deme for folks from working-class backgrounds who did not wish to leave the past behind. That was the price of the ticket" (p. 36). However, others, such as Lubrano (2004), suggest that straddling allows one to honor both their poor or working-class roots and their middle-class education or profession. Even when individuals pursue higher education, it does not mean they desire to alter their class identity or participate in class mobility. This is why academic and economic capital are only two of the many aspects of class identity; just because someone has earned a degree or finds themselves with a middle- or upper-class income does not mean they cannot retain their poor or working class of origin, or its other forms of capital, as their current, felt class identity.

In this paradox of different lived class experiences, particularly when pro-fessionals consider themselves as renegades or double agents (i.e., straddlers), the action of code-switching is used to navigate between the home and higher education environments. Because there is an array of class differences ranging from food and language to expectations and ways of being, professionals from poor and working-class backgrounds develop the fluency in their class of origin and in their middle-class work environment. Throughout their time in higher education they learn to speak and act in ways that are the norm in their current middle-class work world, although this can result in feeling inadequate or inauthentic. Whether it is a survival technique or merely an adjustment, code-switching allows those who straddle to effectively exist in differing class surroundings.

Regardless of the self-identity or code one chooses, there is a cost, which frequently results in not feeling at home in either environment; being ostracized by both home and higher education environments; and being identified as a model of meritocracy, or proof that "if you work hard, you can do anything." As poor and working-class folks are earning degrees and seeking staff and faculty roles in colleges and universities, higher education needs to pay attention to how job search processes and job fit characteristics may be limiting poor and working-class folks' ability to obtain positions and find success in the field of higher education.

CLASS AND THE JOB SEARCH

The higher education job search process is a time-consuming, emotional, and logistical endeavor (Ardoin, 2014). Job searching for roles with colleges and universities involves many nuances and contains unwritten rules about the social construct of professionalism and the determination of what, and who, matters. Professionalism can itself be viewed as a form of oppression that favors upper-class, White maleness (Rios, 2015). Class identity can intersect with many aspects of the job search, including but not limited to an individual's alma mater and degrees, style of dress, and negotiation skills.

Institutional Types and Academic Capital

While *class* and *education level* are sometimes used as interchangeable, synonymous terms, this is a limited, narrow way to view class identity. Education level, also described as *scholastic capital*, is only one aspect of many capitals that comprise class identity (Yosso, 2005). Academic capital, aspirational capital, economic capital, and navigational capital can influence if and where an individual attends higher education and how they experience it. As Soria (2016) indicates, many poor and working-class individuals are steered toward community colleges and public, four-year institutions as more economical options and "are less likely to have graduated with prestigious credentials" (p. 131). They also choose institutions close to home, often within 50 miles, which many times limits the number and type of institution available (Higher Education Research Institute, 2007; Stricker, 2014). Given the variables of cost, location and prestige, Stricker (2014) shares, "I applied only to the university closest to my home, fully unaware of the opportunities I was missing by not seeking out institutions based on academic reputation" (p. 107). This reflects poor and working-class individuals' lack of understanding of the various forms of capital involved in higher education as well as the degree of capital depending on the prestige and reputation of the particular campus. Additionally, many higher education graduate programs at some institutions offer tuition remission along with graduate assistantships, which can drive poor and working-class individuals' graduate school decisions. Further, if one is making their college choice based on finances, they may pay less attention to the way their degree is designated—masters of education versus masters of science and doctor of education versus doctor of philosophy—which can influence perceptions of academic rigor, prestige, and job preparedness (Soria, 2016).

Thus, institutional types and types of degree can impact an individual's job search process. Some institutions believe it is essential to hire someone with experience at their specific institutional type. Other institutions are concerned with hiring graduates from peer or aspirational institutions, which are "comparison groups" for their finances, enrollment, selectivity, and other measures (Fuller, 2012; Warnock, 2016). These comparison institutions are often based on institutional reputation and rankings and, if used as a hiring measure, could, for example, limit the ability of professionals at community colleges or comprehensive institutions from being considered for employment at research institutions. Both of these practices can create barriers for those poor and working-class individuals who had less access—for a variety of reasons—to small, private, or highly ranked institutions. Additionally, if we only hire "our own," how do we expect our staff and faculty to reflect our student body, some of whom are poor or working class?

Professional Dress

One of the questions people will be asked when approaching the job search process is about their clothes. Both job seekers and their supporters inquire about suits, ties, dresses, accessories, shoes, and bags in an attempt to ensure that "appropriate attire" is worn for the interview process. Graduate school programs and supervisors try to educate on appropriate professional dress and how to be perceived as "put together." As Lubrano (2004) points out, "The right picture is imperative. Clothes, then, become vital for the proper office portrait" (p. 130). In this requirement to look put together, achieving professional dress can come at a literal cost, one that job seekers may not want or be able to pay. In addition, wearing this type of attire may also come at the figurative cost of making an individual feel uncomfortable or inauthentic. This combination of sacrifices can cause emotional and financial stress that often goes unaddressed in order to support the systemic middle- and upper-class norms of "professionalism."

Higher education job seekers have to make a decision of whether to conform to class norms or showcase their resistant capital (Yosso, 2005) because, as highlighted by a participant in Hurst's (2007) study, "If you don't have the nice shoes, if you don't have the nice clothes, and the cute hair, then you're gonna be made fun of and ostracized" (p. 91). Despite others' reactions to an individual's dress, Rios (2015) points out that "none of the work that [we] do is impacted by what [we're] wearing, and the work [we] do should speak much more loudly than how [we] look" (para. 12). So, the question is, Does professional dress really matter in the field of higher education or are we just creating a "visual hierarchy" as a way to sort people by class and other dimensions of identity (Rios, 2015)?

Negotiating Salary and Benefits

Even after professionals from poor and working-class backgrounds land a job offer in higher education, their class identity can show up in the negotiation process. Negotiation can often be a challenge for individuals from poor and working-class backgrounds because their navigational capital (Yosso, 2005) is often different from that of academia. Institutions may have an expectation that individuals will negotiate, while poor and working-class individuals may assume they are being offered the maximum salary available, feel uncomfortable talking about money, or be unaware of inquiring about benefits not typically provided, such as parking passes, recreation center memberships, meal plans, moving expenses, and so on. This can create a gap between those who know to ask, or feel comfortable asking, for more and those who may not realize they should be asking or know what benefits to negotiate. It is unfair to assume that all individuals understand the process of negotiation; thus, institutions of higher education should be more forthright with their job offers and determine salary and benefits based on equitable experiences and contributions, rather than one's knowledge and practice of negotiation.

CLASS AND JOB FIT: HOW WORDS, LOGOS, AND "RUBBING ELBOWS" INFLUENCE BELONGING

Class identity shows up not only in the job search process but also in whether the individual and their colleagues perceive the job as a good fit. *Job fit* is a term used to assess an individual's suitability for the position, office, and institution. It can also be used as a euphemism to conceal others' dislikes, stereotypes, or "-isms" toward an individual. So, while job fit can sometimes be awry for legitimate reasons, it can also be a disguise for thinking or feeling that someone is not well matched for a position or institution because of one, or more, dimensions of identity. Class identity can influence many aspects of job fit, including but not limited to stereotypes and discrimination, language and word choice, supervisory relationships, office or university gear and events, professional socializing, and professional development opportunities.

Given these potential dynamics associated with class, there is a professional responsibility to develop and maintain the foundational outcomes related to the social justice and inclusion competency established by American College Personnel Association (ACPA) and NASPA-Student Affairs Administrators in Higher Education's (2015) *Professional Competency Areas for Student Affairs Educators*. The foundational competencies most critical to directly supporting class identity on an individual level include

- identifying systems of socialization that influence one's multiple identities and sociopolitical perspectives and how they impact one's lived experiences;
- understanding how one is affected by and participates in maintaining systems of oppression, privilege, and power; and
- engaging in critical reflection in order to identify one's own prejudices and biases. (p. 30)

It is critical for supervisors and colleagues to raise their awareness of the dynamics and complexities of class. When we are able to do so, we can better support professionals from poor and working-class backgrounds to navigate within the system of higher education, which is often unfamiliar and can be marginalizing through unwritten rules and norms. Additionally, building class consciousness among all staff and faculty is equally important to not only learn about class identity on individual, group, and systemic levels but also support people from poor and working classes of origin who may face struggles in the workplace yet feel unable to say anything due to their desire to fit in the environment.

Class Stereotypes and Discrimination

Because "class difference and classism are rarely overtly apparent, or they are not acknowledged when present" (hooks, 2000, p. 5), higher education professionals may not realize the class identities of their colleagues or not choose to engage around issues of class in their workplaces. Colleagues and students may make thoughtless comments or perpetrate microaggressions related to class identity and not recognize the impact it has on those from poor or working-class backgrounds. Soria (2016) shares how microaggressions leave her feeling that she is "but a working-class novelty in [higher education's] middle-class culture . . . an imposter in the ivory tower" (pp. 132–133). For example, colleagues can make sarcastic comments about one's professionalism, assumptions about one's ability to purchase the latest book or technological gadget, or joke about the "ghetto" or "trailer park trash." hooks (2000) illustrated this sentiment:

> I, like most of my working-class peers, was not prepared to face the class hierarchies present in academia. . . . When class was mentioned at the school, . . . negative stereotypes about poor and working class people were the only perspectives evoked. (p. 42)

Language and Word Choice

Rivera (2015) points out that success in employment can depend on talking and writing like a middle-class person, highlighting how language comes in varying styles, with some types holding more value than others. Grammar and communication that are viewed as "proper" are those used by the middle class (Streib, 2016), with examples of *proper* being comfortable, palatable, "formally" educated, and not containing slang or profanity. In addition to society's general preference for middle-class language, higher education has its own academic discourse. Each college and university has its own vernacular particular to that institution, comprising jargon and acronyms that create in-groups and out-groups (Ardoin, 2013). Lubrano (2004) notes that language is critical to fitting in: "Central to the whole thing is language. If you don't talk like them, they won't give you the time of day" (p. 10). Individuals from poor and working-class backgrounds possess linguistic capital (Yosso, 2005) that is likely different from the general higher education environment and the particular institution; they may also be unaccustomed to the manner in which the language and message is communicated. Thus, they may be misperceived as less informed about the position, office, and institution, unless their colleagues and students recognize that a diversity of dialect, accents, and word choice bring additional richness and perspective to both the work environment and the institution.

In addition, staff and faculty are expected to have tact with their language choice, speak in political or roundabout ways, and refrain from using profanity. These expectations are often challenging for poor and working-class individuals who grew up in environments where honesty and directness were preferable and four-letter words showed passion (Lubrano, 2004). Arner (2016) notes that even when people are aware of their language difference, it is "extraordinarily difficult to alter," particularly in environments such as higher education which tend to value language patterns that exhibit "male privilege and [middle- or upper-]class privilege" (p. 60). Supervisors and colleagues need to discuss why knowing a particular vernacular and speaking in a specific way may be thought of as prerequisites for job fit. Higher education should honor an individual's ability to communicate in multiple forms and allow time for folks to learn another language.

Supervisory Relationships

A significant part of the perception of job fit is a person's relationship with their supervisor (Tull, 2009). Class identity can become a factor in this relationship when the supervisor and supervisee have different expectations about how the relationship should be created, defined, and managed. For many poor and working-class individuals, patience for office politics is scarce, directly speaking their mind is natural, challenging authority is commonplace, and authenticity is highly valued (Lubrano, 2004). They may struggle with why supervisors may refrain from providing direct communication, explaining precisely what is expected, and providing transparent feedback. Lubrano (2004) illustrates:

If the boss is wrong, you tell [them]; you think the assignment is stupid or the editing bizarre? Just say it. . . . Growing up, blue-collar types have no reason not to speak their minds; there's nothing to lose when you're on the bottom. We tell you what we feel rather than what you want to hear. (p. 131)

The need to be tactful in order to be "professional" can create strains between poor and working-class professionals and their middle- or upper-class colleagues, supervisors, or supervisees. Not learning to communicate with "professional tact" can, unfortunately, lead to middle- and upper-class professionals viewing their colleagues from poor and working-class backgrounds as tactless and "unprofessional." In addition, supervisors from poor and working-class backgrounds who may identify as renegades or double agents (Hurst, 2007) may attempt to redefine *class* for poor and working-class supervisees, which can also lead to supervisory struggles.

Many times, even with the best intention, there are different languages being spoken by both parties (Welsch, 2005). This can become an issue of fit if the supervisor views these behaviors through a lens of insubordination rather than class and capital difference—particularly linguistic and resistant capitals (Yosso, 2005). Through relationship building, supervisors can role model the importance of class identity by sharing stories of their own class of origin and its alignment or misalignment with their current, felt class identity. As class is often invisible and assumed, this sharing is valuable to create space for those from various class backgrounds to convey their own story, particularly for those from marginalized identities. To effectively support employees from poor and working-class backgrounds, supervisors need to have conversations with them about class identity, particularly class identity of origin. In doing so, supervisors can better determine if supervisory challenges are really an issue of fit or merely a difference in how one was taught to approach communication and collaboration.

Office and University Gear

Similar to professional dress, which carries over into characteristics of job fit, there can be an expectation that staff and faculty will obtain and promote their institution through both office and university gear—shirts, hats, water bottles, lapel pins, and so on. While some people receive free items from their workplaces, others do not. Thus, there can be pressure to purchase items to wear for job-related events, "wear your colors" days, and general university functions. With collegiate licensing fees and campus bookstore upcharges, this gear can become very pricey. Poor and working-class individuals are faced with the decision whether or not to spend money on attire they might not otherwise purchase—but feel compelled to buy—just to fit in with their colleagues and campus. As a field, why do we place so much value on what people wear and whether they have the "right" logo on their items? Are individuals unable to do their jobs well without having a university or college logo on their polo? This is something to consider and reflect upon as new staff and faculty are hired and socialized into the campus environment.

Office and University Events

Along with having the right gear, the student affairs field also has expectations that staff and faculty will be present on campus for a number of office and university events, whether or not they are designated to work at those events. From fund-raisers and sports games to lectures and art exhibits, staff and faculty are often asked and pushed to make appearances on behalf of their office or division. While tickets and entry fees may be waived in some instances, this is not always the case. In addition, events may require particular attire or costumes not readily available to the individual being asked to attend.

Regardless of cost, individuals from poor and working-class backgrounds may have little interest in attending these events—for numerous reasons. Possessing different cultural and familial capital (Yosso, 2005) than some of their colleagues, they may not enjoy these kinds of events or the family of the individual may not be welcome to join. These events, often considered "highbrow" in the eyes of the poor or working-class person, can also generate anxiety or discomfort in not knowing how to operate in the environment: "The idea of choosing the right fork in a fancy place has always tripped up [poor and working-class folks] and it's amazing how many describe trepidation about cutlery" (Lubrano, 2004, p. 83).

Additionally, they may not want to spend their free time at events that are not necessarily work but carry similar expectations or responsibilities. Not to mention, with the typical combination of accumulated debt from obtaining degrees and being underpaid, these same professionals may hold a part-time job to cover expenses and, thus, have limited time available for such events. Gauging fit for jobs based on how much time and presence people have on campus outside of their actual job or their comfort level with formal events is misguided because this marker views institutional commitment and community engagement from a narrow perspective.

Professional Socializing

With a reputation of being a highly social field with many extroverted personalities, higher education staff and faculty are often expected to socialize with their colleagues in a variety of formats. If one does not participate, it may reflect negatively on their interest in collegial connection and collaboration. However, professional socializing is often an out-of-pocket cost that poor and working-class individuals may not be able to afford or may not find value in spending their time and money on, perhaps being "allergic to false gaiety" (Lubrano, 2004, p. 147). A participant in Hurst's (2007) study aptly illustrated this concept: "I don't want to have to explain everything, like why I can't afford to go to the movies" (p. 91). Four examples of professional socializing that frequently arise for higher education professionals include meeting up for coffees, lunches, potlucks, and happy hours.

Socializing often begins in the morning, with coffee. When colleagues ask to meet over coffee, they are often inviting the individual to join them at a campus or community coffee shop that sells $5 to $8 cups of coffee. For individuals from poor and working-class backgrounds, the coffee meeting can be uncomfortable not only because of the expectation that everyone drinks expensive coffee but also because it infers that business needs to be conducted in a particular, social way. Additionally, in this simple act of grabbing coffee, there is an assumption that one has knowledge about types of coffee and the variety of coffee drink combinations (Black, 2005). Why not consider having the same meeting in an office or conference room space or over a walk around campus—all at no cost both economically and psychologically?

The pressure to socialize continues at noontime when colleagues often invite one another out to lunch. This is seen as a way to get off of campus and have a more casual meeting to discuss topics that may be more sensitive or social in nature. While lunch away can have its perks and create connection, it also can require time and money that can be a strain on poor and working-class individuals. For those who are in hourly or unionized positions, lunch has to occur during a strict 30-minute or 1-hour block. It also likely comes at a cost of $10 or more, depending on the location.

Rather than going out for lunch, colleagues sometimes decide to stay near the office and host potluck events where each person is asked to provide something to share with the rest of the group. Poor and working-class individuals may feel stress around potlucks because they may have dining habits or food preferences that differ from their colleagues or do not fit into middle class standards, or they may not have the extra funding to purchase food for large groups that are not family members or close friends. Instead of assuming colleagues do not fit in because they decline lunch or potluck invitations, consider asking if they would like to chat over whatever lunch they brought from home; it can be eaten outside on a nice day or in a quiet corner of the student union.

Then there are after-work pressures to participate in happy hour. While there are a host of concerns with happy hour as a form of socializing in higher education, the concern of interest here is the pressure to join colleagues after work for a beverage of choice to rehash the day, debate an issue, or celebrate a success. In addition to the financial cost of happy hour for poor and working-class individuals, there could also be a familial or social cost (Yosso, 2005). For people who need to pick up children, focus on family dinner and evening activities, work a second job, or attend to a personal hobby or social engagement, happy hour can present a struggle between feeling part of the team or community and taking care of personal and family business after work.

There may also be an unawareness or discomfort around what is appropriate to drink at a work happy hour; as Lubrano (2004) describes, "The whole beer-versus-wine thing could be a problem too" (p. 84). With professional socializing there is a distinction of activities across class, with some being considered more professionally appropriate than others. In a study by Svoboda (2012), a participant shares her experience while attending a professional association conference. One night she went out with colleagues for drinks. On the ride back to campus the next day with other colleagues she remembers them discussing the "tacky, unprofessional girls" that went out the previous night. All the while the participant felt ashamed and guilty because, "I did not confess I was one of them. . . . I also did not call out their hypocrisy, as they had been busy consuming wine all night at the hotel bar, but felt it was okay to judge the beer drinkers in the group" (Svoboda, 2012, p. 84). To reduce discomfort and judgment, another option for connecting with colleagues over challenges and celebrations is to ask the individual how and when they prefer to connect.

Professional Development Opportunities

Higher education is a field focused on lifelong learning. This learning happens in a variety of ways—from formal degrees and conference opportunities to university human resource department trainings and reading literature (Ardoin, 2014). Many would argue it is necessary to continue one's growth and development as an essential element to job fit and career success. Some colleges and universities pride themselves on being highly engaged with professional associations—calling themselves an "ACPA campus" or "NASPA campus"—and convey expectations to their employees that they should be involved with local, regional, and national associations; hold volunteer positions with these associations as a form of service to the institution and profession; and present sessions at conferences to showcase institutional efforts and market the division and institution. Doing so increases forms of cultural and social capital, which inadvertently reinforces classist dynamics.

The concern is that many times professional development is a significant financial investment because webinars, trainings, institutes, and conferences typically require registration fees, travel, lodging, meal, and time costs (Ardoin, 2014). Some institutions allot funding for this purpose, while others do not. For those who do have it, it is often the first item to be eliminated when budget cuts arise. Even when the funding is not an issue, these opportunities often result in time away from both work and family responsibilities and raise issues of professionalism, professional dress, and professional socializing. Because of these financial, time, and professional requirements, poor and working-class individuals' aspirational, familial, social, navigational, and resistant capital (Yosso, 2005) may steer them away from the "traditional" national conference scene. In addition, being in the spotlight as presenters or facilitators can be challenging for poor and working-class individuals who were often taught to value humility and not boast of accomplishments (Soria, 2016).

What does this mean in terms of others' perception of their fit? If an institution is looking for employees who are on the regional or national "scene" and who present and network at conferences, then choosing not to engage in this way could hinder poor and working-class individuals' advancement or value to the institution. This often reflects the notion of networking as a learned, or coached, class behavior that is not natural or comfortable for individuals from poor and working-class backgrounds. As such, poor and working-class folks may struggle to find the value in professional development or networking and find themselves with less social capital to utilize for themselves and their institutions. The question becomes this: Does higher education value employees for their work ethic in their position or do they expect employees to do their job well while also elevating the reputation of the institution?

CONCLUSION

Higher education is a microcosm of society and many of the identity challenges are illuminated on college and university campuses. This is true not only for students but also for staff and faculty at the institution. Staff and faculty from poor and working-class backgrounds can be perceived as having a learning curve at an institution in order to have any chance at becoming part of the community. However, institutions, and those who inhabit them, need to be reminded that poor and working-class individuals bring many forms of capital to the table (Yosso, 2005) and enrich the higher education environment—even before socialization occurs. As Casey (2014) illustrates: "I learned to speak a new [educated] language that my family does not share. . . . Yet the working-class culture I came from is also a part of me, by far the most formative piece of all" (p. 95).

It is time to shift the viewpoint of class identity as a deficit to one of value and recognize that "[poor and working-class folks] are hybrids. That duality is their strength and their struggle" (Lubrano, 2004, p. 29). Let us not be quick to determine that poor and working-class individuals do not fit; rather, let us intentionally take time to get to know our colleagues and their valuable forms of class capital—and share our own—in order to recognize additional ways of functioning across class identity as colleagues, educators, and, ideally, friends.

REFERENCES

American College Personnel Association, & National Association of Student Personnel Administrators. (2015). *Professional competency areas for student affairs educators*. Professional Competencies Task Force. Washington DC: Authors. Retrieved from https://www.naspa.org/images/uploads/main/ACPA_NASPA_Professional_Competencies_FINAL.pdf

American Council on Education (ACE). (2012, March 12). *Leading demographic portrait of college presidents reveals ongoing challenges in diversity, aging*. Retrieved from http://www.acenet.edu/news-room/Pages/ACPS-Release-2012.aspx

Ardoin, S. (2013). *Learning a different language: Rural students' comprehension of college knowledge and university jargon* (Doctoral dissertation). Retrieved from North Carolina State University Libraries Repository.

Ardoin, S. (2014). *The strategic guide to shaping your student affairs career*. Sterling, VA: Stylus.

Arner, L. (2016). Strategies for working-class women as junior faculty. In A. L. Hurst & S. K. Nenga (Eds.), *Working in class: Recognizing how social class shapes our academic work* (pp. 49–64). New York, NY: Rowman & Littlefield.

Barratt, W. (2011). *Social class on campuses: Theories and manifestations.* Sterling, VA: Stylus.

Begert, A. A. (2005). Sonia Apgar Begert. In K. A. Welsch (Eds.), *Those winter Sundays: Female academics and their working-class parents* (pp. 161–172). Lanham, MD: University Press of America.

Black, L. J. (2005). Laurel Johnson Black. In K. A. Welsch (Ed.), *Those winter Sundays: Female academics and their working-class parents* (pp. 58–68). Lanham, MD: University Press of America.

Bourdieu, P. (1986). The forms of capital. In J. G. Richardson (Ed.), *Handbook of theory and research for the sociology of education* (pp. 241–258). New York, NY: Greenwood.

Casey, J. (2014). A box from my grandfather. In C. Collins, J. Ladd, M. Seider, & F. Yeskel (Eds.), *Class lives: Stories from across our economic divide* (pp. 92–95). Ithaca, NY: Cornell University Press.

Collins, C. (2014). Afterword: The power of story. In C. Collins, J. Ladd, M. Seider, & F. Yeskel (Eds), *Class lives: Stories from across our economic divide* (pp. 211–213). Ithaca, NY: Cornell University Press.

Collins, C., Ladd, J., Seider, M., & Yeskel, F. (2014). *Class lives: Stories from across our economic divide.* Ithaca, NY: Cornell University Press.

Fuller, A. (2012, September 12). In selecting peers for comparison's sake, colleges look upward. *Chronicle of Higher Education.* Retrieved from http://www.chronicle.com/article/in-selecting-peers-for/134228

Higher Education Research Institute (HERI). (2007). *A profile of first-generation college students at four-year institutions since 1971.* Los Angeles, CA: Author.

hooks, b. (2000). *Where we stand: Class matters.* New York, NY: Routledge.

Hurst, A. L. (2007). Telling tales of oppression and dysfunction: Narratives of class identity reformation. *Qualitative Sociology Review, 3*(2), 82–104.

Hurst, A. L. (2010). *The burden of academic success: Loyalists, renegades, and double agents.* Lanham, MD: Rowman & Littlefield.

Lubrano, A. (2004). *Limbo: Blue-collar roots, white-collar dreams.* Hoboken, NJ: Wiley.

Rios, C. (2015, February 15). You call it professionalism; I call it oppression in a three-piece suit. *Everyday Feminism.* Retrieved from http://everydayfeminism.com/2015/02/professionalism-and-oppression/

Rivera, L. (2015). *Pedigree: How elite students get elite jobs.* Princeton, NJ: Princeton University Press.

Rosenblum, A. (2014). Coming clean. In C. Collins, J. Ladd, M. Seider, & F. Yeskel (Eds.), *Class lives: Stories from across our economic divide* (pp. 193–197). Ithaca, NY: Cornell University Press.

Soria, K. (2016). Working-class, teaching class and working class in the academy. In A. L. Hurst & S. K. Nenga (Eds.), *Working in class: Recognizing how social class shapes our academic work* (pp. 127–139). Lanham, MD: Rowman & Littlefield.

Streib, J. (2016). Lessons learned: How I unintentionally reproduce class inequality. In A. L. Hurst & S. K. Nenga (Eds.), *Working in class: Recognizing how social class shapes our academic work* (pp. 79–90). New York, NY: Rowman & Littlefield.

Stricker, K. (2014). Hitting the academic class ceiling. In C. Collins, J. Ladd, M. Seider, & F. Yeskel (Eds.), *Class lives: Stories from across our economic divide* (pp. 105–107). Ithaca, NY: Cornell University Press.

Svoboda, V. (2012). *Constructing class: Exploring the experiences of White women student affairs educators from working class backgrounds* (Doctoral dissertation). Retrieved from University of St. Thomas Research Online.

Tull, A. (2009). Supervision and mentorship in the socialization process. In A. Tull, J. Hirt, & S. Saunders (Eds.), *Becoming socialized in student affairs administration* (pp. 129–151). Sterling, VA: Stylus.

Warnock, D. M. (2016). Capitalizing class. In A. L. Hurst & S. K. Nenga (Eds.), *Working in class: Recognizing how social class shapes our academic work* (pp. 173–183). Lanham, MD: Rowman & Littlefield.

Welsch, K. A. (2005). Kathleen A. Welsch. In Welsch, K. A. (Ed.), *Those winter Sundays: Female academics and their working-class parents* (pp. 36–48). Lanham, MD: University Press of America.

Yeskel, F. (2014). Introduction: Caviar, college, coupons, and cheese. In C. Collins, J. Ladd, M. Seider, & F. Yeskel (Eds.), *Class lives: Stories from across our economic divide* (pp. 1–12). Ithaca, NY: Cornell University Press.

Yeskel, F., & Leondar-Wright, B. (1997). Classism: Curriculum design. In M. Adams, L. A. Bell, & P. Griffin (Eds.), *Teachings for diversity and social justice: A sourcebook* (pp. 231–260). New York, NY: Routledge.

Yosso, T. (2005). Whose culture has capital? A critical race theory discussion of community cultural wealth. *Race Ethnicity and Education, 8*(1), 69–91.

6

Finding Fit as an "Outsider Within"

A Critical Exploration of Black Women Navigating the Workplace in Higher Education

Stacey D. Garrett and Natasha T. Turman

THE EXPERIENCES OF BLACK women in higher education are often conveyed in a manner that perpetuates and reinforces a dominant narrative with ways of knowing, standards of beauty, and standards of professionalism that are White, Western (i.e., Eurocentric), and often male. Based on the stereotypes surrounding Black women in the United States, the experiences of Black women are reduced to critiques of their appearance (e.g., choices in hairstyle or comments on their body type); their education (e.g., educational background); or their ability to lead, teach, or mentor students (Ladson-Billings, 2009). These standards have been normed in U.S. educational systems and in the workplace, and they are often used to delineate the idea of fit in the job search process. Various constructions of fit, informed by this dominant narrative, are used to discriminate against, devalue, or exclude people who do not match such norms or, essentially, fit in. This chapter seeks to center the experiences of Black women by exploring the job search process and workplace experiences from the standpoint of Black women. Critical race feminism and the concept of community cultural wealth serve as the frames for and lenses through which these experiences are presented. These theoretical frames will allow us to illuminate the power, perspectives, and unique experiences of Black women in higher education.

In this chapter, we discuss the job search process, from recruitment to onboarding, from the perspective of employers and candidates, particularly in predominantly White institutions (PWIs). At each step of the process, Black women make intentional decisions and considerations as they navigate the unspoken rules, or hidden curriculum, of institutions of higher education. We intend to problematize the idea of fit and its use as a means for institutionalized oppression and exclusion. First, we provide background for the topic, including our positionality as authors and the social location of Black women in society and higher education. Second, we define *fit*. Third, we provide an overview of the theoretical frameworks that ground our perspectives. Fourth, we review the decision points and challenges of navigating the hiring process. Fifth, we discuss the opportunities and challenges once one is hired and formally on the job. Sixth, we close with implications and recommendations for how the information presented can inform the policies and cultures of academic and student affairs departments, along with encouragement for Black women seeking work in the academy.

BACKGROUND

As scholars in the field, it is important to note our personal connection to and experience with this topic.

Positionality of the Authors

We both identify as Black, cisgender women with varying privileged and marginalized identities. Our research agendas focus on women of color (WOC) and their experiences in higher education. We have professional experiences in student affairs serving in housing positions, fraternity/sorority advising, academic advising, leadership development, and multicultural affairs. We have served on department search committees, training committees, and hiring committees in our combined 10+ years of experience in the field, and we have participated as candidates in various hiring processes. We have yet to formally work within departments of human resources (HR), but we have interacted with HR departments and researched this topic to prepare this conceptual chapter. This chapter is based on our research and observations and is evaluated from a critical perspective.

Throughout this chapter, we speak exclusively from the position of cisgender, Black women. We acknowledge there may be differences for transwomen of color as well as cisgender women with different racial/ethnic identities. We have chosen to focus on cisgender, Black women for this chapter based on our research and personal experiences. Additionally, we have chosen to intentionally and sparingly use the word *we* when referring to Black women. While we identify as and with Black women, we want to maintain a more neutral tone and refer to Black women in the third person or in the collective. Our goal is to present our ideas and thoughts on this topic from a researched, scholarly lens rather than a personal one. In the recommendations section, we chose to communicate directly with Black, female readers and utilized a conversational style.

Social Location of Black Women

We center the voices of Black women in this chapter because we possess a unique standpoint in society and in the higher education environment. While we share a distinct social location (i.e., the groups people belong to because of their position in history and society, often characterized by gender, race, social class, age, ability, religion, sexual orientation, and geographic location; Collins, 1986), our experiences may converge or diverge at different points. This chapter should not be reviewed and applied to all Black or African American women. Our goal is to provide a general explanation of experiences, not to offer a definitive rule. Black women are socially positioned at the intersection of their race and gender, trammeled by the historical marginalization, discrimination, and oppression Black people and women have experienced and continue to experience in U.S. society (Carter, Pearson, & Shavlik, 1996; Crenshaw, 1991; Graves, 1990; Turner, 2002). Within the higher education environment, the experiences of Black women in higher education are directly influenced by this positionality. Although the literature illustrates that all women in higher education face gendered norms and expectations, the experiences of WOC are compounded by racialized and gendered perceptions of their identities, ultimately impacting how they engage with and experience many facets of the academy.

According to the most recent *Digest of Education Statistics* from the U.S. Department of Education's National Center for Education Statistics (2014), Black women comprise 13.2% of student affairs, academic affairs, and other education services roles across institutions of higher education in the United States. Within the ranks of faculty, Black women represent 8.3% of the 752,750 women faculty in U.S. institutions of higher education (U.S. Department of Education, National Center for Education Statistics [NCES], 2014). Although these numbers have increased over the years, they have done so at a very unremarkable pace, only up 2% since 2004 for each respective group (U.S. Department of Education, NCES, 2003–2004). Several scholars have lamented these dismal numbers, reiterating that although statistical data are useful to measure quantity, numbers fail to illustrate the quality of one's experiences in higher education (Graves, 1990; Patitu & Hinton, 2003; Turner, 2002; West, 2015).

As we attempt to deconstruct ideologies to understand how Black women traverse the job search process, we do so with a keen awareness of how one's multiple, and intersecting, social identities inform and shape that process. Patricia Hill Collins (1986) suggested that Black women possess an "outsider within" standpoint, emphasizing that while Black women are granted access to and are present in majority White spaces, they are not fully members of those spaces. An outsider-within standpoint causes Black women at PWIs to experience a nearness and remoteness simultaneously; granted access but still lacking voice to effect change. This unique tension is paramount to consider when critically examining fit in higher education student affairs.

Throughout the chapter, we refer to employers, departments, and institutions. Please note that these groups are contextualized within PWIs rather than historically Black colleges and universities (HBCUs) or other minority-serving institutions (MSIs). We will focus on PWIs as the context for this chapter, given that the issues around fit for Black women are most evident at PWIs. We define *PWIs* as colleges and universities where White men and women make up the largest percentage of students, faculty, and professional staff. These institutions have historically excluded people of color (POC).

Diversity in higher education is not a new question or issue for university leaders. By adopting a critical race feminist lens, we accept and approach this topic with the belief that racism, sexism, and classism are endemic to U.S. society. Since institutions are microcosms of larger society, these institutions can also perpetuate racism and sexism. PWIs, by design, have historically been spaces of incongruence for women and POC. As such, an exploration of fit for Black women at PWIs will provide much-needed insight into how to bolster congruency in the stated values and hiring processes of staff and faculty and improve the overall experiences of this group within the higher education environment.

FIT DEFINED

Fit is an abstract construct used to describe how things are connected in a given setting. In higher education, fit refers to how people, ideas, and perspectives align with a department or institution. There are norms that inform what physical appearance (e.g., dress, hairstyles), educational pedigree, and ways of knowing are deemed appropriate. Within the context of PWIs, *fit* has had a monolithic definition. Historically, these spaces were created with White men in mind, lacking diverse representation from women and POC (Dayton, 2015). Our definition of *fit* comprises two parts: institutional and individual notions of fit. Both pieces are critical to the success of candidates and employers finding what they are looking for in the job search/hiring process. Unfortunately, these two definitions rarely align with each other and, thus, cause the tensions we currently see in the field.

On the institutional side, fit has become coded language for finding someone with similar attitudes, beliefs, and maybe even identities. Subconsciously and consciously, we, as human beings, gravitate toward and attract those who we believe (i.e., assume) to be like us. Also known as *homophily*, this principle is seen in social networks and stems from attributing certain characteristics or behaviors to certain groups (McPherson, Smith-Lovin, & Cook, 2001). We naturally surround ourselves with those who share the same categorical identities, or in this context, social identities, thus reinforcing the belief that those who look like us also behave like us (McPherson, Smith-Lovin, & Cook, 2001). In the hiring process, departments at PWIs often say they "welcome applicants from diverse backgrounds" or that "women and minorities are encouraged to apply." The motivation behind these general statements around diversity can be difficult to trust, especially when the institutional demographic does not reflect this commitment. As a result, candidates must find a way to determine whether the department is sincere in its quest for a diverse pool or simply complying with the conditions of an equal employment opportunity office. Given that homophily subconsciously prevents an individual from believing that someone from a different social identity will behave or think like that individual, Black women must overcome the unconscious biases of hiring managers with varying social identities.

On the individual side, as candidates, Black women may be looking for a space in which their multiple and intersecting social identities are welcomed and appreciated. This is a space where she can be her authentic self (i.e., a self-defined true expression of identity) without consequence, where she can make suggestions, challenge processes, and call out archaic or oppressive practices

(Jones, Kim, & Skendall, 2012). She may be seeking a space where she will feel supported and appreciated, while being developed and encouraged in her aspirations. However, this is not always easy for Black women, who daily navigate essentialized notions of social identities like race, gender, class, and sexual orientation that have been socially constructed and promulgated (Wiley, 1994).

As it pertains to job fit in higher education, struggles around identity politics manifest around the notions of authenticity and impression management/code-switching. What and who an individual expresses externally, versus what they keep to themselves, is at the center of authenticity (Jones, Kim, & Skendall, 2012). Often used interchangeably, *impression management* and *code-switching* reflect tactics that are used to help people navigate unfamiliar spaces and elicit from others a perception of fit in that space (Kacmar & Carlson, 1994). Tactics such as adjusting language, appearance, style, and behavior are the deliberate exhibition of a preferred image—an image of acceptance within a space.

When fit is discussed, there is a natural assumption that this reflects a seamless alignment or a perfect balance that meets all an individual's personal and professional needs. The reality for most people is that there are elements of the self that are either relegated to the periphery or suppressed to fit in. As Black women seek fit in the higher educational context, they often engage in dialectical thinking—holding two seemingly different ideas simultaneously—being their authentic selves and emulating the prescribed roles and duties as defined within the institutional culture.

Defining *fit* from both an institutional and individual lens demonstrates the varied expectations of the candidate and employer in the search process. When institutional and individual definitions of *fit* collide, Black women suffer. We argue that instead of requiring Black women to change, institutions should make room for and incorporate the distinct identities and contributions of Black women in order to evolve with the changing landscape of higher education. The next section outlines the theoretical frameworks used to situate the distinct experiences of Black women as they seek fit at PWIs.

THEORETICAL FRAMEWORKS

To reconcile the tensions of institutional and individual fit in higher education for Black women, we use two liberatory frameworks: critical race feminism (Wing, 1997) and community cultural wealth (Yosso, 2005). Together, these theoretical approaches acknowledge those who reside in the margins, interrogate the places of power within the higher educational environment, and elevate Black women's standpoint to disrupt dominant ideologies around fit in higher education.

Critical Race Feminism

Critical scholars have acknowledged that the experiences, needs, and ways of knowing that individuals from marginalized positions possess are "different from but equally valuable to those experiences of the dominant discourse" (Somers & Gibson, 1994, p. 54; see also Lorde, 1984). Critical race feminism (CRF) is one such theoretical framework to elevate the voices and experiences of WOC in higher education. According to Sulé (2011), CRF provides a lens through which social identity can be examined at both the societal and institutional level. As an extension of critical race theory (CRT), CRF honors the intersectionality and multiplicity of WOC's social identities and acknowledges that WOC's lived experiences are influenced by their gender and racial identities (Sulé, 2011; Wing, 1997). Zinn and Dill (1996) posited race is "a power system that interacts with other structured inequalities to shape genders" (p. 324). Historically, the experiences and needs of WOC have been examined from either a gender-focused or race-focused framework, neglecting the fact that WOC have intersecting and compounding social identities that cannot be siphoned out or examined individually and manifest within systems of inequality (Crenshaw, 1991; Collins & Bilge, 2016; Evans-Winters & Esposito, 2010; Sulé, 2011; Wing, 1997).

A CRF perspective allows for a deeper, critical examination of Black women's professional experiences in higher education. Evans-Winters and Esposito (2010) highlighted several benefits for using CRF to examine the experiences of African American women in higher education. They posited that CRF recognizes the unique experiences and perspectives of WOC, acknowledges multiple forms of oppression and marginalization that daily impact WOC, honors the multiplicity and intersectionality of identity and thought of WOC, and strives to dismantle gender and racial oppression. Through CRF, we can investigate the experiences of Black women while acknowledging how those experiences are mitigated by multiple forces.

Community Cultural Wealth

Along with CRF, we view this topic through the lens of community cultural wealth. Yosso (2005) describes community cultural wealth as "an array of knowledge, skills, abilities, and contacts possessed and utilized by communities of color (COC) to survive and resist macro and micro-forms of oppression" (p. 77). As we discuss fit in higher education, community cultural wealth is used as a framework to investigate how Black women convert their sociocultural assets into social, cultural, and professional capital necessary to navigate the job search process and persist in a new position. We provide examples of how Black women use various forms of cultural capital to successfully navigate the higher educational environment.

When describing the experiences of Black women in the job search process, we will refer to *navigational capital* and *social capital*. Yosso (2005) defines navigational capital as the skills to move through systems created without POC in mind. Black women must adapt to a process that was designed for White, middle-class citizens. The process values Western, Eurocentric forms of knowledge and education (Delgado Bernal & Villalpando, 2002) and defines professionalism around White, heteronormative standards of dress and beauty. Social capital refers to "networks of people and community resources" (Yosso, 2005, p. 79). Black women utilize navigational and social capital when traversing spaces that were not designed for them and to make up for the financial capital to which they may not have access.

Aspirational capital and *resistant capital* are used to describe how Black women persist and function on the job. Aspirational capital refers to the ability of Black women to maintain a sense of hope for a better future despite clear barriers to their success (Yosso, 2005). Resistant capital describes the tools formed through "oppositional behaviors" (Yosso, 2005, p. 80). With resistant and aspirational capital, Black women learn how to use their whole selves to be oppositional toward race, gender, and class inequality (Yosso, 2005). These undervalued forms of capital allow Black women to succeed in the face of opposition, as well as transform hostile environments.

CRF and community cultural wealth are two useful tools to interrogate dominant constructions of fit in higher education. With these frames, we place Black women at the center of the conversation and give value to the skills and abilities they possess to navigate the workplace. Often, the experiences of Black women are encompassed by research focused on all African Americans or all women (Crenshaw, 1991; Sulé, 2011; Wing, 1997). However, the intersectionality of Black female identities creates a unique experience, particularly in higher education, that has yet to be told. Our goal is to illuminate the unique experiences of Black women and to highlight the benefits of the various forms of capital Black women possess. The next section will examine how Black women navigate the hiring process, exploring nuanced differences as they pertain to recruitment efforts and the interview.

BLACK WOMEN NAVIGATING THE HIRING PROCESS

When Black women begin the process of job searching in higher education, there are multiple points at which they must make a conscious choice about how they proceed. Institutions also must make some decisions when they begin to recruit for a position. In this section, we highlight decision points that can create or prevent a mismatch between Black women and institutional hiring managers engaging in a hiring process. We discuss these decision points from the perspective of Black women as candidates as well as the perspectives of institutional hiring managers, employees, and search committee members.

Starting the Job Search

When evaluating a job posting, there may be subtle indications regarding the type of person a department is looking to hire. Black women must interrogate the words of a job description to understand the goals of the department. Institutions may choose to list certain qualifications that could be viewed as coded language. For example, when recruiting for a position in fraternity/sorority affairs, a department may say it is specifically looking for candidates that are members of fraternities or sororities that were founded to serve POC. This may imply that the department is looking for a person of color, because it is more likely that they will belong to these organizations. Contrarily, a job posting may privilege those with membership in or experience advising historically White sororities. This communicates to applicants that their different fraternity/sorority experience may not be valued or seen as transferable in advising a predominantly White student population.

Additionally, for some Black women the espoused mission and values of a department may be considered signs of appreciation for diversity and inclusion. Unfortunately, public statements of a commitment to diversity do not always translate to a reinforcement of this commitment internally (Barnett-Johnson, 2010). With diversity included in the mission of a university, one would reasonably assume that a commitment to diversity is a foundational element of the university (Smith, 2015). Black women may feel more positively toward an organization with diversity included in the guiding principles (i.e., mission and values) and seriously consider applying for a position. Wolf-Wendel (2000) found women of all races, at a variety of institutions, experienced positive effects from being at institutions with a clear mission they believed was inclusive of them. Chickering and Reisser (1993) substantiated this further when they posited, "a strong sense of shared values and purpose is the foundation for institutional coherence and integrity" (p. 480). With this espoused position, Black women can reasonably assume that their contributions and they, themselves, will be valued in those spaces.

Black women may also consider the surrounding area and the university town for signs of diversity among the general population. For example, the distance an individual must travel for their preferred stylist or a grocery store that stocks specialized ingredients could influence one's decision to apply. Black women consider the surrounding community context in ways that differ from others. Most people will think about the type of college setting in which they would like to be—urban, rural, and so on. Black women wonder if they will be underrepresented in the larger community and what limitations that will place on their quality of life. Being the only person to represent an underrepresented group or identity in a college setting generally leads to a tokenizing experience—being called out to speak on behalf of that group or to serve as the "diversity" on committees, a physically low-risk endeavor. However, being the only person of an underrepresented group or identity in a housing community or neighborhood is generally not a positive experience and could become a physically high-risk, unsafe environment. For Black women, evaluating the area surrounding an institution digs deeper than evaluating the social scene or identifying the closest retail area. The evaluation process for Black women involves questions around physical safety, ability to find comfortable housing, and connecting with a community of people where they will be accepted.

In addition to the institutional context of the position, Black women also take an internal assessment of their experiences and qualifications before applying for a position. Women, in general, are socialized to be rule-followers and to believe that career success is based on meritocratic achievements (Mohr, 2014). This socialization results in women believing they must have all the listed qualifications for a position in order to apply. For Black women, adding on layers of imposter syndrome can create additional barriers to initiating the application process. Hiring managers may have a difficult time recruiting Black women given the self-doubt, fear, and apprehension that Black women strive to overcome before choosing to apply. Thus, a commitment to recruiting a diverse pool means that hiring managers must take additional steps to communicate with potential candidates exactly who or what they want in a new employee.

In some situations, it may be necessary to create positions with the purpose of diversifying one's department when a diverse pool cannot be created in the traditional sense. For example, in faculty hiring processes, special hires are utilized to intentionally recruit a candidate that brings certain identities to the department. Special, or targeted hires, can be a way to create a diverse pool outside of expected fields such as ethnic studies and women or gender studies (Smith, 2015). The targeted hiring practice intentionally recruits and selects candidates that represent particular identities. These hires are sometimes solely an effort by the department to show their interest in diversity at a surface level. Generally, the structural diversity achieved through special hires is sufficient for complying with many diversity requirements.

Departments that purely focus on structural diversity are most likely not looking for what comes with that individual (e.g., different perspectives, experiences, cultural capital, and motivations for their work). A department may be looking for someone who will increase their diversity numbers without actually diversifying the department mind-set. This can create a mismatch later in the hiring process. Black women may approach a position believing that, if hired, the department will welcome their perspectives, opinions, and approaches to the work. However, if the department is looking only to create visible, or representational, diversity rather than opening themselves to incorporate new ideas, then the new employee will soon experience her own issues of fit.

Getting to the Interview

The first review of applications is an opportunity for search committees to uphold or challenge their implicit biases and prototypes (i.e., images) of an ideal candidate (Kacmar & Carlson, 1994; Krieger & Fiske, 2006; Staats, 2014). These biases and prototypes may be based on their understanding of the position, the actual duties and expectations outlined in the job description, how a candidate would fit within the institutional culture, and their personal mental scripts that inform how they view and understand the world around them. Based on these factors, many individuals are selected for a job when they come closest to fitting the prototype envisioned by hiring personnel. When search committees lack representation from individuals with diverse social identities, educational backgrounds, and career experiences, these biases can go unchecked. Often, with the underrepresentation of POC in any single department, it is difficult to create a diverse hiring committee. While Barnett-Johnson (2010) recommends that hiring committees comprise members that represent varied identities, often there is a burden placed on a single person of color to speak for all underrepresented racial identities.

In the initial review, the HR department, or the hiring committee will ensure that applicants have met the minimum standards for the position. A closer look at the résumé begins, which may involve a discussion about the type of institution from which a candidate has earned their degrees. Delgado Bernal and Villalpando (2002) discussed the current Eurocentric standard for knowledge. The dominant narrative in U.S. higher education is that the education received at a four-year, PWI is superior to other institutions simply based upon Eurocentric ways of knowing, learning, and creating knowledge. In terms of educational background, hiring committees today privilege degrees that come from institutions that closely mirror the institutions from which the committee members graduated. Committee members may privilege candidates with degrees from institutions of similar rigor, prestige, or classification. When educational background is subjectively reviewed, hiring committees can systematically exclude those who do not fit into the current context of the department. A potential, and often likely outcome of this systematic exclusion is the overrepresentation of POC in culturally specific positions like multicultural affairs and the underrepresentation of POC in more "mainstream" positions that work with the larger student body.

Faculty members face similar challenges. The research agenda of Black women is subjectively reviewed in comparison to Eurocentric ways of knowing, which influences the initial review of their application materials (Delgado Bernal & Villalpando, 2002). The scholarship of POC is often deemed less rigorous based on the types of epistemologies and research designs that prioritize the experiences of POC (Delgado Bernal & Villalpando, 2002; Thomas & Hollenshead, 2001). The experiences of White people and truths deduced from quantitative, empirical research are more readily accepted as viable sources of knowledge in U.S. society (Delgado Bernal & Villalpando, 2002). Thus, when Black women utilize critical theory or constructivist perspectives to investigate the experiences of Black women or other POC, their research is viewed as personal research as opposed to legitimate knowledge. This is most harmful in faculty job searches where one's scholarship is evaluated for rigor and significance. Additionally, search committee members may deem the findings from research focused on the experiences of POC as not transferable to a larger, predominantly White student population.

During the application phase, the implicit biases of hiring committee members can negatively affect the advancement of Black women. Often, a hiring committee's prototypical candidate does not include the varying identities, experiences, and epistemological orientations of Black women as evidenced by the lagging representation of Black women in higher education. Therefore, when an organization's ideal candidate prototype is void of the qualities that Black women possess, it becomes very difficult for Black women to find fit.

The Interview

After the application phase, Black women face a new set of decisions and considerations during the interview. While Black women are managing others' impressions of them throughout every phase of the hiring process, they engage in a considerable amount of impression management during the interview stage. To fit the institution's ideal candidate, Kacmar and Carlson (1994) suggest that individuals engage in a variety of impression management strategies. These tactics allow individuals to present themselves in a way that appears as though they fit perfectly with the job description and institutional culture. Impression management also allows a person to conceal aspects of themselves that they believe may hinder their chances of securing the position. Much of the existing research on impression management in the hiring process speaks to the difference in tactics between men and women. For example, several scholars have noted that women alter their appearance, language, and nonverbal behavior to better reflect what they believed to be the ideal candidate the organization desires (Kacmar & Carlson, 1994; von Baeyer, Sherk, & Zanna, 1981).

While this is useful insight, these studies fail to consider the compounding effects of both gender and race when engaging in impression management, a reality that Black women navigate daily. Feminist scholar Anzaldúa (1990) captured the art with which WOC engage in impression management. Although her work centers the experiences of Chicana women, the phenomenon of impression management still holds true for women across marginalized racial/ethnic identities. Anzaldúa (1990) posited that, in order to survive and navigate dominant culture, "to become less vulnerable to all these oppressions, we have had to change faces. . . . Some of us who already wear many changes/inside our skin (Audre Lorde) have been forced to adopt a face that would pass" (p. xv).

This tension reflects the ever-present physical and sociopolitical identity politics Black women traverse in many facets of their lives. Esposito (2011) captured this dialectic, noting the following:

> Regardless of social context, . . . bodies are sites of struggle and power (Foucault, 1979); they speak social codes (Grosz, 1995); and these codes are continually contested and resignified. . . . Our everyday practices and bodily inscriptions not only reproduce gender and race, but they also help to produce what gender and race signify. (p. 144)

The stereotypes about Black women are vast and plentiful and unfortunately inform many of the cognitive scripts organizational members reference as they engage in the hiring process. Many stereotypes about Black women label them as aggressive, boisterous, overly confident, outspoken, and "the angry Black woman" (Evans-Winters & Esposito, 2010, p. 12). Collins (1986) noted that many of the characteristics that comprise Black women stereotypes are "actually distorted renderings of those aspects of Black female behavior seen as most threatening to White patriarchy" (p. 17). As Black women seek positions at PWIs of higher education, many of which are bastions of patriarchy and hegemonic norms and values, they find themselves engaging in strategic impression management. Several studies have shown that WOC find themselves downplaying elements of their racial and/ or cultural identities to fit in/assimilate to the institutional culture and environment (Dawson, 2006; Fearfull & Kamenou, 2006; Wyatt & Silvester, 2015).

From the way they elect to wear their hair (e.g., in its natural state versus straightened) during the interview to the way they articulate their words, Black women are cognizant of these historical and socially constructed stereotypes and strive to intentionally disrupt them. Impression management is an arduous task, making it difficult for Black women to reflect their authentic selves in the hiring process. If Black women must constantly engage in code-switching and impression management, regulating their level of authenticity, true job fit cannot be attained.

ON THE JOB

The onboarding and acclimation process is unique and, at times, challenging for Black women as they juggle being their authentic selves with managing others' preconceived notions of their abilities, intellect, and social identities. Like most people starting a new job in a new environment, there are things they must learn to better fulfill their duties. Within the context of higher education, new hires must learn the culture of the institution and the department. This can comprise deeply rooted norms, assumptions, values, and beliefs that inform and shape practice and behavior (Museus & Harris, 2010).

Navigating the Hidden Curriculum

As Black women traverse their new positions in higher education, they begin to learn the institutional and departmental culture and understand how well they fit into that culture. Along with learning the explicit institutional culture, they must navigate the hidden or implicit cultural norms, values, "common sense" rules, and expectations—the "hidden curriculum" (Esposito, 2011, p. 143; Jackson, 1968; Margolis, 2001; Margolis & Romero, 1998). Navigation of the hidden curriculum informs how individuals operate and exist within the environment (Esposito, 2011; Margolis & Romero, 1998; Thomas & Hollenshead, 2001). While there is emergent scholarship that examines how WOC students in higher education navigate the hidden curriculum (see Esposito, 2011; Margolis & Romero, 1998), there is scant literature that looks at navigating the hidden curriculum in higher education from the standpoint of professional WOC. Regardless, many of the elements of the hidden curriculum for WOC students can be applied to WOC professionals in higher education. Margolis and Romero (1998) suggested that the environments and mechanisms in which the hidden curriculum manifests include departmental culture, meetings, professional relationships, duty allocations, cliques, and promotion practices, among others.

At PWIs of higher education, WOC and other marginalized individuals are often not privy to this hidden curriculum, but they must learn it quickly to thrive and be successful in these spaces. WOC professionals in higher education must learn the nuances of their job roles and expectations while simultaneously learning "how their bodies fit into larger political, social, and cultural contexts" (Esposito, 2011, p. 144). The hidden curriculum can manifest in myriad ways. However, at the core, these implicit lessons are designed to maintain existing culture and practice, uphold privilege, and retain the interests and knowledge of the dominant group (Apple & King, 1977; Margolis & Romero, 1998). Acknowledging and learning the curriculum can be the difference between thriving and floundering in one's new role.

Disrupting the Curriculum

Although this may seem fatalistic and paint a picture that Black women are not successfully navigating the higher education environment professionally, many are in fact thriving and excelling by tapping into navigational capital (Yosso, 2005). Ingeniously, Black women have learned how to disrupt the curriculum. They have discovered how to transform spaces and situations to meet their needs by employing resistant and aspirational capital (Yosso, 2005). The skills and insights acquired through oppositional positioning, coupled with the persistence necessary to reach future goals, allow Black women to successfully circumvent barriers, adversities, or ill-fitting positions. Both capitals are "forms of cultural wealth" (Yosso, 2005, p. 81) rooted in communities of color to empower self and progress toward social and racial justice.

Resistant Capital

Sulé (2011) suggested that some Black women resist marginalization inside and beyond higher education's walls by embodying "oppositional positions" (p. 170) that allow WOC to acknowledge their marginalized identities while actively resisting and undermining daily personal and collective subordination. Oppositional positions manifest when Black women enter spaces and challenge perceived constructs of Black women's lived experiences. Earlier work from WOC scholar bell hooks (1990) also speaks to the transformative power of using marginality as a place to resist. hooks (1990) explained that when marginality is used as a site of resistance, it "offers to one the possibility of radical perspective from which to see and create, to imagine alternatives, new worlds" (p. 50).

For example, there has been an increase in the use of critical frameworks and pedagogy by Black women faculty, graduate students, and scholar-practitioners to undergird their work. These frameworks interrogate places of power, privilege, and systematic oppression and allow the lived experiences and voices of Black women and other WOC to take center stage. This oppositional position allows Black women in the academy to "affirm their identity and social position" (Sulé, 2011, p. 170), going beyond just being physically present and contributing to compositional diversity, but instead embodying action that challenges the status quo.

Tools of Resistant Capital Fostering Navigational and Social Capital

Audre Lorde (1984) proclaimed, "The master's tools will never dismantle the master's house" (p. 111). As such, when Black women manifest oppositional positions in higher education, they acknowledge that a new or reimagined set of tools are required and look within their locus of control to foster empowerment and change. One such tool has been mentoring relationships. There is considerable literature that speaks to the benefits of mentorship in higher education. Most of that literature looks at the importance of mentoring for students in college. However, mentoring has been a useful tool for Black women to assist them in successfully navigating the academy.

When Black women serve as mentors for one another, a pipeline of WOC in higher education is created. Guinier (1997) suggested WOC mentors empower through feedback, guidance, and sharing. Their outsider-within statuses allows WOC mentors to be both advocate and member, strategically assisting others (DuBois, 1903/1994; Guinier, 1997; Collins, 1986). For Black women in the academy, mentoring relationships can increase their social capital by expanding their network and access; navigational capital by helping them understand the institutional and/or departmental culture; and aspirational capital by validating their perspectives and affirming their personal and professional goals. When Black women mentor one another and assist each other in navigating the academy, they foster a community that can collectively dismantle systematic oppression in higher education and help one another find their true fit.

Aspirational Capital

Yosso (2005) noted that each form of cultural capital does not stand alone, but works synergistically, building on one another as a collective community of cultural wealth. As such, when Black women engage in resistant capital, drawing on oppositional positions daily to resist micro- and macro-oppressions in higher education, they increase their aspirational capital as well. An element of aspirational capital is having the ability to dream, hope, and be inspired for the future even when barriers seem insurmountable. Ray (2006) suggested that aspirations emerge within an "aspiration window" (p. 409), where dreams and future behaviors are inspired. Through aspiration windows, Black women can establish aspirations and find inspiration from the experiences, accomplishments, and ideals of the lives of those who exist in their aspiration window. When Black women engage with other WOC professionals in higher education, whether in a mentoring relationship or as a colleague, these interactions serve as visual correlations between image and possibility—becoming an "aspirational window to help them envision possibilities for themselves and their future" (Zell, 2014, p. 9).

As Black women strive to find fit within the higher educational environment, they continually draw on their aspirational capital to persist and thrive. When an incongruence of fit is acknowledged, Black women can use their aspirational capital to elevate themselves to more congruent and better-fitting positions. These tactics include developing clear and attainable goals, setting pragmatic time lines, executing their work beyond expectations, maintaining self-discipline, exuding confidence, sustaining hope, concentrating on outcomes, and, finally, seeing themselves in their future possibilities (Zell, 2014). These approaches allow Black women to simultaneously engage in oppositional positions while using their aspirational capital to resist and maintain hope despite perceived barriers or fit incongruence.

Even when the curriculum is concealed, Black women continue to employ resistant and aspirational capital to successfully navigate institutions of higher education that may not always be spaces of safety, support, or fit. Using their "outsider within" status, Black women have engaged in strategic resistance, tapped into their spheres of influence to harness meaningful relationships to navigate spaces, and disrupted the curriculum by challenging the status quo. As we seek to understand how Black women find fit in the higher educational context, we do so with the recognition that even if the spaces Black women enter have not been designed with us in mind, we do, in fact, still rise.

RECOMMENDATIONS

In the sections to follow, we provide suggestions for department managers and university leaders looking to diversify their institutions and reminders for Black women as they navigate careers in higher education.

Recommendations for Institutional Members

Before the start of any search process, department leaders should reflect on the institutional and departmental mission, values, and goals. These espoused beliefs should inform the presentation of a transparent and authentic context for the position. A commitment to diversity should be well aligned with the institutional mission (Smith, 2015). The centrality of a diversity commitment may be shaped by institutional type, but it should be acknowledged prior to creating or advertising a vacancy. Often, when institutions acknowledge a commitment to diversity, they simply mean they are open to, or are specifically recruiting, POC. However, what is unclear is if there is a commitment to shifting the culture of the university to become a space in which POC are full members of the community, rather than conditional guests (Ahmed, 2012). Ahmed (2012) suggested, "The word 'diversity' invokes difference but does not necessarily evoke commitment to action or redistributive justice" (p. 53). We believe structural (i.e., increasing the representational diversity) and integrative (i.e., creating a cultural climate that embraces various perspectives, beliefs, etc.) measures of diversity are necessary, but not every institution is designed with or prepared to make such a commitment. Thus, reflection and admittance of what the institution values is the best place to start for hiring managers. Moving forward in the hiring process will be easier once all parties understand the priorities for the department.

After reflecting on the mission, departmental leaders can determine what is needed in a new hire. If looking to recruit and create a diverse pool of applicants, search committee members must understand their charge. The hiring manager should communicate their expectations for a diverse pool and support the committee in effective recruitment strategies. This starts by creating a job description that explicitly discusses the mission and values of the department as well as the goals for the position. The level at which diversity is prioritized in the department can be communicated through the job description and reflected in other public materials, such as a department website. Institutions can use inclusive language (i.e., neutral pronouns); articulate an emphasis on developing innovative practices; and employ a staff representing diverse backgrounds, educational training, and perspectives.

Next, hiring managers should develop evaluation standards for use by search committee members. Standards for evaluation should match the minimum qualifications outlined in the job description. Training should be held to ensure search committee members can objectively review and evaluate applications to create diverse pools. If you want to establish parameters around type of degree and quality of degree, make sure that information is explicitly listed in the job description. You may also add years of experience, or prior experience executing certain responsibilities, as a requirement to communicate the expectations for a new hire with only paraprofessional-level work experience. Providing training for how to adjudicate and value educational and work experiences that may be different from one's own will further reduce undue bias in the review process.

Moreover, hiring managers should be prepared to challenge their own implicit biases surrounding fit and the prototypical candidate. Hiring team members should become comfortable questioning and naming the biases of one another to aid in the disruption of dominant narratives that pervade the higher education context. The reality, unfortunately, is that individuals are not always comfortable calling themselves or others out on their biases. There is inherent risk involved with the sensitive nature of attending to bias; it can create tension, distrust, and hostility. However, attending to bias is necessary to create a hiring process in which difference is acknowledged, valued, and appreciated. Regardless of the questions asked and the statements made around diversity, the most dangerous aspect of the hiring process for Black women lies in the unknown minds of her evaluators. Guided reflections and opportunities to explore and name one's own biases will alleviate some of the potential bias in the hiring process, but a continual process of checking one's beliefs must be maintained.

Recruitment from the institutional perspective requires a high level of intentionality. This requires hiring managers to adopt new strategies that go beyond including a statement in their job description saying they welcome applications from women and underrepresented minorities. Recruiting a diverse pool by utilizing the standard strategies is inefficient. A reasonable person would not go to an apple orchard with the hopes of buying a pumpkin. Recruiters should not solely rely on posting their jobs to the job board of their PWI and think Black women will find it. Organizations truly committed to creating a diverse applicant pool should consider strategies that will place their job advertisement in the hands of diverse candidates. Job advertisements can be distributed through the affinity groups within various professional associations, journals, publications, and social media outlets that focus on issues relevant to people of varying identities.

Finally, department leaders must prepare their employees to welcome and integrate a new member once a candidate is hired. Preparation includes outlining what the onboarding process will look like for new hires: "Organizational socialization, or onboarding, is a process through which new employees move from being organizational outsiders to becoming organizational insiders" (Bauer & Erdogan, 2011, p. 51). Engaging new hires at the beginning of their employment influences their retention, job satisfaction, and overall effectiveness (Bauer & Erdogan, 2011). From the employer perspective, successful onboarding activities include formal orientations, acceptance by organizational members, assisting new employees with role clarity, and sharing information related to organizational culture (Bauer &

Erdogan, 2011). Current employers may require additional training to support new employees, but minimally, department leaders should outline the expectations for current employees to assist with the onboarding process. While the new employee has some responsibilities for their own successful socialization, the organizational members need to commit to supporting and engaging new employees in the work of the department.

The success of new employees is directly connected to support from colleagues through mentoring and openness to their contributions (Smith, 2015). To increase the chance of positive connections among colleagues with differing identities, institutional and department leaders can create opportunities to explore individual's similarities across identity. Depending on the departmental or institutional culture, development sessions may include facilitated dialogues around social identities and systems of oppression and privilege. Department members could present their research or discuss their philosophies around working with students, staff, and faculty in department meetings. Supervisors should be held responsible for creating inclusive work environments for the benefit of all department members.

Onboarding Black women means communicating acceptance in a way that acknowledges and challenges the raced and gendered status quo of higher education. It is important that department heads connect with Black women to discuss the goals of the department to diversify in a way that impacts the core functions of the department. Telling the new employee how their role will help move the department forward will communicate value in their experience and presence beyond the role of token. Connecting Black women to networks of individuals across the university will appeal to the community-oriented mind-set of WOC and counter feelings of isolation that may affect a successful onboarding process, ultimately increasing their resistant and aspirational capital.

Recommendations for Black Women in Higher Education

In this section, we feel it is important to be in community with Black women and speak in the collective voice. Speaking from this perspective, we own our positionality as Black women and honor our commitment to center our collective voices and experiences. The previous section demonstrates that colleges and universities must commit to and create space for Black women in higher education. The recommendations we offer are meant to empower, encourage, and elevate you as Black women and are in no way an indication that we believe Black women must fix a system they did not create. We want to be explicit and say that Black women and our education and experiences are not liabilities, but unique and valuable assets.

When we consider what is required to traverse the higher education hiring process and to find fit, we must tap into our cultural wealth to dismantle spaces not designed with us in mind. We must own that we are holders of each form of capital outlined throughout this chapter. Next, we must be comfortable using that capital. Based on Yosso's (2005) six forms of community cultural wealth, we offer recommendations for you as Black women through the lens of each form of capital.

Social Capital

Given that Black women experience PWIs as racialized and gendered environments, mentoring and professional development opportunities will support your success in these spaces. Inquire about resources, networking opportunities, and guidance that may be provided as a part of the socialization process. Additionally, it is critical you play an active role in your own socialization to the organization. This means choosing to engage with your colleagues, learn about the culture and goals of the department, and participate in current practices (Bauer & Erdogan, 2011). Finally, make sure that you network; find your community within and outside of your institution (i.e., "your people"); and use those networks to help you find jobs, prepare for interviews, and learn the hidden curriculum.

Navigational Capital

The hidden curriculum is real. You *must* learn it to figure out fit. It is paramount you determine what is real and what is institutional politics. This can only be done once the blinders are removed. Although many of these spaces were not designed with you in mind, navigating these spaces with a level of authenticity is ideal. Start your search process with honest reflections on negotiable and nonnegotiable aspects of the position, department culture, institutional priority, and location. Determine for yourself how or if you will navigate racialized and gendered environments and at what cost to your personal well-being and professional advancement.

Resistant Capital

Audre Lorde (1984) reiterates that sometimes you will stand alone, unpopular because of oppression and marginalization. The oppositional position you hold as a Black woman allows you to resist these forces to affect change. For example, during the interview process, be prepared to ask about the culture and climate of the department and university to assess what your experience as a Black woman may be in those spaces. You may ask specifically for those with whom you are meeting to describe the culture and climate. You may ask indirect questions, such as, "How do folks feel after one or two years working here? How are departmental decisions made? How are employees groomed or prepared for their next position while working here?"

You must assume that there will be spaces where new perspectives and ideals will be received with skepticism. For example, not all institutions have embraced the idea of diversity with the same level of importance as embracing technology (Smith, 2015). Be comfortable asking questions related to institutional priorities, the role of the position in the larger department, and your ability to create change within the department and institutional community. Questions you ask could be directed toward search committee members or the direct supervisor during the interview process. Although asking questions directly related to diversity efforts and institutional change may seem intimidating due to the personal and professional risks of seeming combative or difficult, it is essential for you to make informed decisions about fit.

Aspirational Capital

Every job opportunity is a stepping-stone for a new opportunity. If fit is not obtained, stay the course and use your aspirational capital to seize the next opportunity. Use your personal and professional goals to motivate you to greater heights and to spaces that will value all that you bring to the table. The networks you have created and the curriculum you have learned to traverse are all tools in your toolbox to help you achieve the next opportunity.

While navigating the job search can be overwhelming and seemingly inauthentic, as a Black woman you should feel confident and encouraged to bring your whole self to the application, interview, and job. The burden should not be placed on you as the applicant or new hire to change the traditions of a racialized and gendered system while seeking employment or starting your new position. However, once you have integrated into the organization, you can then begin to challenge the status quo and push for change as needed.

CONCLUSION

Throughout this chapter, we examined the contexts and considerations of establishing fit in higher education for Black women. From hiring managers and search committee members to department heads, everyone has a role to play in creating an inclusive environment that works for all constituents. The main source of mismatches in fit is a lack of authenticity in the job search process. Black women should feel comfortable and confident in who they are and share that during the interview process. Institutions should be clear about their priorities and not pretend to be more open than they are. Organizational leaders at PWIs can no longer maintain a White, male, heteronormative standard of professionalism and expect to create diverse environments. Similarly, organizational leaders can no longer afford to avoid creating diverse environments without risking their status as viable institutions (Smith, 2015). Organizational leaders must embrace diversity as a mission-critical advancement to stay relevant in the competitive higher education market.

Hiring managers in education should use the scholarship found in the field of industrial/organizational psychology and human resource development to understand the processes needed for recruitment, onboarding, and talent management. The first 6 weeks of the college experience is crucial to a new student's success and retention at their institution (Woosley, 2003). In the same way, an individual's job fit, congruence, and overall satisfaction are influenced by their experiences in the first 90 days or less. Supervisors and department members must fully engage in onboarding processes to support all new organization members.

The cycle of diversification (i.e., the desire to increase visual representation of social identities) grants Black women some access to predominantly White spaces, but not full access; creating the "outsider within" status and hindering true fit from being obtained. The first step in creating spaces for Black women to engage and advance as professionals is to commit to valuing their experiences and contributions. Department members must embrace an inclusive appreciation for diversity that goes beyond numbers and truly value all that Black women have to offer for them to find fit in higher education.

REFERENCES

Ahmed, S. (2012). *On being included: Racism and diversity in institutional life*. Durham, NC: Duke University Press.

Anzaldúa, G. (Ed.). (1990). *Making face, making soul: Haciendo caras: Creative and critical perspectives by feminists of color.* San Francisco, CA: Aunt Lute Books.

Apple, M. W., & King, N. P. (1977). What do schools teach? In R. H. Weller (Ed.), *Humanistic education* (pp. 29–63). Berkeley, CA: McCutchan.

Barnett-Johnson, K. R. (2010). Moving heaven and earth: Black women in admin searches. *Women in Higher Education, 19*(8), 13–14.

Bauer, T. N., & Erdogan, B. (2011). Organizational socialization: The effective onboarding of new employees. In S. Zedeck (Ed.), *APA handbook of industrial and organizational psychology: Vol. 3. Maintaining, expanding, and contracting the organization* (pp. 51–64). Retrieved from http://psycnet.apa.org.libproxy .clemson.edu/books/12171/002.html

Carter, D., Pearson, C., & Shavlik, D. (1996). Double jeopardy: Women of color in higher education. In C. Turner, M. Garcia, A. Nora, & L. Rendon (Eds.), *Racial & ethnic diversity in higher education* (pp. 460–464). Needham Heights, MA: Simon & Schuster Custom Publishing.

Chickering, A. W., & Reisser, L. (1993). *Education and identity* (2nd ed.) (p. 144). San Francisco, CA: Jossey-Bass.

Collins, P. H. (1986). Learning from the outsider within: The sociological significance of Black feminist thought. *Social Problems, 33*(6), S14–S32.

Collins, P. H, & Bilge, S. (2016). *Intersectionality.* Malden, MA: Polity Press.

Crenshaw, K. (1991). Mapping the margins: Intersectionality, identity politics, and violence against women of color. *Stanford Law Review, 43*, 1241–1299.

Dawson, G. (2006). Partial inclusion and biculturalism of African Americans. *Equal Opportunities International 25*(6), 433–449.

Dayton, J. (2015). *Higher education law: Principles, policies, and practice.* Bangor, ME: Wisdom Builders.

Delgado Bernal, D., & Villalpando, O. (2002). An apartheid of knowledge in academia: The struggle over the "legitimate" knowledge of faculty of color. *Equity and Excellence in Education, 35*(2), 169–180. doi:10.1080/713845282

DuBois, W. E. B. (1994). *The souls of Black folk.* New York, NY: Dover Publications. (Original work published 1903)

Esposito, J. (2011). Negotiating the gaze and learning the hidden curriculum: A critical race analysis of the embodiment of female students of color at a predominantly White institution. *Journal of Critical Education Policy Studies, 9*(2), 143–164.

Evans-Winters, V. E., & Esposito, J. (2010). Other people's daughters: Critical race feminism and Black girls' education. *Educational Foundations, 24*(1–2), 11–24.

Fearfull, A., & Kamenou, N. (2006). How do you account for it? A critical exploration of career opportunities for and experiences of ethnic minority women. *Critical Perspectives on Accounting 17*(7), 883–901.

Graves, S. (1990). A case of double jeopardy? Black women in higher education. *Initiatives, 53*, 3–8.

Guinier, L. (1997). Of gentlemen and role models. In A. K. Wing (Ed.), *Critical race feminism: A reader* (pp. 73–87). New York, NY: New York University Press.

hooks, bell. (1990). *Yearning: Race, gender, and cultural politics.* Boston, MA: South End Press.

Jackson, P. W. (1968). *Life in classrooms.* New York: Holt, Rinehart, and Winston.

Jones, S. R., Kim, Y. C., & Skendall, K. C. (2012). (Re-)Framing authenticity: Considering multiple social identities using autoethnographic and intersectional approaches. *The Journal of Higher Education, 83*(5), 698–723.

Kacmar, K. M., & Carlson, D. S. (1994). Using impression management in women's job search processes. *The American Behavioral Scientist, 37*(5), 682–696.

Krieger, L. H., & Fiske, S. T. (2006). Behavioral realism in employment discrimination law: Implicit bias and disparate treatment. *California Law Review, 94*, 997–1062.

Ladson-Billings, G. (2009). "Who you callin' nappy-headed?": A critical race theory look at the construction of Black women. *Race Ethnicity and Education, 12*(1), 87–99.

Lorde, A. (1984). *Sister outsider: Essays and speeches.* Berkeley, CA: Crossing Press.

Margolis, E. (Ed.) (2001). *The hidden curriculum in higher education.* New York, NY: Routledge.

Margolis, E., & Romero, M. (1998). "The department is very male, very White, very old, and very conservative": The functioning of the hidden curriculum in graduate sociology departments. *Harvard Educational Review, 68*(1), 1–32.

McPherson, M., Smith-Lovin, L., & Cook, J. M. (2001). Birds of a feather: Homophily in social networks. *Annual Review of Sociology, 27*, 415–444.

Mohr, T. S. (2014). Why women don't apply for jobs unless they're 100% qualified. *Harvard Business Review.* Retrieved from https://hbr.org/2014/08/why-women-dont-apply-for-jobs-unless-theyre-100-qualified

Museus, S. D., & Harris, F. (2010). Success among college students of color: How institutional culture matters. In T. E. Dancy II (Ed.), *Managing diversity: (Re)Visioning equity on college campuses* (pp. 25–43). New York, NY: Peter Lang.

Patitu, C. L., & Hinton, K. G. (2003). The experiences of African American women faculty and administrators in higher education: Has anything changed? *New Directions for Student Services, 104*, 79–93.

Ray, D. (2006). Aspirations, poverty and economic change. In A. Banerjee, R. Bénabou, & D. Mookherjee (Eds.), *What have we learnt about poverty?* (pp. 409–422). New York, NY: Oxford University Press.

Smith, D. G. (2015). *Diversity's promise for higher education: Making it work* (2nd ed.). Baltimore, MD: Johns Hopkins University Press.

Somers, M. R., & Gibson, G. D. (1994). Reclaiming the epistemological "other": Narrative and the social construction of identity. In C. Calhoun (Ed.), *Social theory and the politics of identity* (pp. 37–99). Cambridge, MA: Blackwell.

Staats, C. (2014). *State of the science: Implicit bias review 2014.* Kirwan Institute. Retrieved from http://kirwaninstitute.osu.edu/wp-content/uploads/2014/03/2014-implicit-bias.pdf

Sulé, V. T. (2011). Restructuring the master's tools: Black female and Latina faculty navigating and contributing in classrooms through oppositional positions. *Equity & Excellence in Education, 44*(2), 169–187.

Thomas, G. D., & Hollenshead, C. (2001). Resisting from the margins: The coping strategies of Black women and other women of color faculty members at a research university. *The Journal of Negro Education, 70*(3), 166–175.

Turner, C. S. V. (2002). Women of color in academe: Living with multiple marginality. *The Journal of Higher Education, 73*(1), 74–93.

U.S. Department of Education, National Center for Education Statistics, Integrated Postsecondary Education Data System (IPEDS). (Spring 2014). Table 314.40. Employees in degree granting postsecondary institutions, by race/ethnicity, sex, employment status, control and level of institution, and primary occupation: Fall 2013. *Digest of Education Statistics: 2014.* (Table prepared March 2015.) Washington DC: Author.

U.S. Department of Education, National Center for Education Statistics Integrated Postsecondary Education Data System (IPEDS). (Winter 2003–2004). Table 225. Employees in degree granting institutions, by race/ethnicity, primary occupation, sex, employment status, and control and type of institution: Fall 2003. *Digest of Education Statistics: 2004.* (Table prepared March 2005.) Washington DC: Author.

von Baeyer, C. L., Sherk, D. L., & Zanna, M. P. (1981). Impression management in the job interview: When the female applicant meets the male (chauvinist) interviewer. *Personality and Social Psychology Bulletin, 7*(1), 45–51.

West, N. M. (2015). In our own words: African American women student affairs professionals define their experiences in the academy. *Advancing Women in Leadership, 35*, 108–119.

Wiley, N. (1994). The politics of identity in American history. In C. Calhoun (Ed.), *Social theory and the politics of identity* (pp. 130–149). Cambridge, MA: Blackwell.

Wing, A. K. (1997). Introduction. In A. K. Wing (Ed.), *Critical race feminism: A reader* (pp. 1–9). New York, NY: New York University Press.

Wolf-Wendel, L. E. (2000). Women-friendly campuses: What five institutions are doing right. *The Review of Higher Education, 23*, 319–345.

Woosley, S. A. (2003). How important are the first few weeks of college? The long term effects of initial college experiences. *College Student Journal, 37*(2), 201–207.

Wyatt, M., & Silvester, J. (2015). Reflections on the labyrinth: Investigating Black and minority ethnic leaders' career experiences. *Human Relations, 68*(8), 1243–1269.

Yosso, T. J. (2005). Whose culture has capital? A critical race theory discussion of community cultural wealth. *Race Ethnicity and Education, 8*(1), 69–91.

Zell, M. C. (2014). Converting capital: The experiences of Latinas/os in graduate health care programs. *The Qualitative Report, 19*(43), 1–26.

Zinn, M. B., & Dill, B. T. (1996). Theorizing difference from multiracial feminism. *Feminist Studies, 22*(2), 321–331.

7

Code Word *FIT*

Exploring the Systemic Exclusion of Professionals of Color in Predominantly White Institutions

Heather O. Browning and Patrice M. Palmer

W HEN IMAGINING YOUR fit in a space not designed for you, consider the analogy of the oval. Even though an oval is rounded in shape, it is not quite a circle. In trying to align itself with the outline, parts of it will match up, but the entire oval will not fit in its circular space. People of color represent this oval, this object that is circular in shape but is not a circle. The fit narrative is that circle, the standard through which all things must pass. We have been socialized to achieve circle status; we have been bombarded by theory that has told us to reshape our oval design in order to achieve success. As professionals of color, we want to fit. However, do we give up our authenticity to achieve that?

Embarking on this journey of writing about job fit is personal to us. We, the authors of this chapter, write from our differing identities and perspectives, while recognizing where those intersect through our experiences as professionals of color in student affairs. As a Black, cisgender woman, I (Heather) have experienced trials and challenges in building my own foundation of professional authenticity within student affairs. Reflecting on my experiences, I recognize that my socialization into the field as a professional of color lacked insight into how to critically examine my environments to determine how they were, or were not, set up to support me. I can distinctly recall the dissonance I felt during my transition from graduate school to my first professional position, including internalizing the challenges I experienced as something that was a fault of my own. I tried to fix my professional way of being instead of understanding the complexities of my environments and learning how to navigate them while staying true to myself.

I (Patrice), a transmasculine AFAB (assigned female at birth), bring the intersections of trans, Black, and Queer, with all of their ups and downs. Each salient identity works in tandem as I navigate the world. Even introducing pronouns such as sHE and HEr can be very intimidating to a society that I experience as seeing presentation and assumption as one in the same. My trans identity is acknowledged only in a medically transitioning way, and not as the umbrella term that I encompass. I am Black *unapologetically*, I am Queer *absolutely!* Does that affect the way I'm seen professionally? *Yes, indeed!* The way I dress, speak, and "show up" are predicated on my feminine name (which is actually unisex; thanks, Mom) and the characteristics assigned to it. I don't fit in the binary, so how can I look to fit in an environment that sees my gender—or lack thereof—and my Blackness as assets? I meet the diversity niche, but only because my identities are visible. That visibility is also marked by invisibility when salient identities are exploited to make departments "look" more diverse. My "why" is embedded in my exclusion within a predominantly White institution (PWI), while I am looked at as fulfilling a specific value within my university objective; I feel I am seen only through the eyes of diversity as it relates to filling a quota.

This chapter equips the reader with an understanding of how the interconnectedness and influence of race and racism, individual characteristics, and sociocultural factors shape interactions, decision-making, and the lens through which job culture, and fit, are constructed. We offer clarity and validation to professionals of color who may find themselves challenged with similar struggles of showing up authentically in their respective work environments. We will provide general insight for those looking to understand the workplace challenges many student affairs professionals of color experience in order to create critical conversations and thoughts around the concepts of job fit and professionalism. Within the profession of student affairs, it is imperative to understand the experience of professionals of color within our own institutional contexts to create environments where professionals can thrive.

Institutional environments contribute to excluding professionals of color, and limit their abilities to be authentic, in the workplace at PWIs. We will examine the multilayered environments that influence a person's experience at work, including the individual and contextual factors that play a role in creating and shaping job fit. Bronfenbrenner's (1994) ecological theory provides a useful framework for describing human conditions and how human development is influenced by a series of interactions between the social systems that structure individuals' day-to-day realities (Neville & Mobley, 2001). We also weave in critical race theory (CRT), which offers a counterstory and communicates the experiences and realities of communities of color (Ladson-Billings & Tate, 1995). CRT tells us that the experiences professionals of color have are real and valid, and there is power in naming these realities. Professionals of color are often isolated on PWI campuses and internalize their experiences as faults of their own rather than outwardly acknowledging the systems of inequity built without them in mind.

The journey to developing professional authenticity is an overarching theme in this chapter. As the authors of this chapter, we believe authenticity is unique to each individual. Drawing on the works of Brené Brown (2010), authenticity is not something you are or are not. It is not something you have or don't. It is a daily, conscious choice of how you want to live, a cultural, social, and physical expression of your true self. In holding true to our authenticity as authors, we will be sharing our personal stories and journeys. Part of this is sharing in unconventional ways to preserve and validate our identities and who we are. Honoring the uniqueness each of us brings begins to break the cycle that causes problems within the complex construct of fit. Although speaking in the ways that we do throughout this chapter may not align with expectations of academic writing, academia does not always align with the fluidity of the gender binary. We decided to write in first person to personalize our stories and experiences and honor our respective identities.

HISTORICAL FORMATIONS OF WHITE SUPREMACIST NORMS IN HIGHER EDUCATION

To understand the concept of fit, we must unpack the narrative from which fit has emerged. In the context of the United States of America, higher education spaces were first created for elite, White, heterosexual, cisgender men. Wilder (2013) writes of an unknown slave referred to only as the Moor, "The birth of slavery in New England was also the dawn of slavery at Harvard. . . . He remains the first enslaved Black person documented in the colony, and his life more tightly braids the genesis of slavery in New England into the founding of the college" (p. 29). White cultural ideology is historically embedded in the language, cultural practices, and traditions of higher education institutions (Gusa, 2010). Therefore, discussing the central role that race has played in creating social, political, and economic systems of inequalities is essential to understanding current conceptualizations of professionalism and job fit (Guess, 2006). Ignoring the influence of race as a factor denies the systemic complexities and disadvantages that student affairs professionals of color face in their work experiences.

Racial stratification was constructed as a way to separate inherent superiority and inferiority of groups based on racial distinctions and is guided by a White, elite power structure (Guess, 2006; Neville & Mobley, 2001). Whiteness can best be understood as a category of privilege or access held by Whites, which is "a system of opportunities and benefits conferred upon people simply because they are White" (Solórzano & Yosso, 2002, p. 27). Whiteness defines the norms and values through which our society operates, creating socially significant consequences for communities of color that fall outside of this defined normalcy (Chubbuck, 2004; Guess, 2006). Whiteness implicitly excludes Blackness and Brownness (Thompson, 2001).

Critically examining the historical oppression of communities of color by institutions of higher education provides a glimpse into how Whiteness has left lasting impacts that we still see functioning today. The more ways that professionals of color find themselves differing from the White norm, the more their social interactions within the university are affected (Turner, 2002). While being authentic may seem like an easy choice, there are reasons why being authentic can feel like a dangerous risk for some professionals of color. If a professional of color shows up as their authentic self in a workplace that devalues the qualities that make them authentic, will they be seen as a good fit? Will being authentic at work impact external perceptions of their work performance, professionalism, and ability for upward movement and mobility? We must dismantle the systems that were created to reinforce a workplace culture designed with Whiteness as the norm.

Dismantling an institution's historical legacy of exclusion can assist in understanding the present campus climate and how that climate influences current practices, revealing an embedded culture of systematic oppression that may still exist (Hurtado, Milem, Clayton-Pedersen, & Allen, 1998). It is important to consider the complete historical context of an institution, which may uncover how the process of creating a culture of fit translates to continued exclusion of people of color today. Historic institutional oppressions may directly affect the ways in which an institution currently operates. Dartmouth College, for example, is well known for its support of Native American education, but the institution has a history rooted in Whiteness and cultural erasure. As a result, Dartmouth demonstrates how an institution can take ownership to reconcile its tainted history and create better environments for the constituents it aims to serve.

Dartmouth was founded as a school to train Native Americans as Christian missionaries as a means of salvation for Native populations (Jaimes, 1999). In turn, the college served to contribute to the forced cultural erasure and suppression of Indigenous culture rather than providing an institution to serve their educational needs (Jaimes, 1999). Today, Dartmouth's commitment to Indigenous education has evolved through the establishment of Native American academic and social programming ("The Native Legacy," 2016). According to its Native American Program's website, nearly 700 Native Americans from over 200 tribes have attended Dartmouth to obtain a higher education since the institution took intentional steps to name its mistreatment of Native American communities about 50 years ago ("The Native Legacy," 2016). Now that Dartmouth has named its oppression against Indigenous communities, it can work to heal and restore the relationships damaged by centuries of colonialism and institutionalized oppression.

SURVIVING VERSUS THRIVING: THE IMPACT OF ENVIRONMENT ON ABILITY TO THRIVE

Understanding an institution's norms, traditions, policies, and practices is important to deeply examine the environments that impact a professional's day-to-day interactions and their ability to thrive. These experiences cannot be fully understood without understanding how environmental, individual, and contextual factors play a role in the creation and shaping of job fit. From our perspectives, to fit is to possess a professional and personal identity that aligns with institutional norms and values without nuance. When deconstructing the layers of a work environment, we see how fit is interconnected to Whiteness. This is perpetuated by cultural norms created within work environments. Here, we apply Bronfenbrenner's (1994) ecological model, which breaks down environments into various levels depending on their sphere of influence on the individual, relationships, institutions, and society at large. By examining fit and race through this lens, we are able to better examine, understand, and conceptualize the interactions between professionals of color and their work environment at different scales.

Take, for example, the interactions between the work and home environments. If a professional of color has a home environment with a particular value system (e.g., behavior, mannerisms) but then finds different expectations in their work environment, the professional must find ways to transition between these two spaces on a consistent and daily basis. I (Heather) grew up in a household where the needs of family were valued over the individual. This collectivist thought meant that there was no such thing as "self-made" because each family member contributed to the successes of the others; everyone played a role. Translating this into the workplace, I am very team-oriented. I believe that it is a team's responsibility to care for and to look out for each other. Our own success is bound in each other's success. I am more focused on the process of how the work impacts individual members than focusing solely on the end results achieved by individuals. I have found myself thriving, and fitting, into work environments that value this type of approach. On the other hand, it is a struggle in environments where the emphasis is purely on individual performance, creating an underlying culture of competition with no emphasis on team unity or group care. Growing up in a collectivist environment, and seeking that in a workspace, has a direct impact on my ability to fit (or be seen as a fit) with environments that do not center, but rather omit, my cultural way of being.

The reality for many professionals of color is a systematic tension between their authentic selves (i.e., cultural way of being) and who the profession demands that they be (Browning & Weiser, 2015). Professionals of color, much like ourselves, are often challenged with negotiating aspects of their identities and true selves in order to fit the norms of the workplace, particularly at PWIs. In order to gain social acceptance and be treated as social equals within the workspace, we have had to adopt White modes of being (Ogbu, 2004). When seeking to fit, professionals of color will change in order to hide behind the masks of conformity. For me (Patrice), my speech and disposition went first. Then clothing and hair until "they" felt I had transformed into a "professional" and not a diverse analog of ideas, abilities, and experiences wrapped in a melanated package. The shedding of that insecurity and need to fit has been a long and tedious process that continues to this day.

Looking beyond the interactions between the home and work environments, there are settings and events in which professionals are not directly involved, but which nonetheless have a direct influence on their experiences. Examples include an institution's racial campus climate and decisions made on behalf of an employee without their input, such as campus policies and norms. While the individual does not necessarily have control over these aspects, they still directly impact their work experience. This can also show up around racial representation. Browning and Weiser (2015) discussed how student affairs professionals of color often find themselves navigating the unfair burdens of racial representation and are asked to take on the bulk of diversity work at PWIs. Even though this work may fall outside of their job role and responsibilities, limited staff diversity on campus results in professionals of color being consistently tapped. These workload additions are coded in underlying expectations influenced by a person's racial identity. This invisible labor is often undervalued and is not rewarded in ways that are beneficial toward a professional's career advancement (Williams, 2015). Rather, it causes professionals of color to feel overburdened or tokenized.

Reflecting on my (Heather's) own experiences, I have found myself assigned responsibilities and asked to use my expertise, with the additional tasks coded as a part of my work. In one instance, this occurred without additional compensation in a setting where White counterparts doing the same work were being compensated. When I spoke up about it, I experienced a lack of support and understanding in how these added responsibilities were impacting my day-to-day work, keeping me from completing my other (paid) tasks in a timely manner. In the end, this bled into and affected my work/life balance and ability to thrive.

In the work setting, the university (and society/dominant culture as a whole) implements the overarching policies that can influence and change department/campus culture. The dissonance between the authentic self and the inauthentic self (behavior that we adapt to be deemed a "good professional") poses an internal conflict in professionals of color that leads us to make a decision to assimilate or to remain true to ourselves. The result of this conundrum is more complex than a binary, so professionals of color often end up playing two different roles at once: the self demanded by the workspace and the true self who shows up regardless of whom the workspace is demanding. We must take into account that a person lives within a society where identities and sociocultural values are stratified by a hierarchical system dominated by Whiteness and an unspoken set of rules, putting professionals of color at a disadvantage (Neville & Mobley, 2001).

THE ELEPHANT IN THE ROOM: FIT AS CODED LANGUAGE

There is an unspoken set of rules that dictates how professionals of color should show up in the workplace. The concept of *performativity* can be used to further understand this. Performativity is the reiteration or repetition of societal norms that have been established and reinforced over time (Butler, 1993). It implies historical conditions that were created, yet still impact the current day. Though Butler speaks about performativity as it relates to the socialization and social constraints of gender, this notion can be applied to how Whiteness confines professionals of color into the rigidity of fit.

Professionals of color are often asked to show up in ways that make White people feel comfortable. Though we may not be asked directly to change who we are, the indirect messaging is structured in a way that leaves little room for interpretation. Whiteness constructs a dominant framework, or code, that creates an embedded system of standards and language that influences the ways in which professionalism and fit are upheld (Gusa, 2010; Solórzano & Yosso, 2002). We, the authors of this chapter, have both experienced the impact of coded language.

When viewed through the lens of Whiteness, the policing of the vernacular—and what is deemed as acceptable or not acceptable in work environments—aims to distinguish the professional from the nonprofessional. As someone who has been described as loud and boisterous, I (Patrice) have been advised to "tone down" in professional environments. For some it may seem like proper etiquette, easily forgetting whose standard of (White) etiquette we are comparing it to. In hopes of not being the outsider, I silenced myself. I retreated to isolation when confronted with the "suggestion" to change. In that isolation, I became reserved, bitter, and silently angry. My presence was tainted with the notion that my authentic self was not welcomed, so to survive, I shut down. I internalized the notion that, in order to be a professional, I must silence a part of myself that made others uncomfortable.

Even the tone and sound of a professional of color's voice are impacted by fit. Since Whiteness normalizes what is deemed as acceptable work language, professionals of color often have to negotiate the way they sound in order to be considered for a role (Deprez-Sims & Morris, 2010). We may find ourselves lightening our voices to sound less threatening or more "feminine." To some it may sound absurd, but to many professionals of color who have been accused of being angry or intimidating based on how others perceive the sound of our voices, it matters. As a person who has what others may describe as a heavy voice, I (Patrice) have been told by White colleagues/students that I "talk too loud" or I "always sound mad." When I once (sarcastically) asked how to change the sound of my voice so that others felt more comfortable, it was met with "talk like a lady." The implication that my Black female voice was somehow innately masculine caused me to change my tone to make my words have a more upward inflection in order to make others feel comfortable and to fit into my surrounding environment. This voice change was met with smiles and affirmation. I personally knew what "ladylike" was coded to mean: *Sound White. Sound female. Sound anything other than what you are because your authentic tone makes me uncomfortable.*

As another example, many professionals of color speak one way at home and another way at work, a concept known as *code-switching*. Code-switching describes how people act or talk more like those around them in order to fit in. The socialization that occurs within cultural communities where the use of particular vernacular and/or slang can serve as indicators of ethnic affiliation and cultural belonging (De Fina, 2007; Young, 2009). The way that some professionals of color naturally communicate in their authentic environments can cause a sense of alienation in White spaces.

One of my (Heather's) experiences stems from a job interview for a position at a large, public PWI within their office of career services. Walking into the interview, I immediately noticed that the office staff appeared to be all White-identified women. Though I felt the interview went well, ultimately I did not receive an offer for the position. Wanting to gain feedback to improve on future opportunities, I set up a follow-up phone call with the interviewer. They told me that although my qualifications were solid, I was very animated in the interview, talked loudly, and spoke too much with my hands. Ultimately, they thought that would not have been a good fit for the office. My initial reaction to this feedback was to internalize it and ask myself how I could have been more "reserved" in how I showed up. I am grateful to have had a mentor, a woman of color, who was able to help me understand what was coded in the language of being "animated" and "speaking too much with my hands." She helped me decode the feedback and understand the problems in what the interviewer was actually saying without saying it. This experience also demonstrated to me the importance of mentorship. Without the perspective of a professional who understood what was happening, I would have been left in a state of dissonance and questioning my individual characteristics as they pertained to professional expectations of the field.

I (Patrice) recall my experience interviewing for a job in housing at a PWI. For the interview, I wore a suit and tie, my preferred style of dress and expression. Arriving at the interview, I was met with confused faces, which I did not take as a good sign. I received criticism from the interviewers in a joking manner for being "overdressed" for the interview. It soon became very clear to me that my authentic manner of expression through what I chose to wear was coded as being overdressed. This continued to show up throughout the interview process. After the rejection e-mail, I reached out to ask what could have been done differently. I was told to smile more and that I seemed intimidating, unapproachable, and "mean." I was also told to dress for my audience. The department has a more laid-back atmosphere and a suit and tie seemed a little "uptight" and again, "unapproachable."

Unlike Heather, I did not have a mentor of color at this time to process my experience. I carried this experience with me for quite some time. I dressed differently by not wearing a suit jacket and tie when I interviewed. I always made sure to have a smile on my face no matter the situation. I tried my best to ensure others felt comfortable with me by stepping back or looking for permission to take up space. The coding of "unapproachable," "mean," and "intimidating" were all phrases used to mask the interviewers' discomfort with my gender expression. Their discomfort made "fitting" impossible because there is nothing that I could have done to make them feel completely comfortable with my authentic self. I was made to choose between my authenticity or changing parts of myself. Thriving versus surviving. I chose the latter. I changed who I was, I went to work, and I was miserable every day. For years I wrestled with this. When I finally chose to be authentic over just being employed, I began to thrive. I realized my identity and sense of self were far more important.

By showing up authentically, however, I knew I was putting myself at risk, a risk that set me outside the norm of my peers and placed a spotlight on my gender expression. As a Queer person of color who expresses outside the gender binary, I had to choose how I would represent and advocate for myself in spaces that I didn't feel wanted *all* of me. By *all* I mean my Blackness, Queerness, and transmasculinity. I have found my identities to be compartmentalized and called upon depending on the needs of the workplace. There has been little room for the intersections of my identities to work together, which makes it challenging for me to show up authentically as my whole true self. For example, there were spaces where I was asked to support Black students but was also told in various ways to leave my transmasculinity at the door. In others, I would show up for Queer and Trans constituents, but my

Blackness was not recognized in those spaces. I no longer wanted to just be a monolithic being in accordance with others' needs depending on the space I was in. I wanted the right to be all those things in every space because that is who I am, in all of my totality. When I stopped looking to fit with my counterparts, I began to thrive in my work. My interactions with students became more authentic, and my ability to advocate for myself came from a place of power and self-worth, not fear.

Our experiences demonstrate how a professional of color experiences dissonance in institutional environments. When environments are not inclusive of identities outside of Whiteness, and Whiteness is positioned as the norm, the internal negotiation of a person of color's sense of identity and purpose is disrupted (Gusa, 2010). Showing up authentically in the ways that we did essentially cost us career opportunities. We were not seen as a fit for the roles solely based on who we are.

While there is no one way of being authentic, the narratives of authenticity are saturated in the dominant structural systems of what it means to embody Whiteness. The internalization of what is "normal," coupled with the external navigation of personally and professionally carving out a space to exist, can create tension that is both physically and emotionally cumbersome. CRT reinforces the notion that the system is flawed. It centers the narratives and experiences of professionals of color rather than blaming them for their inability to conform (Iverson, 2007; Yosso, 2005). CRT puts the ownership on the institutions that center Whiteness as the measurement of fit, contributing to how professionals of color internalize their inability to fit into professional spaces. The reality is that institutional structures, environments, and their practices are systematically influenced by race and racism (Yosso, 2005). Those who identify as White may find more fluidity fitting into professional spaces specifically as it relates to their racial identity and professional appearance because Whiteness is positioned as the norm, influencing both how *professionalism* is defined and how the concept of fit is applied (Gusa, 2010). Pushing against the erasure of cultural authenticity as a professional of color is important in order to be able to show up as one's true self.

TOKENIZATION AND THE EXPLOITATION OF CULTURAL CAPITAL

It is exhausting to be one of a few professionals of color at a PWI. We are asked to show up in ways that directly align with our identities, ways in which our White counterparts are not. This includes being asked to be racial representatives on behalf of our communities, asked to creating new programs and initiatives to promote inclusive campus environments, called on when racial or racist incidents occur, and/or seen as experts *only* when it comes to matters of race (Orelus, 2013). Professionals of color are often an active and visible display of the diversity of a department, becoming valuable, yet tokenized, commodities to the workplace. Hurtado and colleagues (1998) define *tokenism* as contributing to the heightened visibility of the underrepresented group, exaggeration of group differences, and the distortion of images to fit existing stereotypes. The value created within institutions ends up assigned to a professional of color's visibility and physical presence, not around our community cultural wealth.

Community cultural wealth is defined as the accumulation of specific forms of knowledge, skills, and abilities that are valued by privileged groups in society (Yosso, 2005). Anything outside of Whiteness does not hold the same value. What may be deemed as valuable to a professional of color does not hold capital within predominantly White work environments. This subtle designation of value further establishes whose knowledge is accepted and whose knowledge is discounted (Yosso, 2005).

We believe that the knowledge, or cultural capital, that professionals of color bring is valued *only* when it benefits the university rather than being seen as a consistent source of expertise. This expertise is tokenized in work environments driven by Whiteness. This impedes our authenticity as we are asked to work in ways that benefit the university, but not us as professionals. CRT tells us that the experiential knowledge of people of color is indeed legitimate, appropriate, and critical to understanding the experiences of professionals of color (Solórzano & Yosso, 2002). It challenges the theories of cultural capital, giving voice to groups that have been repeatedly marginalized and recognizing that the experiential knowledge they hold is essential in understanding their experiences.

Speaking from my (Patrice's) own experiences as a Queer person of color, I have been asked to head numerous committees on Queer professionals of color and Queer ally partnerships, lent my expertise to search committees to ensure inclusive practices were occurring, and attended dinners and other events to visibly represent the department as a showing of departmental dedication. My demanded visibility accounted for longer hours, bigger projects, and added responsibility without additional compensation. Using my lived experiences in these ways made it possible for my White counterparts to be less accountable for engaging in diversity and inclusion work: "Oh Patrice can do it. They are the expert."

Holding the responsibilities of your job while being put in positions to educate others about who you are and how you show up is an example of emotional labor. We define *emotional labor* as the burden of unpaid, unacknowledged, and uncompensated tasks that professionals of color undertake. Consistently trying to explain yourself, your thoughts, and your experiences; showing up to make others comfortable; thinking about how your reactions may land on others; or being described as "angry" or "insubordinate" when you speak up are all examples of this concept. I (Patrice) can speak to the experience of expending emotional labor while working at a PWI with locs.

When meeting with a White colleague who had never seen me with my hair down, she proceeded to run her fingers through my locs, without consent, and commented on "how soft" they were. Taken aback, I did not know how to address being groped by this colleague without my consent, but I also did not want to come across as combative. Instead, I took the time to explain why it was inappropriate to touch my hair without consent when what I really wanted to do was walk away. Upon telling this colleague what they did was wrong, I then had to deal with the guilt and shame they expressed from being called out on their actions. Even though it was my personal space that had been violated, I carried the emotional labor of walking this colleague through the inappropriateness of her actions. It is exhausting to have to carve out space for your identities rather than that labor being taken on by others to carve it out for you. It is also exhausting to have to show up in ways that are not reflective of how you truly feel.

What we are speaking to are the common expectations, or "display rules," of how folks "should" show up in any given field. Ashforth and Humphrey (1993) define *display rules* as "what emotions ought to be *publicly* expressed rather than to what emotions are actually *felt*" (p. 89). These expectations define what are deemed appropriate emotional reactions. In student affairs, we are expected to be empathetic, compliant, accommodating, and flexible, regardless of the situation. The socialization of student affairs professionals teaches us to accept varying forms of harm and to put others before self. We are taught to deal with the emotions of others, but to *not* respond with our own emotions and to "fix" situations, even when there is harm. The violation Patrice experienced left a feeling of obligation to "appropriately" address their colleague by turning it into a teachable moment rather than feeling free to express their true emotions of anger, hurt, and guilt. In contrast to our

White peers, we as professionals of color are often made to feel as though we are combative or "sensitive" as it relates to issue of race.

Emotional management is racialized, and emotional norms vary across race. Professionals of color are prohibited from exhibiting true expressions of emotions, such as anger and frustration, particularly as it comes to issues they may experience in the workplace directly related to their race/ethnicity: "The feeling rules in professional workplaces are not neutral, but are in fact racialized in ways that deny [professionals of color] areas of emotional expression accessible to their White colleagues" (Wingfield, 2010, p. 265).

These are the types of experiences that interface with the White norms of a work environment while making it difficult for professionals of color to be authentic or thrive. There is a lack of discussion, acknowledgement, and training for professionals of color to successfully enter the field of student affairs. We are not prepared to effectively navigate the racialized dynamics and challenges of our work environments.

SOCIALIZED TO FIT

Coming into your professional authenticity means unlearning the socialized norms that you have become accustomed to. Messaging about job fit starts before student affairs professionals even enter the field, and it is important to critically examine the professional socialization that influences how student affairs professionals think about fit in order to understand how individuals make meaning of their professional experiences. Perez (2016) introduced a model for the socialization that occurs in graduate student affairs preparation programs, defining *professional socialization* as both gaining the knowledge and skills needed to succeed and internalizing how the typical practitioner behaves on the job. Student affairs socialization tends to focus on identifying institutional practices (e.g., synergistic supervision and professional development workshops) and conditions (e.g., cultural fit) that lead to "successful" professional socialization outcomes (Perez, 2016) without acknowledging the environmental conditions that are specific to the experiences of professionals of color. What is missing from these graduate programs is the knowledge and skills professionals of color need to evaluate institutional culture and work environments, as well as an understanding of how race shows up in work environments. A professional of color's experience and adjustment is dependent on what they experience day to day in their work environment

(Neville & Mobley, 2001). The strain of continually trying to show up in ways that cater to dominant societal values creates environments that suppress the ability to be authentic.

My (Heather's) own experiences of dissonance during the transition from graduate student to new professional highlight this problem. During my first professional job search, I knew I wanted a position with a direct focus on diversity and social justice, particularly working with underrepresented and marginalized student communities. I received recommendations and advice from faculty, mentors, and current professionals to identify institutional factors—such as university size, type, and academic rigor—that would be ideal for me. I was told to look for, read, and review university, department, and diversity mission statements, as they would provide insight into an institution's commitment to students, staff, and faculty of color. My limited understanding was that if these existed, then there must be a commitment.

The naïveté in my logic exemplifies the rhetoric that catches so many professionals of color off guard once they find themselves in their first jobs. I was not equipped to read between the lines and decode mission and value statements or to ask effective questions in an interview that would offer insight into the lived experiences of staff of color. Unfortunately, despite my efforts to find an institution and position that would allow me to bring my authentic self to work, my first job did not meet my expectations. I began experiencing situations in the role that evoked dissonance between my values and those of the organization, and I began questioning my own professional abilities as the factor for my discomfort.

Through experiences such as these, individuals begin to learn what fit really means for them. They make decisions about whether to give up aspects of themselves to fit in or to challenge the status quo by bringing themselves authentically into the workplace, a decision that is often an unsafe risk for professionals of color. Until we dismantle the systems and socializations that reinforce Whiteness as the workplace norm, determining whether that risk is something worth taking is up to each individual to decide.

FUTURE IMPLICATIONS

This chapter is a starting point for institutions and individuals to begin thinking about how to deconstruct fit and professionalism in their current systems of practice in order to reconstruct environments where professionals of color are able to show up in their authenticity. The system of Whiteness leaves professionals of color unable to fit, or be seen as a fit, in professional environments. To begin to address this, we must name the ways in which we see this show up in our work environments. In order to challenge this, student affairs professionals must self-reflect to understand the ways in which Whiteness has been internalized as it comes to their understanding of fit and professionalism.

For those who are in the position of hiring, remember that fit is a subjective concept with coded language rooted in Whiteness. It is important to unpack the cultural values of your institution and department, and what is meant by fit, before using it to determine someone's candidacy. There is validity to organizational needs. For example, if your department has a cooperative and team-oriented culture, a professional who prefers to work individually and not collaborate with others will not be a good fit.

Hiring professionals of color as tokens does not fix a broken system. It creates what we call the *POC assembly line*. The POC assembly line begins with eager professionals of color who are brought in, often as tokens to increase institutional diversity (by numbers), serve students of color, and impact (in theory) institutional change. Often, these professionals end up working in environments that are not conducive to their growth and development; do not allow them to show up authentically; and exploit their emotional labor, as the institutional commitment is really about creating visible diversity and not about actual institutional change. Quickly, these work environments become toxic. Professionals of color find themselves underrepresented, overworked, unsupported, and undervalued, leading to frustration and exhaustion. Ultimately, they are left with the choice of putting up with it or leaving. Instead of looking at the contributing factors that led to the loss of that professional of color, institutions simply hire the next one, who ultimately goes through the same thing. This is not a healthy or sustainable model for institutions committed to retaining professionals of color. We challenge institutions to review and reflect on the culture that they foster for professionals of color, particularly at PWIs. Are your professionals of color thriving or surviving? Instead of telling them, "You don't fit into the system," the culture needs to shift to be more inclusive and accommodating to folks outside of the dominant norms.

For student affairs professionals of color who find themselves in environments that make it difficult for them to show up authentically, we recommend seeking opportunities that allow you to connect with other staff of color. Speaking for myself (Patrice), I have found support in being part of the multicultural staff and faculty board at my current institution. This space is designed for faculty and staff of color to share ideas and to support and encourage one another. During a brown bag discussion on self-promotion, also known as "bragging," I learned how to quantify my various commitments on campus and seek out recognition and awards.

Prior to attending this discussion, self-promotion was uncomfortable for me. It felt odd and strange to take up space by "bragging." In my family, I was not encouraged to self-promote. It was seen as being rewarded for things you should already be doing. Instead, I was always told to do better. In the work environment, I thought that if my accomplishments were valid, then others would see that and promote me accordingly. Instead, taking on multiple projects and creating and advocating weren't being seen as viable accomplishments that deserved recognition. They became acts of invisible labor, tasks that were assigned to me because of my identities, and they were not given the same value as the work my White counterparts were doing. The multicultural board has provided professional and personal value, creating an environment that feels safe with others who have similar points of reference as myself. Having a space like this on campus is important, but it is also just as important that this initiative is supported by my department, ensuring that I continue to thrive and expand my professional network.

We, the authors of this chapter, have learned to show up unapologetically, fully recognizing and understanding the inherent risk, but knowing that the alternative is a defeated sense of self. We seek environments that value an employee's ability to bring the uniqueness of who they are authentically to the work that they do, and we have learned to do so both by trial and error and in the many other ways outlined throughout this chapter.

To all of our fellow student affairs professionals of color, we hear you and we see you. Know that you are and the work that you do is valid, beneficial, and valuable.

REFERENCES

Ashforth, B. E., & Humphrey, R. H. (1993). Emotional labor in service roles: The influence of identity. *The Academy of Management Review, 18*(1), 88–115.

Bronfenbrenner, U. (1994). Ecological models of human development. In T. Husén & T. N. Postlethwaite (Eds.), *International encyclopedia of education* (2nd ed., Vol. 3, pp. 1643–1647). Oxford, UK: Elsevier.

Brown, B. (2010). *The gifts of imperfection: Let go of who you think you're supposed to be and embrace who you are.* Center City, MN: Hazelden.

Browning, H., & Weiser, S. G. (2015). A campus apart: The lived experiences of student affairs professionals of color. *The Annual Knowledge Community Conference Publication*, 41–42. Retrieved from http://apps.naspa.org/files/2015-NASPA-KC-Publication-Final.pdf

Butler, J. (1993). Critically Queer. *GLQ, 1*, 17–32.

Chubbuck, S. M. (2004). Whiteness enacted, Whiteness disrupted: The complexity of personal congruence. *American Educational Research Journal, 41*(2), 301–333.

De Fina, A. (2007). Code-switching and the construction of ethnic identity in a community of practice. *Language in Society, 36*(3), 371–392.

Deprez-Sims, A., & Morris, S. B. (2010). Accents in the workplace: Their effects during a job interview. *International Journal of Psychology, 45*(6), 417–426.

Guess, T. J. (2006). The social construction of Whiteness: Racism by intent, racism by consequence. *Critical Sociology, 32*(4), 649–673.

Gusa, D. L. (2010). White institutional presence: The impact of Whiteness on campus climate. *Harvard Educational Review, 80*(4), 464–489.

Hurtado, S., Milem, J. F., Clayton-Pedersen, A. R., & Allen, W. R. (1998). Enhancing campus climates for racial/ethnic diversity: Educational policy and practice. *Review of Higher Education, 21*(3), 279–302.

Iverson, S. V. (2007). Camouflaging power and privilege: A critical race analysis of university diversity policies. *Educational Administration Quarterly, 43*(5), 586–611.

Jaimes, M. A. (1999). *The state of Native America: Genocide, colonization, and resistance.* Boston, MA: South End Press.

Ladson-Billings, G., & Tate, W. (1995). Toward a critical race theory of education. *Teachers College Record, 97*(1), 47–68.

Native Legacy at Dartmouth College. (2016, February 24). Retrieved from http://www.dartmouth.edu/~nap/about/

Neville, H. A., & Mobley, M. (2001). Social identities in context: An ecological model of multicultural counseling psychology processes. *The Counseling Psychologist, 29*(4), 471–486.

Ogbu, J. U. (2004) Collective identity and the burden of "acting White" in Black history, community, and education. *The Urban Review, 36*(1), 1–35.

Orelus, P. (2013). The institutional cost of being a professor of color: Unveiling micro-aggression, racial [in]visibility, and racial profiling through the lens of critical race theory. *Current Issues in Education, 16*(2), 1–11.

Perez, R. J. (2016). A conceptual model of professional socialization within student affairs graduate preparation programs. *Journal for the Study of Postsecondary and Tertiary Education, 1*, 35–52.

Solórzano, D. G., & Yosso, T. J. (2002). Critical race methodology: Counter-storytelling as an analytical framework for education research. *Qualitative Inquiry, 8*(1), 23–44.

Thompson, A. (2001). *Summary of Whiteness theory.* Retrieved from http://www.pauahtun.org/Whiteness-Summary-1.html

Turner, C. (2002). Women of color in academe: Living with multiple marginality. *The Journal of Higher Education, 73*(1), 74–93.

Wilder, C. S. (2013). *Ebony and ivy: Race, slavery, and the troubled history of America's universities.* New York, NY: Bloomsbury Press.

Williams, A. (2015, November 8). The invisible labor of minority professors. *The Chronicle of Higher Education.* Retrieved from http://www.chronicle.com/article/The-Invisible-Labor-of/234098

Wingfield, A. H. (2010). Are some emotions marked "Whites only"? Racialized feeling rules in professional workplaces. *Social Problems, 57*(2), 251–268.

Yosso, T. J. (2005). Whose culture has capital? A critical race theory discussion of community cultural wealth. *Race Ethnicity and Education, 8*(1), 69–91.

Young, V. A. (2009). "Nah, we straight": An argument against code switching. *JAC, 29*(1/2), 49–76.

8

Negotiating Fit While "Misfit"

Three Ways Trans Professionals Navigate Student Affairs

C.J. Venable, Kyle Inselman, and Nick Thuot

"People couldn't seem to hear what I was saying over the sound of my body."

—Riki Wilchins, *Queer Theory, Gender Theory: An Instant Primer*

F OR TRANS[1] PROFESSIONALS, THE "sound" of our bodies, and how others react to it, directly impacts our ability to participate in higher education environments while expressing our authentic gender. This causes trans professionals to be akin to misfits, individuals who do not belong or are seen as incompatible with the norms and expectations of a particular environment. Trans people are a varied population and span a vast diversity of gender expressions, from being able to be perceived as a binary cis[2] person to being visibly marked as a gender-nonconforming person. By examining how trans professionals experience a state of fit—a sense of belonging, acceptance, and compatibility—or misfit and then exploring ways to resist and disrupt the systems of oppression currently at play, we posit a reconceptualization of *fit* that more fully includes trans professionals. This reframing of the idea of fit demonstrates how it is presently used to exclude as often as include and draws attention to the need to consider fit in a more critical fashion.

A primary structure central to our analysis is *institutional cisgenderism*, the idea that cisgender identity and appearance is normal, expected, and

167

preferred (Seelman, 2014). Institutional cisgenderism presents trans people as an unacceptable deviation from what is perceived as normal gender identity and expression, due to a "belief that cisgender identities are more 'normal', 'healthy', and 'real', [and thus they] are treated as 'superior' to transgender and gender non-conforming identities" (Seelman, 2014, pp. 619–620). These beliefs become "institutional patterns" (Seelman, 2014, p. 620) that privilege cis people over trans and gender-nonconforming people. Examples of acts seen as transgressive under institutional cisgenderism include

- identifying as a gender other than that assigned at birth or other than man or woman;
- wearing clothing, accessories, or hairstyles seen as unacceptable for one's gender;
- using third person pronouns other than *he* or *she*, such as *they* or *ze*;
- having medical needs that fall outside of the expectations associated with one's gender (e.g., a trans man taking parental leave for pregnancy); and
- seeking recognition of the fluidity of gender as more than a static trait, such as by asking colleagues to use a different name than one they initially learned.

These transgressions may contribute to the sense that trans people do not fit. Ultimately, the idea of transness is "in itself a challenge to gender norms" (Wilchins, 2014, p. 154), and this experience of being perceived as a challenge, intentionally or not, informs our analysis. The "institutional" portion of institutional cisgenderism refers to how cisgenderism permeates college and university culture and influences the "behaviors, goals, norms, and values of higher education institutions" (Seelman, 2014, p. 619). As our intention with this chapter is to critically analyze and offer remedies for the issues of fit that come up for trans professionals in student affairs, we take the presence of institutional cisgenderism as a given.

Administrative violence is also an important consideration when examining trans professionals and fit. Spade (2011) describes administrative violence as a kind of epistemic violence, whereby trans people are made "impossible" through administrative systems that operate only within a rigid gender/sex binary. If trans people are assumed not to exist, there is no need, for example, to create structures to accommodate those who wish to change their gender on official records, to include preferred names different from legal names for professional organization membership, or to offer insurance plans that ensure full coverage regardless of gender. Trans professionals in student affairs regularly experience administrative violence as a result of institutional cisgenderism that assumes they do not and should not exist.

Further, these constructs often show up in the experiences of trans student affairs professionals in the form of microaggressions (Sue, 2010), which are "'othering' messages related to a person's perceived marginalized status" (Nordmarken, 2014, p. 129). It is important to note that Sue's (2010) work on microaggressions has the effect of othering trans people, as he conflates transness with sexual orientation by referring to "LGBTs" (lesbian, gay, bisexual, transgender) when discussing sexual orientation and by not addressing trans people when discussing gender (see Sue, 2010). Other work on microaggressions (Nadal, Rivera, & Corpus, 2010) similarly pays only lip service to trans microaggressions. Regardless, microaggressions contribute to the sense that trans professionals do not fit, as they are consistently, subtly reminded that they do not conform to norms of gender identity and expression in higher education.

AUTHOR POSITIONALITY

In considering how trans professionals experience oppressive structures, we believe it is important to acknowledge our specific positionalities and how they frame our insights. Rather than attempt to justify our analysis as unbiased and objective, we believe it is essential to name the identities and contexts that consciously influence our perspectives. This includes viewing our positionalities as valuable assets in demonstrating experiences of trans professionals, even if it means our narratives are not universally generalizable. In addition, there are likely other contexts that influence our experiences in ways we are not fully aware.

I (C.J.) am a genderqueer person who identifies as trans, as neither a man nor a woman, and I use the singular *they* as my pronoun. During my graduate program, I began to critically interrogate my identities and came to know myself as genderqueer. It was also during this time that I began to gain a deeper understanding of critical and intersectional frameworks for understanding oppression. Presently, I work full time as an academic adviser at a large public university where I am mostly out to students and colleagues as trans. I present at work as a gender-nonconforming professional in my clothing and appearance, but I feel significant internalized pressure to temper or tone down my identity. This internal voice is an important part of my daily experience.

Further, as a White person from a middle-class upbringing with graduate-level education, I am regularly reminded how these identities shield me at work, despite my inability to show up in the fullness of my humanity each day.

I (Kyle) identify as a female-to-male trans person and use the pronoun *he*. I fit into a traditional narrative of experiencing gender dysphoria since early childhood, and in college I transitioned socially, medically, and legally toward male. I find a great deal of salience in my transition and my upbringing as a girl, and I feel most authentic when I have the option to safely be open about this history, regardless of whether I choose to be open in a particular space. While I am often (but not always) perceived as a man, I bend gender expectations in my attire, voice, and demeanor. As a professional, I have navigated the balance between living authentically and negotiating comfort and safety at four institutions, often encountering societal and institutional cisgenderism. My positionality in coauthoring this chapter is also influenced by my Whiteness, middle-class background, and professional role as a career adviser.

I (Nick) use *trans* and *nonbinary* to describe my gender identity. At this time, the pronoun that works best for me is singular *they*; however, I am excited by new possibilities for my gender and my pronouns as I continue to learn more about myself. I have really only come to know my gender over the last couple of years. While completing my degree in student affairs, I worked alongside individuals who understood their genders in ways beyond what I had been socialized to believe were possible. I am eternally grateful for the people that helped expand my possibilities. I currently navigate various levels of outness as a trans person. Presently, I am out professionally, but I have not yet found the ability to be out to family or any friends outside of higher education. My positionality as a contributing author of this chapter is influenced by (but not limited to) my Whiteness, being disabled, and my United States citizenship.

Our mutual Whiteness, educational privilege, and trans identities are points of convergence for us as authors of this chapter. These identities necessarily shape our views and experiences as trans people working in student affairs. We also diverge in important ways, including our particular gender identities, our functional area experiences, our socioeconomic backgrounds, and our geographic differences. These similarities and differences are interwoven in the same way we aim to intertwine our voices as authors and our experiences in higher education. Although we may identify a single author as the voice of specific examples, we largely seek to synthesize our individual perspectives into a coherent analysis of trans fit in student affairs.

PURPOSE OF THE CHAPTER AND CRITICAL FRAMEWORKS

The purpose of this chapter is to critically examine the ways that trans professionals experience fit in student affairs. We illustrate the different kinds of responses that individuals may have that result from the expectation that they fit into institutions that were never intended to include trans people. To model the power of centering trans narratives, we will share examples from our own experiences as trans student affairs professionals. Given the dearth of literature on the lived experiences of trans people at work (e.g., Budge, Tebbe, & Howard, 2010; Schilt, 2010), including those of trans student affairs professionals (e.g., Jourian, Simmons, & Devaney, 2015; Simmons, 2017), we believe that our stories, interwoven with critical frameworks, provide a deeper understanding of how trans professionals can experience fit.

We use several critical frameworks to understand how trans professionals experience fit in student affairs. We are inspired by Spade's (2011) conception of a critical trans politics that looks beyond policies, rights, and laws as ways to improve trans lives. Critical trans politics draws heavily on the traditions of critical legal studies and critical race theory (CRT) in its critique of the idea that legal rights given to minoritized people will be effective in eliminating structural oppression. Instead, critical trans politics demands collective action for justice that goes beyond the actions of individuals to address systems and structures that maintain oppression, including unjust laws and policies.

We must also acknowledge the role of intersectionality (Crenshaw, 1989) on our analysis. Crenshaw specifically examined the compounding oppression of being a woman and being Black in conceptualizing intersectionality. As White student affairs professionals, we lack the insight of those impacted by racialized institutional cisgenderism, administrative violence, and microaggressions. For that reason, to uncritically apply intersectionality to our experiences "would mean altering Crenshaw's arguments about multiple subordinations in order to fit our own needs" (Anders & Devita, 2014, p. 32). Instead, we attempt to highlight instances of racialized oppression and other interlocking oppressive systems that move us beyond single-issue identity politics. This is a necessary, albeit insufficient, step to move toward realizing Spade's (2011) notion of a trickle-up social justice centering the most marginalized.

Finally, *neoliberalism*—a political, social, and economic orientation marked by rugged individualism, including the belief that success is solely a result of individual effort—has a deleterious effect on the capacity for trans people to be seen as fully human. In particular, neoliberalism advances the idea that an individual's value to society is determined by their capacity to provide "productive" labor (Irving, 2008; Pitcher, 2015). Nicolazzo (2017) discussed how neoliberalism within higher education can act to commodify marginalized people, turning "diverse genders and sexualities [into] something one could acquire through participating in a training, educational session, in-service, or class experience" (p. 108). In this framework, trans professionals might only have value to the extent that they are willing to be consumed as an educational experience. Given the constraints that trans professionals experience under the oppressive systems of institutional cisgenderism, administrative violence, and trans microaggressions, neoliberalism seriously limits one's capacity to be "productive" and therefore worthy of value.

Using these frameworks, we discuss how trans professionals negotiate fit both by colluding with institutional cisgenderism—that is, going along with it, though not necessarily willingly—and by resisting collusion with it. We also explore how cis people can resist institutional cisgenderism and create space for trans colleagues to fit within existing organizational systems and structures. We conclude the chapter with a discussion of how to disrupt institutional cisgenderism, addressing both individual actions and underlying systems that create a sense of misfit for trans professionals. Because this is the work of lifetimes, this chapter simply begins the conversation on what student affairs without institutional cisgenderism could be like. It is up to each of us to engage in the work to make that world a reality.

COLLUDING WITH INSTITUTIONAL CISGENDERISM

For trans professionals, we primarily frame collusion through the practice of covering. Yoshino (2007) described *covering* as when an individual "tone[s] down a disfavored identity to fit into the mainstream" (p. ix). Specifying further, Pryor (2015) described the practice as "a performance people utilize in situations when they perceive their identity is stigmatized or their safety is at risk" (p. 443). This performance necessitates following societal norms and rules related to gender: fitting in rather than standing out. As student affairs professionals, we (the authors of this chapter) have felt significant pressure to collude with institutional cisgenderism to secure employment, meet the expectations of our colleagues, and fit into existing higher education cultures. Collusion serves to uphold oppressive systems in the interest of the survival of an individual trans professional. Understanding how and why professionals collude with institutional cisgenderism underscores why it is necessary to resist and eventually dismantle it, particularly within higher education institutions.

What may immediately come to mind when considering covering is being closeted—not disclosing one's trans identity. Grant and colleagues (2011) found that 32% of trans people in the United States reported being forced to present in the wrong gender at work; this could be due to overt pressure from the workplace or a decision made by a trans person out of fear. For trans people who are open about their identity, whether by choice or necessity, covering becomes the task of striking cautious balance in conforming to gender norms while being an out trans person. As Gonzalez and kemp-delisser (2010) explained, "the premise behind covering is that the majority group will accept differences in identity only to the extent that its norms are not confronted with nonconformist behavior" (p. 121). For an out trans professional, this could include practices of not correcting pronoun mistakes or of conforming to gendered norms of dress, behavior, and speech for the comfort of others. One might also "tone down" trans activism or advocacy at one's institution as part of covering, leaving issues unaddressed in order to depoliticize their identity and their body. For example, when I (Kyle) worked in a conservative area, I did not identify myself as a trans person when inquiring about inclusive restroom policies and spaces. While I needed the ability to safely use the restroom at work when the erosion of such rights had begun across the country (i.e., so-called bathroom bills), I was concerned that voicing my need could put me at a greater risk of harm should the wrong person find out about my gender history. Therefore, I asked about a hypothetical student and relied on sharing my expertise about the issue, rather than petitioning from my experiences as a trans employee.

Factors Leading to the Decision to Collude

There are many reasons that some trans people collude with institutional cisgenderism. Foremost is survival. As Edelman (2009) explained, in a society with strict gender norms, "the hyper-embodied trans body must engage in a hyper-normativity in order to gain access to the limited resources available" (p. 167). Though trans people are more likely than the general population to have attended college or graduate school, unemployment rates are at least twice as high, and up to four times as high for Black trans people (Grant et al., 2011). Trans women, particularly trans women of color, face a higher risk of discrimination, harassment, and violence than trans men (Bender-Baird, 2011; Grant et al., 2011). These increased incidents of violence create very real concern and risk for trans individuals, including trans staff in higher education (Seelman, Walls, Costello, Steffens, Inselman, Montague-Asp, & Colorado Trans on Campus Coalition, 2012).

For trans people, one's productivity as a worker, indeed one's worth under neoliberal capitalism, is inextricable from one's transness. Irving (2008) noted that in the early twentieth century, "the majority of medical professionals classified transsexuals as the most damaged—and *damaging*—among nonnormatively gendered individuals," thus "encompass[ing] socially corrosive forms of deviance" (p. 47). This medicalized, deficit view meant that transness, when "framed as a mental disorder, renders the body unproductive" (Irving, 2008, p. 47). Viewing transness as inherently unproductive led to discourse that positions gender transition as means to a productive life; that is, a "damaged" trans individual can contribute to the workforce once "fixed" by medical transition. This discourse allows for some positive workplace inclusion efforts such as benefits covering medical transition. However, Irving (2008) explained that these changes are not focused on full inclusion of the individual, rather inclusion only to the extent that the individual can be exploited for their productivity. This leaves trans professionals who do not conform to cisnormative standards still marginalized, still "unproductive" within systems that require normativity as a prerequisite to functionality.

The pressing issues of physical safety and economic survival under neoliberal capitalism can lead some individuals to collude more than they would prefer in order to gain or maintain employment. Grant and colleagues (2011) found that 90% of trans people in the United States experienced workplace discrimination or "felt forced to take protective actions that negatively impacted their careers or their well-being, such as hiding who they were, in order to avoid workplace repercussions" (p. 56). Even in situations where one is employed, colluding can be a way to secure advancement or success while tempering fear of discrimination.

Minoritized people working in higher education are not immune from the pressure to collude (Reinert & Serna, 2014). I (CJ) chose not to be out or share that I use singular they while I searched for my first professional position after graduate school. My personal and financial situations were precarious enough that I felt I could not share my trans identity without seriously jeopardizing my chances of finding a position before graduation, at which point I would become homeless. This caused my job search to be particularly stressful as I navigated both the complexities of a national search and managing the emotional toll of covering.

We affirm that not all gender conformity is due to fear and that, in discussing collusion, "we must not assume that individuals behaving in 'mainstream' ways are necessarily covering" (Yoshino, 2007, p. 191). For some trans people, what may be perceived as covering may instead be a decision to live stealth (i.e., not disclosing a trans history) due to personal understandings of one's own gender and transness (see Edelman, 2009). Thus, we recognize that perceived gender expression only tells part of the story, and for some trans individuals a normative expression may be an intentional and meaningful way to live.

Regardless of one's personal identity as binary or stealth, there are still pressures to collude for the trans professional who is not out at work. For example, when selecting healthcare benefits, choosing to register as male or female usually means choosing to have some health needs covered and others left uncovered, depending on the insurance policy or the state of residence. I (Kyle) encountered a precarious situation at one institution where the insurance company stated that the sex on my policy must match the sex on the institution's human resources records. Since I was hired as "male," this meant I would need to change my employee file to "female" in order to cover my medical needs; at that institution, this would have required revealing my transition history to my direct supervisor. To keep stealth, I chose not to amend my records; that is, I colluded with the assumption that I was a cis man. Without my insurance set to "female," I spent months appealing the insurance company to cover a routine gynecological exam, initially denied due to my "male" policy. The situation I encountered due to the constraints of the binary system is likely not an isolated incident. Research has found that trans men may avoid regular reproductive care due to discomfort with cisnormative intake processes, which include the question of whether to check the box for "male" or "female" (Dutton, Koenig, & Fennie, 2008). For a trans professional, inquiring which sex would be most appropriate to select when filling out new employee paperwork could necessitate coming out; it can thus be understandable why one might choose to collude rather than raise the issue.

Limitations of Collusion

Collusion is not without limitations, and it does not satisfactorily allow all trans professionals to be authentic at work. The pressure to collude can arise from very real fears, stemming from the larger society or a rigid, cisnormative culture within the workplace itself. Institutions can mitigate some of these fears. Adding gender identity and gender expression to institutional nondiscrimination policies or diversity statements sends a message of inclusion (Taylor, Dockendorff, & Inselman, 2017), as does changing signage on single-stall restrooms to say "all gender" or "gender neutral" (Beemyn, 2003). Though these efforts contribute to a safer atmosphere for trans people on college campuses, the pressure to collude with oppressive systems is great and extends into social norms that constantly other trans people. The visibility of gender and its presumed innateness makes any disruption to social norms highly noticeable and often suspect.

As necessary as colluding is for many trans individuals to secure employment or thrive in their chosen position, colluding through covering does not ensure that institutions celebrate trans staff. Bender-Baird (2011) points out that

> an overemphasis on the need to pass in order to avoid discrimination perpetuates the pressure to present a normative gender expression, ignoring the identities of gender non-conforming people and creating an unnecessary and unhelpful divide . . . between gender-normative people and gender-nonconforming people. (p. 124)

That is, by emphasizing conformity to cisnormative standards of gender as a means of fitting into the workplace, only some trans people are able to fit as themselves. Gonzalez and kemp-delisser (2010) emphasized that "covering attaches certain conditions to [one's] full integration into society" (p. 118) and that "the pressure to cover can be cloaked in the language of inclusion or accessibility" (p. 121). Indeed, even if a trans individual has not experienced overt discrimination, covert hostility toward transness can still lead to serious, negative psychological outcomes for trans people in the workplace (Bender-Baird, 2011; Rood et al., 2016). Ensuring that trans staff are able to bring their authentic selves to work, without feeling that fitting into binary cisnormative standards is necessary for fitting into student affairs, is crucial for creating a space conducive to full participation. For this reason, it is necessary to determine ways that both cis and trans professionals can resist institutional cisgenderism in student affairs.

RESISTING INSTITUTIONAL CISGENDERISM

Trans student affairs professionals have found numerous ways to resist institutional cisgenderism. We define *resistance* as behaviors that deny or subvert the premises of institutional cisgenderism, like the idea that all student affairs professionals are cis or that trans people cannot fit in organizations predominantly composed of cis people. We explore several examples of how cis and trans professionals may resist and highlight individual and collective efforts to do so. However, while acts of resistance have the effect of undermining the power of institutional cisgenderism, they do not necessarily create structural changes that affect deeper levels of organizational norms. We refer to these more profound changes as *disruption* of institutional cisgenderism, which we examine in the final section of this chapter. For now, we explore three key potential sites for resistance: pronoun usage, professional attire, and critical problematization. These are not the only options, or perhaps even the most important ones, but they are ones with which we have extensive experience. Resisting institutional cisgenderism in these domains can help trans professionals to fit more readily.

Pronoun Usage

For cisgender people, pronouns may seem as natural an identifier as one's name, with no confusion and little chance of being *mispronouned* (referred to with the incorrect pronouns) or *misgendered* (assumed to be a gender other than one's identified gender). This is not always the case for trans people. Some trans people who pass as a binary gender do not have to seriously consider pronouns. However, not all trans people pass as cis or identify with a binary gender and, in these circumstances, being mispronouned or misgendered can be a regular, painful occurrence. Here, correcting others on their assumptions or their incorrect use of pronouns can be seen as subversive or even aggressive.

When trans people are forced to correct others after being mispronouned, they are reminding those they correct that their assumptions regarding both the individual in question and the larger system of gender are wrong. This can be disorienting for someone who understands gender in a static, binary way and requires a monumental paradigm shift. It takes practice for individuals to become familiar with new pronouns, particularly if one is not familiar with the variety of pronouns in use today. Commitment to using correct pronouns for a trans person is an indicator that resisting institutional cisgenderism is an acceptable practice.

When I (Nick) started in my first professional role, I recall feeling fear and shame regarding wanting to change pronouns within my department. As someone who is generally perceived by those I interact with to be a cis male, I found myself greatly concerned with the perceptions of my peers and supervisors. It was not until three of my peers stumbled through sharing their pronouns in a meeting with a campus partner that my transness began to feel possible rather than impossible (Spade, 2011), even if for a brief moment. As the months rolled by, sharing pronouns in introductions became relatively common among those who cared that I felt included. This small act helped me feel accepted and valued when I needed it the most.

For some people, this shift is vehemently resisted. Trans people may be repeatedly misgendered by a colleague or student who says, "I just see you as a man, so I use those pronouns" or "I don't think an individual person can use *they* as a pronoun." Nationally, 45% of trans people "reported having been referred to by the wrong pronouns 'repeatedly and on purpose' at work" (Grant et al., 2011, p. 62), a dehumanizing microaggression that serves as a reminder that one does not fit. Intentional mispronouning because someone is upset with a trans person or their job performance becomes a form of retaliatory behavior.

The focus within neoliberalism on performance can lead to the perception that focusing on one's gender causes one to be "unproductive." Irving (2008) discussed one incident wherein a doctor viewed a trans man as having "thwarted" his ability to contribute productively and meaningfully "due to his fixation on expressing his masculine identity" (p. 42). Today, trans people continue to be characterized as "fixated" on gender, with gender transition and advocacy for trans rights viewed by some as unproductive distractions from one's "real" work. It is easy for student affairs professionals to sacrifice their personal needs in order to be "productive" in a profession that emphasizes going "above and beyond" to serve others. When a professional attends to personal needs, that can be seen as a misuse of time and resources, or "unproductive," regardless of their actual performance. By designating assertion of one's gender as an "unproductive" personal issue, neoliberalism places an undue burden on trans professionals to advocate for themselves only within the narrow constraints of what their colleagues deem acceptable.

Individuals can resist the oppressive potential of pronouns not only through correcting mispronouning but also by asserting the regular sharing of pronouns as acceptable for all people. This could look like including pronouns as part of one's introductions, requesting that pronouns be listed on business cards, and including pronouns in an e-mail signature or on professional name tags. Cis people, by modeling this same behavior, can reject the cisgenderist assumption that all people are easily assigned a gender on sight. These behaviors demonstrate to trans people that they can fit, regardless of what pronouns they use. However, it is important for cis people to frame such a practice intentionally; as Catalano (2017) reminds us, uncritically adopting pronoun sharing as a best practice may have unintended consequences that ultimately subject trans people to greater scrutiny. Even among well-meaning cis professionals, sharing pronouns can become a situation where gender is scrutinized, and those who do not conform to expectations end up hypervisible rather than normalized. Thus, without critical engagement with the practice and purpose of pronoun sharing, trans people can continue to be made into misfits despite acknowledging pronouns.

Professional Attire

Deeply attached to class[3] and gender, professional attire establishes a standard of dress often linked to expectations of formality, social distance from students and nonprofessionals, and strict gender roles (Yakaboshi & Reinert, 2014). Because of this connection, transgression in professional attire can make a trans professional suspect not only for their fit but also for their professionalism. People whose appearance does not conform to binary, cisgender expectations for their perceived gender may be seen as wearing clothing that is inappropriate for the workplace. This is compounded by the struggle that trans people may have finding professional clothes—which are gendered in size and cut—that look "appropriately" professional. For instance, slacks cut in a "men's" style may appear unprofessionally baggy when worn by a trans man with wider hips and a shorter stature than most cis men.

Resisting institutional cisgenderism in professional dress can vary for different professionals. I (CJ) regularly wear nail polish and beaded necklaces with polos and slacks. This juxtaposition of feminine and masculine sets me apart, occasionally prompting questions about my gender and professionalism. For trans professionals who find ways to maintain a professional appearance while also engaging in gender-affirming dress, concerns that such dress is distracting or represents a lack of professional competence can contribute to a sense that one does not fit (Forbes, 2012). Some trans people may also prefer that fellow trans people assimilate to gendered expectations of professional dress, either to downplay the tensions resistance creates or because they have internalized these expectations as normal and essential for professionalism. Resistance, however, questions the importance of assimilation and instead looks for ways to expand spaces to allow trans people to simply be themselves. While trans people who resist strict gender roles in professional attire may not initially be seen to fit, their resistance aims to change the expectation of what a professional "looks like" (Forbes, 2012, pp. 41–42).

Cis people can resist institutional cisgenderism by questioning the intrinsic value placed on professional attire. Questioning the neoliberal link between the clothes one is expected to wear and the level of competence one is assumed to have resists the negative pressure that professional attire norms exert. While such questioning may be unsettling for cis professionals, examining how these policies have unintended consequences is essential to realizing a trans-inclusive workplace. Removing gender-specific requirements from dress codes could help ameliorate their oppressive function. If professional attire expectations are a guide, rather than a dictum, trans professionals will be able to fit more readily into offices and organizations as equals. As implementing this practice could be perceived as personally, rather than professionally, motivated for trans professionals, we suggest that cis supervisors especially consider taking this type of action.

Critical Problematization

Ahmed (2010a) discussed how naming a problem can turn the person who names the problem into a problem themselves. Being a *killjoy*, in Ahmed's terms, can have material consequences for those who bring up problems. Consider, for example, a housing department with a set of residence halls that will accept requests for gender-inclusive housing (GIH). A living-learning community exists for students in specific majors, located in a building that does not provide GIH. This means that a trans student must choose between housing that affirms their gender identity and housing that includes the benefits of additional support for their major. This seemingly inclusive housing policy still leaves trans students with fewer opportunities than their cis peers. When a professional points out this limitation, they may be "killing the joy" of their colleagues, who are pleased that they have created GIH on campus at all. While the professional is resisting institutional cisgenderism by calling attention to a problem, they are also calling attention to themselves and how they fit with what is seen as "good" in their department (Ahmed, 2010b).

Often, simply questioning how policies and procedures affect trans people has the effect of problematizing those policies and procedures. Asking questions makes power dynamics visible that often go unquestioned or even celebrated. Because of how institutional cisgenderism operates, questioning established policies for their effects on trans people can be seen as threatening. Particularly if coming from a new professional, repeated questioning of the effects of established norms can make one a killjoy and contribute to a perceived lack of fit—that is, a lack of willingness to fit in established expectations and procedures. However, resisting oppressive systems is about both calling attention to how institutional cisgenderism expresses itself and attempting to carve out space where transness can fit into the norms, traditions, and values of an office or institution.

It is possible for both trans and cis professionals to ask these kinds of questions, but for out trans people, there is the added risk that they will be seen as inserting their own identity into their work, unable to "separate the personal from the professional" (Simmons, 2017, p. 278). Cis professionals who are willing to interrogate institutional cisgenderism do face some risk of being seen as misfit or having their gender questioned, but the bulk of these risks are borne by trans people. Where trans professionals might be seen as engaging in identity politics when addressing trans issues at their institutions, cis people are often praised for being progressive and cutting edge for raising the same issues. This differential attribution of meaning can perpetuate marginalization by further alienating trans professionals while their cis colleagues are lauded for doing the same work. The fact that out trans people make up a small proportion of students, staff, and faculty on any given campus compounds this issue; professionals may experience additional resistance from colleagues for attempting to illuminate institutional cisgenderism because they are told "there are no trans people here." This too makes resistance dangerous—a stealth or closeted trans person who wishes to create a more trans-affirming environment on their campus risks being questioned about why trans issues are so important to them and being outed in the process.

In our experience, however, fulfilling the duty of killing joy, of problematizing spaces and calling attention to the insidious ways that institutional cisgenderism appears in our everyday work, is liberatory. Despite the personal risk, it can also have the effect of carving out space, creating somewhere to fit, even when the systems in place within an office or institution do not provide such space.

Factors Influencing the Ability to Resist

A constellation of factors influences the ability to resist institutional cisgenderism in the ways we have described. For us, Whiteness is a key factor that informs our ability to enter spaces and engage in acts of resistance. Within higher education as a whole, Whiteness provides protection, legitimacy, and power (Bondi, 2012). As White professionals, we are often assumed to be experts, to be reliable and trustworthy, and to be capable of success, rather than inexperienced, unproductive, and generally suspect. Because race is such an important consideration for the safety and success of trans people, intersectional approaches to understanding institutional cisgenderism are essential (Anders & Devita, 2014; Pitcher, 2015; Spade 2011).

While concerns for physical safety are on the minds of many trans people, violence disproportionately affects trans women of color (Grant et al., 2011). Beyond the safety and security of one's body, race shows up within institutional cisgenderism in many other ways. For example, in addition to gendered aspects of professional dress, a Black trans woman must also confront the expectations placed on her regarding the professionalism of her hair or other racialized facets of her body. This is due to the combined effects of institutional cisgenderism and misogynoir (Bailey, 2013), intersectional oppression specific to Black women. Professionals with multiple marginalized identities, including trans people of color, trans people with disabilities, and poor trans people, experience additional hurdles when attempting to resist institutional cisgenderism and simultaneously stay employed (Stryker, 2008). This makes coalitional work that goes beyond single-issue, single-identity politics an essential part of dismantling institutional cisgenderism (Spade, 2011).

Environments also play a major role in influencing whether professionals feel they can push back—in subtle or obvious ways—against systems that center and prize cisgender and binary identities. A supportive campus climate is important, through both nondiscrimination policies and professionals who are visibly engaged in efforts to resist institutional cisgenderism. These two often must work together to create a welcoming environment for trans people. For example, Vaccaro (2012) found that trans workers "described a climate as positive only if they found acceptance and support from colleagues in their department or work unit" (p. 438). Geographic region and locale are also important considerations. Campuses and cities with strong queer and trans networks can help create a supportive system that may allow trans professionals to resist institutional cisgenderism more consistently at work. Given that there is no national legislation that explicitly protects trans people, professionals are at the mercy of state and local ordinances to determine whether they have legal recourse when they experience transphobic discrimination or violence. Measures like the Public Facilities Privacy & Security Act in North Carolina (H.R. 2, 2016), also known as House Bill 2, and the political retaliation of H.R. 2248 (2016) that defunded the Office of Diversity and Inclusion at the University of Tennessee, Knoxville, and prevented the use of gender neutral pronouns (H.R. 2248, 2016), send a strong message to trans professionals that they should not resist institutional cisgenderism if they wish to fit and succeed.

These factors are important in considering how individuals can resist the pressure of institutional cisgenderism on their campuses while still presenting resistance as a process of individual action. The resistances we have illustrated here are attempts to carve out a place for trans people in offices and universities, but they do little to create deeper changes that make trans people fit in higher education by design. Still, these actions can be first steps toward that work. The next section will examine ways that institutional cisgenderism can be dismantled, allowing trans people to both fit and thrive in higher education.

DISRUPTING INSTITUTIONAL CISGENDERISM

We define *disruption* as any act or effort that seeks to deliberatively interrupt the dominant narrative of cisgender identity as unquestioned, normal, and preferred. While we advance some possibilities for disrupting these narratives and systems, we acknowledge that there are many possible ways to disrupt institutional cisgenderism. These will inevitably be informed by one's constellation of identities and the specific contexts of one's environment. Actions taken by individuals must continue to evolve and expand toward liberation. If our actions remain stagnant, the environments in which we find ourselves will continue to be stagnant as well and perhaps become further entrenched in these oppressive systems.

Within the context of neoliberal capitalism, pressures from stakeholders and an often-hostile campus climate for trans people push professionals toward developing strategies that will not be met with much resistance. The guise of making *some* progress for those individuals can have dire implications, reinforcing the idea that trans people are a problem to be ameliorated. These types of strategies passively reinforce the dominance and normativity of cis individuals by focusing on what is comfortable for those in positions of dominance to concede.

We share Pitcher's (2015) concerns that "the notion that one could develop best practices, or that it is even desirable to do so, only seeks to advance a neoliberal logic that emphasizes palatable, and therefore marketable, ways to address perennial issues in higher education" (pp. 20–21). Advancing a rigid, one-size-fits-all approach to addressing institutional cisgenderism can be an act of resistance but not of disruption or liberation; best practices are thus insufficient. Best practices cannot be utilized uncritically, without consideration of the context in which they will be applied, regardless of their success at other institutions or their cachet as buzzwords within higher education. For example, a common best practice is to implement gender-neutral restrooms alongside gendered restrooms. However, the idea that gender-specific restrooms are needed at all serves to uphold a binary conception of gender and the disciplining of bodies into two distinct, disjointed categories. Creating a limited number of gender-neutral restrooms does nothing to reject this cisnormative process and can mark nonbinary trans people as "other." Multi-stall all-gender restrooms for everyone to use are a much more radical proposal, one that seeks to disrupt institutional cisgenderism by reorienting everyone toward more gender-liberatory practices. While it can be uncomfortable and disorienting to create and advance solutions that surpass uncritical best practices, such discomfort must be embraced in search of liberation.

Finally, it is also vital to interrogate the possibilities that emerge through the lens of considering "who is not in the room, who is alone, and whose voice is not being heard" (Wilchins, 2014, p. 166). We must avoid engaging in nonperformatives—actions that aim to "change perceptions" rather than "change . . . organizations" (Ahmed, 2012, p. 34). Commitment to action without taking action creates good feelings about diversity and change without serious threat to the systems that are in place. Without deliberate consideration by policymakers of how intersecting identities create unique needs, "inclusive" policies that are ultimately exclusive to the most marginalized will be inevitable. By envisioning actions through these lenses, we can advance strategies that enhance the lives of trans people and begin disrupting institutional cisgenderism.

We invite readers to consider what role you could play in the implementation of disruptive strategies. For truly liberatory solutions to be implemented, we must be radically committed to addressing the local context and moving beyond simple solutions to complex problems. In the following sections, we detail examples of disruptive practices in professional organizations, professionalism, and graduate preparation programs.

Professional Organizations

Student affairs professional organizations have taken some actions to resist institutional cisgenderism, such as including all-gender bathrooms at national conferences and highlighting Trans 101 breakout sessions. However, there have been few actions that seek to center the voices of trans professionals in these organizations and actively dismantle the systems that cause trans people to not fit. In response to this situation, *T* Circle*, "a dialogue for, by, and with trans* educators" (Jourian et al., 2015, p. 432) occurred at the 2014 American College Personnel Association's (ACPA) annual convention. This dialogue offered counternarratives to the dominant nonperformative paradigm that permeates the student affairs field (Jourian et al., 2015). By engaging in conversation about the experiences of trans professionals without allowing audience members to ask questions, *T* Circle* created space for trans people to fit unconditionally, without a need to justify themselves as trans or as professionals. Rather, this was a space to name issues related to "systemic issues of genderism within and beyond higher education" (Jourian et al., 2015, p. 437). Continuing to create spaces that center the voices and experiences of trans people in a deliberately intersectional and cross-sectional way could be a powerful commitment to the idea that trans professionals indeed fit in student affairs. Simply focusing on introductory-level trans breakout sessions year after year is insufficient.

Further, Jourian and colleagues (2015) noted potential milestones for trans inclusion in student affairs, including "increasing visibility of trans* educators, particularly trans* women of color [and for] research to be expanded, deepened, and driven by trans* people" (p. 437). Professional organizations should commit to solutions that do more than simply fit trans people into existing structures; rather, they should reform those structures such that all people can fit naturally. These changes, done in an intentional way, could begin to change the face of the field to one in which trans professionals can see themselves in our organizations, in our canon of literature, and in our institutions. Without doing so, our collective commitment to social justice and inclusion will remain hollow.

Notions of Professionalism

Another step that could have a profound impact on the field would be to reexamine and redefine *professionalism*. Our field's current understanding of professionalism has its roots in the oppressive structures that we seek to dismantle. Within student affairs,

> the markers of "professionalism," the way that people speak, dress, and interact, are all deeply based in hegemonic systems of oppression that were intended to distinguish between those who belong and those who don't. At its

core, the concept of "professionalism" is as much about dictating behavior and appearance as it is about exclusion. (Baptista, 2015)

The current system of professionalism provides benefit to those already privileged by systems of oppression; it is vital for us to consider how a disproportionate impact is felt by those who hold multiple marginalized identities. Beginning a dialogue on how to separate professional practice from professionalism will allow us as a field to begin to construct a world without these hegemonic systems, including institutional cisgenderism.

One of the ways this could be enacted is through a more radical reimagining of dress expectations that goes beyond resistance through flexibility with professional attire, such as the elimination of dress expectations altogether. A move in favor of individual professional judgment would not be without precedent, as it is already seen in some industries through a growing "dress for your day" approach (Greenfield, 2016), wherein professionals can modify their attire to match the needs of their agenda for the day. For example, a professional who has no formal meetings may prefer to wear attire for their after-work plans. Within student affairs, dress expectations currently vary greatly depending on functional area, institution, geographic region, and supervisor preference, with some professionals wearing jeans and logo wear and others dressing daily in slacks and collared shirts. These variations are also shaped by one's race, ability, and gender, thus holding individuals within the field to a plethora of standards. For these reasons, this transformation should be viewed as a less oppressive possible future, dependent upon context and systemic change.

Student Affairs Professional Preparation

It is imperative that cisnormative expectations of who we consider to be competent, qualified, and welcome be challenged as well. One possible method to achieve this is through trans-inclusive education within student affairs graduate programs. Ensuring that a critical mass of student affairs practitioners entering the field have at least a foundational level of knowledge regarding transness moves us closer to Talbot and Viento's (2005) assertion that "to be credible as well as ethical, faculty and graduate programs must model the values that the student affairs profession endorses" (p. 79). Given that two of us (CJ and Nick) first became aware of our trans identities during our graduate studies, it is also important for faculty in student affairs graduate programs to avoid assumptions of static gender identity and expression in their students.

In a study on classroom experiences of transgender students, Pryor (2015) found that participants experienced a "chilly" (p. 452) classroom environment, with mixed experiences of faculty and peer support within academic settings. I (Kyle) have experienced some of this "chilly" environment in my own graduate studies. Even with departmental faculty supportive of my trans identity, I often had to seek out research about lesbian, gay, bisexual, transgender, and queer (LGBTQ) students on my own and encountered situations where my otherness as trans created discomfort for both peers and faculty/staff across my institution. This resulted in pressure to be an educator on trans issues, something many trans students feel (Inselman, 2017). Had LGBTQ concerns been built into the curriculum in each of my departments, my speaking up—an act of resisting institutional cisgenderism—would not have been necessary for trans topics to be given due attention. Intentionally educating graduate students about trans people will look different at each institution given the vast diversity of student affairs professional preparation programs. However, equipping emerging and advancing student affairs professionals with tools to disrupt institutional cisgenderism should be an essential charge of these programs.

Ultimately, these possibilities go beyond nonperformatives and demand deeper changes to culture and practice in order to disrupt institutional cisgenderism. These transformative solutions cannot be implemented quickly and must consider the individuals involved and the histories and cultures of the places where they are enacted. Sustained dialogue about how our cultures, policies, and practices uphold institutional cisgenderism is necessary to understand how pervasive these systems are and to devise long-term solutions to dismantle them. The suggestions we have presented are possibilities to consider; professionals on every campus have the potential to devise other solutions that can advance the goal of disrupting institutional cisgenderism. We must sustain our efforts to look beyond simple solutions and contextual best practices in order to reimagine student affairs without institutional cisgenderism.

CONCLUSION

While we have demonstrated that institutional cisgenderism is both prevalent and interwoven into the fabric of our profession, we also hold that student affairs professionals have an opportunity and an obligation to disrupt this narrative of dominance. More importantly, we hope the frameworks we have described will begin to empower individuals to engage in practices prioritizing inclusion and liberation of trans professionals at all of our dynamic intersections. While this will look different at every institution, learning to identify what Johnson (2006) called "paths of least resistance" (p. 80) regarding institutional cisgenderism is the duty of every student affairs professional. These paths are what allow us to maintain oppressive systems by simply going along with what is already in place, rather than breaking out and demanding that substantive, liberatory changes be made.

Addressing the multiplicity of ways that institutional cisgenderism appears in student affairs is essential to creating solutions that do more than simply treat the symptoms. Learning to identify when and how individuals are pressured to collude with institutional cisgenderism can provide an opportunity to disrupt the conditions that create such pressures. Creating environments where professionals are free to express the wholeness of themselves, including their gender identity and expression, lessens this pressure. Although neoliberalism creates expectations of impersonal productivity, resistance and disruption of institutional cisgenderism can lead to more liberatory workplaces for trans student affairs professionals. Additionally, engaging in resistive and disruptive behaviors is in line with even the foundational expectations that have been established regarding social justice in student affairs (ACPA & NASPA-Student Affairs Administrators in Higher Education [NASPA], 2015).

Finally, student affairs professionals must seek justice beyond our campuses. The field must move beyond managing gender diversity and subvert the belief that trans people are a problem to be solved. As we have discussed throughout this chapter, professionals have the ability to resist and disrupt in myriad ways. While working toward liberation is a lengthy and complicated process, individuals have the agency to begin to make changes that undermine the power of institutional cisgenderism every day. We must not let the complexity of liberation keep us from taking action now, even if the actions we take are small and individual. These actions can help build networks to move toward sustained actions that address both individuals and systems. Through our collective action, we can create more liberatory environments for trans professionals—places where we fit by design.

NOTES

1. *Trans* in Western contexts refers to anyone "identifying as a sex and/or gender different than [that] assigned at birth" (Inselman, 2017), including nonbinary and genderqueer persons. Because language describing the diverse ways individuals

experience gender is constantly evolving, we use *trans* as an overarching category, sensitive to the fact that not every person included in our definition uses this label. We additionally acknowledge there are non-trans, gender-nonconforming individuals who experience gender oppression. Thus, while our chapter focuses on trans professionals, we maintain solidarity with those who are harmed by institutional cisgenderism (Seelman, 2014) however it manifests.

    2. *Cisgender* or *cis* refers to individuals who are not trans.

    3. For a more thorough examination of class and fit, see chapter 5, this volume.

REFERENCES

Ahmed, S. (2010a). Feminist killjoys (and other willful subjects). *The scholar and feminist online, 8*(3), 1–8. Retrieved from http://sfonline.barnard.edu/polyphonic/ahmed_01.htm

Ahmed, S. (2010b). *The promise of happiness.* Durham, NC: Duke University Press.

Ahmed, S. (2012). *On being included: Racism and diversity in institutional life.* Durham, NC: Duke University Press.

American College Personnel Association & National Association of Student Personnel Administrators. (2015). *Professional competency areas for student affairs educators.* Professional Competencies Task Force. Washington DC: Authors. Retrieved from https://www.naspa.org/images/uploads/main/ACPA_NASPA_Professional_Competencies_FINAL.pdf

Anders, A. D., & Devita, J. M. (2014). Intersectionality: A legacy from critical legal studies and critical race theory. In D. Mitchell, C. Y. Simmons, & L. A. Greyerbiehl (Eds.), *Intersectionality & higher education: Theory, research, & praxis* (pp. 31–44). New York, NY: Peter Lang.

Bailey, M. (2013). New terms of resistance: A response to Zenzele Isoke. *Souls: A Critical Journal of Black Politics, Culture, and Society, 15*(4), 341–343.

Baptista, R. D. (2015, April 9). Critical reflections on the rules of "professionalism" [Blog post]. Retrieved from http://www.myacpa.org/entity/standing-committee-women/blog/critical-reflections-rules-professionalism

Beemyn, B. G. (2003). Serving the needs of transgender college students. *Journal of Gay & Lesbian Issues in Education, 1*(1), 33–50.

Bender-Baird, K. (2011). *Transgender employment experiences: Gendered perceptions and the law.* Albany, NY: SUNY Press.

Bondi, S. (2012). Students and institutions protecting Whiteness as property: A critical race theory analysis of student affairs preparation. *Journal of Student Affairs Research and Practice, 49*(4), 397–414.

Budge, S. L., Tebbe, E. N., & Howard, K. A. S. (2010). The work experiences of transgender individuals: Negotiating the transition and coping with barriers. *Journal of Counseling Psychology, 57*, 377–393.

Catalano, D. C. J. (2017). Resisting coherence: Trans men's experiences and the use of grounded theory methods. *International Journal of Qualitative Studies in Education, 30*(3), 234–244.

Crenshaw, K. (1989). Demarginalizing the intersection of race and sex: A Black feminist critique of antidiscrimination doctrine, feminist theory, and antiracist politics. *University of Chicago Legal Forum, 1989*(1), 139–167.

Dutton, L., Koenig, K., & Fennie, K. (2008). Gynecologic care of the female-to-male transgender man. *Journal of Midwifery and Women's Health, 53*(4), 331–337.

Edelman, E. A. (2009). The power of stealth: (In)visible sites of female-to-male transsexual resistance. In E. Lewin & W. L. Leap (Eds.), *Out in public: Reinventing lesbian/gay anthropology in a globalizing world* (pp. 164–179). Oxford, UK: Wiley-Blackwell.

Forbes, K. (2012). "Do these earrings make me look dumb?": Diversity, privilege, and heteronormative perceptions of competence in the academy. In A. F. Enke (Ed.), *Transfeminist perspectives in and beyond transgender and gender studies* (pp. 34–44). Philadelphia, PA: Temple University Press.

Gonzalez, J., & kemp-delisser, k. (2010). Two student affairs professionals' journeys to (un)cover. *The Vermont Connection, 31*, 118–127.

Grant, J. M., Mottet, L. A., Tanis, J., Harrison, J., Herman, J., & Keisling, M. (2011). *Injustice at every turn: A report of the National Transgender Discrimination Survey*. Washington DC: National Center for Transgender Equality & National Gay and Lesbian Task Force.

Greenfield, R. (2016, April 5). The office workers left behind by the casual dress revolution. *Bloomberg.* Retrieved from http://www.bloomberg.com/news/articles/2016-04-05/the-office-workers-left-behind-by-the-casual-dress-revolution

H.R. 2248, 109th Gen. Assem., Reg. Sess. (Tenn. 2016).

Inselman, K. (2017). *Differences in use of campus resources for gender transition and support by trans college students: A mixed-methods study* (Unpublished master's thesis). University of Utah, Salt Lake City, UT.

Irving, D. (2008). Normalized transgressions: Legitimizing the transsexual body as productive. *Radical History Review, 2008*(100), 38–59.

Johnson, A. (2006). *Privilege, power, and difference* (2nd ed.). New York, NY: McGraw-Hill.

Jourian, T. J., Simmons, S. L., & Devaney, K. C. (2015). "We are not expected": Trans* educators (re)claiming space and voice in higher education and student affairs. *TSQ, 2*, 431–446.

Nadal, K. L., Rivera, D. P., & Corpus, M. J. H. (2010). Sexual orientation and transgender microaggressions: Implications for mental health and counseling. In D. W. Sue (Ed.), *Microaggressions and marginality: Manifestation, dynamics, and impact* (pp. 217–240). Hoboken, NJ: Wiley.

Nicolazzo, Z. (2017). *Trans* in college: Transgender students' strategies for navigating campus life and the institutional politics of inclusion.* Sterling, VA: Stylus.

Nordmarken, S. (2014). Microaggressions. *TSQ, 1*(1–2), 129–134.

Pitcher, E. N. (2015). Another world is possible: Envisioning an intersectional social justice student affairs praxis. *Journal of Critical Thought and Praxis, 4*(1), 1–32.

Pryor, J. T. (2015). Out in the classroom: Transgender student experiences at a large public university. *Journal of College Student Development, 56*(5), 440–455.

Public Facilities Privacy & Security Act, H.R. 2, 2016-3 Gen. Assem., 2d Extra Sess. (N.C. 2016).

Reinert, L. J., & Serna, G. R. (2014). Living intersectionality in the academy. In D. Mitchell, C. Y. Simmons, & L. A. Greyerbiehl (Eds.), *Intersectionality & higher education: Theory, research, & praxis* (pp. 88–98). New York, NY: Peter Lang.

Rood, B. A., Reisner, S. L., Surace, F. I., Puckett, J. A., Maroney, M. R., & Pantalone, D. W. (2016). Expecting rejection: Understanding the minority stress experiences of transgender and gender-nonconforming individuals. *Transgender Health, 1*(1), 151–164.

Schilt, K. (2010). *Just one of the guys? Transgender men and the persistence of gender inequality.* Chicago, IL: University of Chicago Press.

Seelman, K. L. (2014). Recommendations of transgender students, staff, and faculty in the USA for improving college campuses. *Gender and Education, 26*(6), 618–635.

Seelman, K. L., Walls, N. E., Costello, K., Steffens, K., Inselman, K., Montague-Asp, H., & Colorado Trans on Campus Coalition. (2012). *Invisibilities, uncertainties, and unexpected surprises: The experiences of transgender and gender nonconforming students, staff, and faculty at universities & colleges in Colorado.* Denver, CO: Authors.

Simmons, S. L. (2017). A thousand words are worth a picture: A snapshot of trans* postsecondary educators in higher education. *International Journal of Qualitative Studies in Education, 30*(3), 266–284.

Spade, D. (2011). *Normal life: Administrative violence, critical trans politics, and the limits of law.* Brooklyn, NY: East End Press.

Stryker, S. (2008). *Transgender history.* Berkeley, CA: Seal Press.

Sue, D. W. (2010). *Microaggressions in everyday life: Race, gender, and sexual orientation.* Hoboken, NJ: Wiley.

Talbot, D. M., & Viento, W. L. E. (2005). Incorporating LGBT issues into student affairs graduate education. In R. L. Sanlo (Ed.), *Gender identity and sexual orientation: Research, policy, and personal* (New Directions for Student Services, no. 111, pp. 75–80). San Francisco, CA: Jossey-Bass.

Taylor, J., Dockendorff, K., & Inselman, K. (2017). Decoding the digital campus climate for prospective LGBTQ+ community colleges students. *Community College Journal of Research and Practice.* doi:10.1080/10668926.2017.1281177

Vaccaro, A. (2012). Campus microclimates for LGBT faculty, staff, and students: An exploration of the intersections of social identity and campus roles. *Journal of Student Affairs Research and Practice, 49*(4), 429–446.

Wilchins, R. (2014). *Queer theory, gender theory: An instant primer.* Bronx, NY: Magnus Books.

Yakaboshi, T., & Reinert, L. (2014, June 12). Professional dress and authenticity [Blog post]. Retrieved from https://studentaffairsfeminists.wordpress.com/2014/06/12/professional-dress-and-authenticity/

Yoshino, K. (2007). *Covering: The hidden assault on our civil rights.* New York, NY: Random House.

9

"You'll Fit Right In"

Fit as a Euphemism for Whiteness in Higher Education Hiring Practices

Kyle C. Ashlee

H IRING PRACTICES IN HIGHER education are in need of critical evaluation. Committees of professionals from various departments are often thrown together with little direction, aside from the job description or discussion about viewpoints or preferences of the committee members. Rarely do these committees receive any training on how to conduct a search, let alone how to overcome unconscious bias that may impact their choice of candidates. Ultimately, a handful of résumés are selected and preference is often given to those candidates with either personal connections to the institution or professional experiences that reflect those represented on the hiring committee. After the obligatory round of phone interviews, on-campus interviews, and reference checks, a candidate who may or may not be the most qualified person for the position is finally selected.

One of the most consistent failures of hiring practices in higher education is the inability to identify and select candidates of Color. In a critically honest *Washington Post* article, Professor of Higher Education at the University of Pennsylvania and Director of the Penn Center for Minority Serving Institutions Marybeth Gasman (2016, September) commented, "The reason we don't have more Faculty of Color among college faculty is that we don't want them. We simply don't want them." The same can be said for the hiring of professionals of Color in student affairs. As Gasman points out, racially minoritized candidates are often unfairly eliminated from searches because it is thought that they will negatively impact the "quality" of the hiring pool. In addition to this blatantly racist excuse, an inadequate pipeline of diverse applicants is often cited as a reason for the continued hiring of white[1] candidates (Antwi-Boasiako, 2008; Jackson, 2008; Kayes, 2006).

A common practice for higher education and student affairs search committees is to identify candidates who are a good fit for the institution. It is assumed that when the hiring committee finds the person who fulfills this mysterious and elusive criterion, a mutually beneficial and long-lasting relationship between applicant and institution will naturally evolve. Indeed, the word *fit* has become ubiquitous in higher education hiring practices, masking the racist assumptions embedded within.

This chapter aims to uncover the hidden agenda of racism in higher education hiring practices, specifically the pervasive notion of fit as a euphemism for white supremacy at colleges and universities. To illuminate this problem, I offer a personal example of the ways in which I have benefitted from white supremacy in higher education hiring practices through a reference to fit during a job interview. From there I explore the problem through an analysis of literature and ultimately draw connections between scholarship and my own story. Reviewing the history and context of higher education, I uncover the depths of racism and white supremacy in higher education hiring practices as well as the culture of whiteness that exists at most colleges and universities in the United States. Delving deeper into literature related to hiring practices, I demonstrate how *fit* is a coded term used by many college and university hiring committees that benefits white people and negatively impacts candidates of Color. Finally, I offer several recommendations for moving beyond fit in order to prioritize racial justice for candidates of Color and combat the white supremacy entrenched in higher education hiring practices.

THE DAY I GOT OFFERED A JOB BECAUSE I'M WHITE

Looking down at my solid black Stafford suit from JC Penny, I felt the knot in my stomach tighten. I never thought I would feel so inadequate wearing a suit. I was waiting in the reception area of the alumni relations office at a small, private, Ivy League college in the northeast United States. In just a few minutes, I'd be called into a sizeable office filled with mahogany wood and glass ornaments. I fiddled with my faux leather padfolio and noticed a large area where the plastic covering had chipped away, revealing the foamy soft interior. The voice in my head shrieked as I stuffed the worn folder under my chair.

The waiting area was filled with cushy sofas and a massive south-facing window that looked out onto an endless sea of rolling New England evergreens. The vastness of the trees coupled with the reputation of Ivy League grandeur left me feeling small and insignificant. I couldn't stop thinking about my cheap suit and old padfolio. Growing up in a working-class family and navigating higher education as a first-generation college student had not prepared me for this moment. Try as I might to look the part, a nagging doubt chipped away at my confidence and caused me to question whether I would be considered a good fit for the job.

I had never worked in alumni relations, but I had a lot of experience planning events for colleges, which is exactly what the job entailed. It was certainly a long shot, but my options were limited. After moving to the area for my wife's new job at the same school, I'd been scouring the university's website for any position that I was even remotely qualified for. The next closest university in the area was over an hour and a half commute by car, which I was hoping to avoid. Despite my lack of experience for the position, I was hoping that my transferrable skills would allow me to get a foot in the door and gain valuable experience in a new functional area.

As I waited to be called in for the interview, my mind began to wander. I couldn't help but think about how unemployment in student affairs seemed to reveal some of the most glaring incongruences between the field's espoused values and the behaviors of professionals in the field. I can't tell you how many positions I applied for that fall, both at the Ivy League school and beyond, where I never received a response. I didn't get a single "thank you for your application" or a "we'll be in touch soon" e-mail, and certainly not an "it was a difficult decision" or a "we're sorry to inform you" message. In a profession that prides itself on transparent communication and authentic dialogue, you'd think courteous professional notifications would be the norm, rather than the exception.

During these long waiting periods during the search, I was always encouraged to "trust the process." As an experienced facilitator of small group discussion and intergroup dialogue, I am very familiar with the notion of "trusting the process" and in that context, it is an adage that I espouse. There is something powerful about navigating through the discomfort that comes when people are pushed to the edge of their comfort zones during difficult dialogue. But having a conversation about race or spirituality in an educational setting is not the same as applying for a job. The learning that comes from hearing someone else's worldview is different from the learning that results from not being able to pay the bills. The bargain JC Penny suit I was wearing that day was a small reminder that, more than an educational moment, I needed this interview and the salary that would come with being hired.

These were the thoughts that swirled in my head as I sat waiting for the chance to pitch myself and plea for a position that I needed. But despite my frustration with the flawed job search process in student affairs, I didn't have to wonder whether the challenges I faced were somehow related to my race. The radio silence I often received after applying for a job was attributed to a lack of consideration rather than a manifestation of subtle racism. For People of Color on the student affairs job hunt, racial politics is likely always a consideration that weighs heavy when not hearing back from a potential employer. And let's not forget that after many months of searching, I had still landed an interview. Looking around the Alumni Relations office, I noticed that all of the staff was white and wondered if my getting that interview was about more than just my experience and credentials.

A gentle voice called my name and I was ushered into the office of the alumni relations director. I shuffled in, leaving my tattered padfolio under the chair in the reception area. Whatever helpful information I wrote inside that folder was not worth the risk of being found out as an Ivy-League fraud. Despite my lackluster suit, I still had a sliver of hope of convincing them that I could do the job. Underlying this hope was the assumption that, despite my differences in social class, I could still belong at an Ivy League school. While it wasn't obvious to me at the time, this assumption was undeniably connected to my social identities. Although I was not incredibly familiar with this elite school, I did know that I could comfortably walk around campus because nearly everyone I encountered looked like me.

After the formal round of questioning was finished, the director asked me if I had any questions about the position. The one thought that kept bouncing through my head was about how I would relate to the university's alumni population given that I did not attend the school myself. "Will it be a problem that I didn't graduate from this college?" I asked. "No, I really don't think that will matter," said the director flippantly. "Most of the alumni that you would be working with will be much older than you, so they won't necessarily know that you didn't graduate from here. Besides, you look like a younger version of most of these guys. You'll fit right in," she replied with a smile.

As the director walked me to the main exit, an administrative assistant shouted from his desk, "Oh, I think you forgot this," waving my ragged padfolio high in the air for everyone in the office to see. I hurried over to the desk and snatched the folder, thanking the man for looking after it for me. With one final handshake, I said goodbye to the director and escaped through the enormous glass doors. As I slid down the seat in my Ford Focus, I let out an exasperated sigh. Even with the director's appraisal of my potential ability to fool the Ivy Leaguers into thinking I belonged at their elite institution, I still felt like an imposter. The more I thought about her comment, the more it puzzled me. My rural working-class Midwest background felt so foreign and out of place in this environment. How could she think that I would "fit right in" among such wealthy East Coast elites?

Then it hit me. Replaying her words in my head, I began to think about what aspects of my identity would allow me to "fit right in," as she so confidently asserted. Thinking back to the school's homecoming festivities that I had attended just weeks before, I remembered being shocked at the overwhelming number of white people I saw on campus. While I could not relate to their sports cars and expensive Italian leather shoes, my race gave me the only qualification I needed to work with these privileged graduates.

A knot of disgust formed in my stomach. The director's comment revealed her unbridled preference for candidates who could relate to the white alumni of the college. Certainly, my gender was at play here as well, but given the prevalence of white women in higher education (Knapp, Kelly-Reid, & Ginder, 2010) and the ways in which they tend to benefit from affirmative action policies (Bell, 1987), I had to conclude that the director's preference for a candidate that looked like me was more about my race than anything else. If that was true of this position, what did that say for professionals who might work with the current student population, which hasn't changed much over the years? And, if an office director at an Ivy League institution could so blatantly acknowledge her bias toward white candidates, what does that mean for the preferences of search committees at other Ivy League institutions? What does it mean for job searches at any college campus?

On that day, I learned that the term *fit*, when referencing higher education hiring practices, is a euphemism for whiteness. By *whiteness* I mean "a position of structural advantage," a "place from which to look at oneself, others, and society," and "a set of cultural practices" (Frankenberg, 1993, p. 54) for white people that is often unnamed, unacknowledged, and unexamined. Embedded in the word *fit* is a world of bias, discrimination, and prejudice that results from whiteness and benefits white applicants. Now when I hear someone on a higher education search committee say, "They'll be a great *fit* for the job," what I hear is a thinly veiled preference for white candidates.

THE PROBLEM OF WHITENESS IN HIGHER EDUCATION HIRING PRACTICES

My personal narrative demonstrates one example of a much larger and more pervasive problem in higher education. The unrestrained preference for a white candidate that the director of Alumni Relations so openly shared with me when she uttered the word *fit* is not a localized phenomenon of individual bias. Rather, this personal story is one example of racism and bias in higher education hiring practices. My narrative is a scholarly attempt to illuminate and interrogate systems of racial oppression. And, if one requires further evidence of the epidemic that is white supremacy in higher education hiring practices, they need only read the literature.

Indeed, studies from various areas of higher education demonstrate the implicit racial bias in hiring practices that results in white racial self-segregation (e.g., Flowers & Jones, 2003; Jackson, 2008; Williams & Williams, 2006). In 2009, white people made up 75.6% of full-time staff at all federally funded degree-granting institutions in the United States (Knapp et al., 2010). Despite mandates and strategic plans, "efforts to diversify . . . continue to be amongst the least successful elements of campus commitments to diversity" (Turner, 2002, p. 14). This failure to recruit and retain candidates of Color is both fueled by and contributes to white supremacy in higher education, establishing institutional expectations for who applies, who is considered, and who is hired (Bonilla-Silva, Goar, & Embrick, 2006).

Delving further into the problem, there are several myths and assumptions that contribute to a general ignorance of racist hiring practices in higher education (Kayes, 2006). The mere proclamation in favor of hiring racially diverse staff does not necessarily result in the proposed outcome. Regardless of institutional diversity statements, many search committees have no training on implicit racial bias nor have they discussed the many benefits of hiring more faculty and staff of Color. In fact, racism in higher education search committees materializes through doubt in candidates' seriousness, a perception of professional invisibility for candidates of Color, the devaluing of professional experiences, and the expectation that candidates of Color would only be competitive for positions related to race and diversity (Sagaria, 2002).

Another assumption that leads to racist hiring practices in higher education is the notion that there are not enough racially diverse candidates to
choose from in applicant pools (Kayes, 2006). Despite intentional efforts to
develop robust pools of qualified candidates of Color, from grow-your-own
strategies to institutional exchange programs, higher.education continues to
hire mostly white faculty and staff (Gasman, 2016, October). A 2016 survey from HigherEdJobs.com found that 31% of the people using the site
for career exploration are from racially minoritized populations. However,
numbers alone in candidate pools cannot account for the dearth of People
of Color selected for professional positions in higher education. Rather, the
problem can be attributed to *aversive racism*, which involves the person hiring finding "a way to hire the white applicant without admitting to himself or herself that racial bias played a role in the choice" (Dovidio, 1997,
p. A60). As opposed to a passive unconsciousness, hiring decisions are often
driven by willful ignorance or intentional decisions to maintain the status
quo (Matias, 2015; Mills, 2007).

Willful ignorance in higher education hiring practices leads to a preference
for white candidates and the proliferation of institutional racism at colleges
and universities. Aside from being unethical, racism in higher education hiring practices is also inefficient and costly. Turnover costs can represent up
to 5% of an institution's overall annual operating budget when accounting
for time spent in the hiring process, the training of new employees, and the
cost of reduced productivity associated with a job search (Waldman, Kelly,
Arora, & Smith, 2004). Indeed, the "revolving door" of faculty and staff of
Color results in the incalculable cost of time and money for individuals and
institutions (Kayes, 2006).

Hiring practices steeped in white supremacy are also detrimental to the
educational environment. Without the unique skills and talents of People of
Color, institutions are impoverished in the scholarship that is produced, the
perspectives that are shared, and the education that is delivered (Mohammed,
2013). Overall student success is negatively impacted by a lack of faculty and
staff of Color who could otherwise offer vital mentorship and support for
many students who might struggle in college environments that were not
built for them (Griffin, Pérez, Holmes, & Mayo, 2010).

Additionally, the continued tendency to hire white candidates under-
mines many of the values of higher education. College mission statements
and professional associations across the country declare the importance of
diversity toward the fulfillment of higher education's goals (Association
of American Colleges & Universities, 2007; American College Personnel

Association & National Association of Student Personnel Administrators, 2015). Hiring mostly white staff and faculty only serves to prevent the progress toward outcomes of racial diversity and inclusion in higher education (Harris & Bensimon, 2007).

Using racist criteria like the notion of fit for making hiring decisions in higher education can have troubling consequences. This word reflects the embedded racism in higher education hiring practices that result in the continued hiring of white faculty and staff over People of Color. The following discussion uncovers the historical and cultural path that resulted in white supremacy in higher education hiring practices as well as the nuanced employment tactics used to perpetuate institutional racism at colleges and universities.

A LEGACY OF WHITENESS

"Most of the alumni that you would be working with will be much older than you, so they won't necessarily know that you didn't graduate from here."

Racism in higher education is not a new phenomenon. Indeed, colleges and universities in the United States were founded on an assumption of white supremacy and are organized by whiteness (Jayakumar & Museus, 2012; Moore, 2008). An assertion from the director of alumni relations during my interview regarding the mentality of older graduates reflects the legacy of both patriarchy and racial oppression in American higher education. The tacit assumption that the white men who graduated in the 1950s would relate to me because I look like them is a clear articulation of higher education's unchanging habitus of whiteness (Bonilla-Silva et al., 2006).

A *habitus of whiteness* is defined as the "racialized, uninterrupted socialization process that conditions and creates whites' racial tastes, perceptions, feelings, and emotions and their views on racial matters" (Bonilla-Silva, 2003, p. 104). The cultural practices, traditions, and customs at colleges and universities all reflect an embedded white institutional presence (WIP), which is rooted in higher education's racist historical underpinnings (Gusa, 2010). Additionally, the statement from the director of Alumni Relations in my story also demonstrates the resilience of white supremacy and the ways in which racism in higher education has remained consistent over time.

Indeed, colleges and universities center whiteness in both explicit and invisible ways (Moore, 2008). The culture of most institutions in higher education reflects a white or Eurocentric perspective, which reinforces the dominance of whiteness through artifacts such as artwork, architecture, rituals, and traditions (Jayakumar & Museus, 2012). These findings should be no surprise considering the racial populations of most colleges and universities. Student, faculty, and staff demographics at most institutions of higher education are dominated by people with white skin (Ginder, Kelly-Reid, & Mann, 2014; Knapp et al., 2010). Both drawn to and responsible for the self-segregating culture of whiteness, white people at colleges and universities maintain an ongoing and resilient ethos of white supremacy in higher education.

The white isolation seen at colleges and universities results in a culture where individuals are conditioned with white racial tastes, perceptions, feelings, and emotions (Bonilla-Silva et al., 2006; Bourdieu, 1984). Examples of white habitus include racial segregation, ignorance about race and racism, and resistance to interracial relationships. This white habitus promotes solidarity with other white people and negative perspectives about People of Color. Given that race is never explicitly discussed, the white habitus establishes a normalcy of white racial segregation, hierarchy, and oppression. Indeed, "because the white habitus creates a space in which whites' extreme isolation is normalized, whites do not experience troubling doubts or second thoughts as to their lack of interaction with Blacks" (Bonilla-Silva et al., 2006, p. 248). Thus, everyday behaviors, like those of hiring committees at colleges and universities, are not seen as being racialized or reinforcing racism by white people.

The fact that white customs, traditions, and epistemologies go unexamined at colleges and universities helps to explain why white supremacy permeates the culture of higher education in the United States (Gusa, 2010). This WIP "is the institutionalized fusion of [w]hite worldview, [w]hite supremacy, and [w]hite privilege" (Gusa, 2010, p. 472). Embedded in this WIP is the dominance of white historical superiority and entitlement, the supposed objective and rational construction of knowledge, racially ignorant colorblindness, as well as the unquestioned estrangement of whites from People of Color. Given that whites constitute 75% of all full-time staff and faculty and 53% of all students at degree-granting colleges and universities, it is no wonder that this WIP so accurately describes the racially oppressive culture in higher education (Ginder et al., 2014; Knapp et al., 2010). In addition to WIP, these figures also help to explain the ubiquitous white habitus in higher education (Bonilla-Silva et al., 2006).

The pervasive nature of white supremacy in higher education has damaging outcomes for the People of Color who struggle every day to survive within the walls of academia. Research demonstrates that People of Color consistently experience their campuses as racially hostile, chilly, and unsafe (Ancis, Sedlacek, & Mohr, 2000; Fries-Britt & Turner, 2002; Harper & Hurtado, 2007; Miller, Anderson, Cannon, Pérez, & Moore, 1998; Rankin & Reason, 2005; Reid & Radhakrishnan, 2003; Watson et al., 2002). Additionally, the Federal Bureau of Investigation reported that schools are the third most-common sites for racially biased hate crimes in the United States (Criminal Justice Information Service Division, 2009). It's no wonder then that students of Color struggle academically and have higher rates of attrition than white collegians (Black, 2004; Cooke, 2002; Harvey-Smith, 2002; Stovall, 2005).

A legacy of whiteness, established through the construction of a white habitus and WIP, has created an environment in higher education that produces racist practices in hiring faculty and staff. Looking to the cohorts of white alumni at the Ivy League school where I was a candidate as a sample, one can understand how whiteness has come to be so firmly entrenched in higher education. For centuries, the culture of higher education has been built by and for white people. This historical perspective reveals the intentionally crafted fog of whiteness that prevents white people at colleges and universities from seeing the racially destructive consequences of their willful ignorance. When put into the context of a legacy of whiteness, the seemingly innocuous term *fit* can be seen for its true nature. Rather than a mechanism for determining the most qualified candidate for a position, *fit* is a coded word that reflects white notions of professionalism and effectively disqualifies candidates of Color in higher education employment processes.

FIT AS A EUPHEMISM FOR WHITE SUPREMACY

"Besides, you look like a younger version of most of these guys. You'll fit right in."

What do we mean when we say that someone is a good fit for a position? Candidates are much more likely to be hired for a job if they share cultural similarities with those in the organization, including aspects of self-presentation, life experiences, and even personal leisure activities (Lareau & Weininger, 2003). More than technical competency, analytical thinking, or communication skills, fit has been cited as the most important criterion when employers make hiring decisions (Reynolds & Rivera, 2012). While the word often goes unexamined, further analysis reveals that *fit* is coded language used to maintain the status quo of whiteness and weed out candidates with different racial and cultural perspectives.

When considering the implications of fit on efforts to diversify staff and faculty in higher education, it's no wonder why organizations struggle. If the way employers actually select candidates is more similar to choosing friends than carefully identifying the most qualified person for a position, there is no mystery why racial diversity is not achieved in workforce hiring (Reynolds & Rivera, 2012). If an organization is predominantly made up of white people with a cultural habitus of whiteness (Bonilla-Silva et al., 2006; Bourdieu, 1984), the prioritizing of fit in hiring decisions is simply a mechanism to uphold whiteness as the norm. In other words, white hiring committees who prioritize fit when selecting job candidates are simply looking to reproduce themselves through their hiring decisions.

Vocational psychologists have been studying the notion of fit for decades, highlighting exactly how pervasive this mentality is in hiring practices. Indeed, Holland's (1959, 1966, 1973, 1985, 1997) theory of vocational personalities is a model commonly used in counseling psychology to help people make career decisions based on six personality types, including Realistic, Investigative, Artistic, Social, Enterprising, and Conventional (abbreviated as RIASEC). Each personality type is characterized by a corresponding set of interests, beliefs, abilities, and values (Nauta, 2010). Holland's (1997) theory suggests that individuals search for and attain jobs that allow them to "exercise their skills and abilities, express their attitudes and values, and take on agreeable problems and roles" (p. 4). According to Holland's RIASEC model, the extent to which an individual's personality type aligns with the characteristics of a job determines what is known as *congruence*. Thus, Holland's theory of vocational personalities provides a framework for the commonly held belief that job satisfaction, stability, and success are related to the fit between someone's personality type and their job.

Holland's notion of fit does not account for cultural or racial identity, only the personality and skills of the individual, as well as the professional classification of the work environment (Fouad & Byars-Winston, 2005). Additionally, the original data set that validated Holland's typology of fit was drawn from a mostly homogenous sample of white men. When higher education hiring decisions are made based on person-environment fit, as they were with the Alumni Relations position I applied for, fit serves as a euphemism for upholding the habitus of white supremacy at colleges and universities. Stated differently, the use of fit in hiring practices influences which job applicants are considered and ultimately hired, resulting in a cycle of white segregated organizations.

In my story about applying for the alumni relations position, my experience and qualifications likely had little to do with whether I was offered the job. In her statement about me "looking like a younger version of most of these guys," the director demonstrated that to be considered, a candidate must resemble the mostly white graduates of the university. Though I did not accept the position, I did end up working at the institution in a different department. I came to discover that the unofficial hiring practices of affirmative action for white people that I experienced in the Alumni Relations search were at play throughout the entire university. In my department, I did not work with a single person of Color during my two years of employment. When attending student affairs divisional meetings, the room was filled with a sea of white faces. Now having worked at several different institutions of higher education, I realize that whiteness is not the exception; it is very much the norm.

Considering that fit is used in hiring practices to perpetuate white supremacy in higher education, it is no surprise how white the field is and how challenging it is for professionals of Color to thrive, or even survive, in these environments (Kayes, 2006; Knapp et al., 2010). If higher education professionals are to fulfill their professed values of diversity, inclusion, and social justice, they must begin to challenge the oppressive hiring practices of how using fit can be a euphemism for maintaining whiteness. Acknowledging and actively resisting white supremacy can transform hiring practices in higher education, resulting in staff and faculty that reflect the racial and cultural makeup of colleges and universities today.

STRATEGIES FOR CONFRONTING WHITENESS IN HIGHER EDUCATION HIRING PRACTICES

If change is to happen in the hiring of staff and faculty, resulting in the racial diversity that higher education claims to value, then there must first be significant efforts made to acknowledge and address the embedded white supremacy in higher education. Specifically, those responsible for making hiring decisions must begin naming the unexamined racist assumptions in institutional hiring practices that result in blatant preference for white candidates. Those responsible for job searches must be vigilant about the relentless prevalence of white supremacy and the ways in which it seeps into every aspect of the hiring process. Additionally, for true transformation to occur in higher education, college and university leaders must look beyond hiring practices and begin acknowledging whiteness at a systemic level.

Becoming Racially Cognizant

To begin this process of naming white supremacy in higher education hiring practices, institutions must

> work to make explicit the unacknowledged [w]hiteness of facially neutral criteria of decision, and adopt strategies that counteract the influence of unrecognized [w]hite norms. . . . Making nonobvious [w]hite norms explicit, and thus exposing their contingency, can begin to define for [w]hite people a coequal role in a racially diverse society. Because the skeptical stance prevents the unthinking imposition of [w]hite norms, it encourages [w]hite decision-makers to consider adopting non-[w]hite ways of doing business, so that the formerly unquestioned [w]hite-specific criterion of decision becomes just one option among many. (Flagg, 1993, p. 957)

In other words, white people in charge of making hiring decisions at colleges and universities must develop the practice of constantly centering race and racism, in the same way that People of Color are forced to do every day (Kivel, 1996).

This type of heedful racial consciousness is an element of *racially cognizant whiteness* (Reason & Evans, 2007). For white professionals making hiring decisions, "a racially cognizant sense of whiteness involves a continuous process of rearticulating the meaning of race" (Reason & Evans, 2007, p. 71). Change in racist higher education hiring practices will not happen until those who make employment decisions are willing to acknowledge and name the many biases, assumptions, and stereotypes that influence their candidate preferences (Kayes, 2006). By embracing the truth about when, where, and how whiteness shows up in the job search process, higher education can begin to actively combat the cycle of racially segregated white culture at most colleges and universities.

Making tangible efforts toward racial cognizance for white professionals at colleges and universities can be challenging. Many white staff and faculty are resistant to training and education efforts geared toward establishing white racial consciousness (DiAngelo, 2011; Kayes, 2006). Additionally, professionals across institutions of higher education are stretched thin with demands on their time and budgets, which can create barriers to effectively making progress. That said, any movement in the direction of white racial consciousness is important in beginning to change practices that reinforce racism and white supremacy. From administering the implicit racial bias test (Greenwald & Banaji, 2013) to developing an intragroup white faculty and staff learning community, there are many possibilities for introducing racial cognizance raising initiatives that are in line with the context of any institution.

USING CRITICAL RACE THEORY AND CRITICAL WHITENESS STUDIES

A useful tool for developing racial cognizance is critical race theory (CRT). CRT is a theoretical framework that emerged from Derrick Bell and Alan Freeman's legal studies in the 1970s (Ladson-Billings, 1998). Specifically, the theory was intended to prioritize and center the experiences of People of Color, while simultaneously acknowledging white supremacy. Since that time, the theory has been applied to various disciplines, including education, to name and address the realities of systemic racism.

Various scholars have outlined and articulated CRT in different ways. Thought leaders, including Delgado and Stefancic (2001), Bell (1987), and Crenshaw (1989), have identified the tenets of CRT, including social constructionism, racism as normal, revisionist history, differential racialization, interest convergence, anti-essentialism, intersectionality, and storytelling. Many of the central ideas in CRT, including intersectionality (Crenshaw, 1989), focus on the ways in which social systems interlock and interact (Collins, 2004) to create individual experiences of oppression. Additionally, other scholars assert that CRT includes tenets related to a critique of liberalism, race as property, the need for interdisciplinary perspectives, and the goal of social justice (Hernández, 2016; Museus & Iftikar, 2013; Pérez Huber, 2010).

Another helpful theoretical tool for developing racial cognizance is critical whiteness studies (CWS), a field of study specifically dedicated to identifying and deconstructing whiteness (Delgado & Stefancic, 1997). Generally, CWS encourages white people to address the historic, social, and cultural realities of white supremacy (Frankenberg, 1993). While there are no specific tenets of CWS, it does provide "a framework to deconstruct how whites accumulate racial privilege" (Matias & Mackey, 2016, p. 34), including material wealth, economic power, and social capital. Higher education professionals who are responsible for employment decisions can develop increased racial awareness in hiring practices by utilizing the tenets found in both CRT and critical Whiteness studies.

Evaluating Racially Coded Language

A concrete place to begin evaluating hiring practices from a racially cognizant lens is the use of words and language in job search processes that express inherent preference for white people. The focus of this chapter is on the word *fit*, which we've seen has detrimental implications when used to justify who is and who is not considered for a faculty or staff job. Beyond this word, however, there is a mountain of coded words and phrases that serve to reinforce values of whiteness and white supremacy.

Professionalism

Right behind fit, the idea of professionalism is another racist hiring measurement used to benefit white candidates and create barriers for candidates of Color. The power of the term *professionalism* lies in its ambiguity. Few can define exactly what the word means, yet there is an undeniable element of whiteness entrenched in this notion. Given that leadership in business, politics, education, and just about every other profession has historically been dominated by white people (Zinn, 1995), examples of what it means to be a professional can often reflect whiteness. Thus, when it is claimed that a job candidate does not display enough "professionalism," the assumption might be that they do not align with the vision and culture of whites who have set the mold of what it means to be a professional.

Qualified

The term *qualified* is often used in conversations about diversifying staff and faculty in higher education. The assumption often made is that considering candidates of Color will automatically decrease the quality of the applicant pool. This notion is false in many ways. First, it should not be assumed that an all-white or nondiverse applicant pool is necessarily more qualified than a racially diverse pool. Depending on the position and the goals of the search, it may be determined that an all-white applicant pool is actually less qualified than one that is racially diverse. Second, why is it assumed that job candidates of Color are less qualified than whites? Considering the systemic challenges that People of Color face in achieving the same professional accomplishments as whites, it can easily be argued that these candidates have additional qualifications. Nearly every higher education position requires candidates to have a set of minimum qualifications, such as number of years of experience and degree attainment, but search committees need to critically evaluate the ways in which these minimum qualifications disadvantage People of Color and benefit white people, who have access to nearly all of society's institutions that contribute to their accumulation. An honest evaluation of this racially loaded term reveals that being labeled as less *qualified* is another way in which higher education hiring practices attempt to police candidates according to white expectations of professionalism.

Attitude

It is likely that many candidates of Color are rejected from job search processes and denied employment because it is thought that they have a "bad attitude." This phrase is linguistically related to the Angry Person of Color trope that is often attributed to any non-white person who expresses emotion in the presence of a white person. Due to white fragility, any interaction between a white person and a Person of Color can result in racial discomfort and stress for the white person (DiAngelo, 2011). Rather than recognizing this stress as their own inability to engage with People of Color, white people often blame People of Color for their feelings of unease. Thus, many candidates of Color might be dismissed under the guise of a "bad attitude" that is merely a symptom of white fragility.

Communication Skills

While the ability to communicate is undoubtedly an important skill for any member of faculty or staff in higher education, the phrase *communication skills* as a criterion for hiring decisions can often be a racially coded term that benefits white people. When a hiring committee indicates that an applicant does not have adequate communication skills, they might be making their judgement based on a white standard of communication. Candidates seeking employment in higher education are expected to speak a specific way and to use a certain vocabulary, all of which reflect and preference the dominant white culture. Any use of regional vernacular, cultural slang, or linguistic accents in an interview can be held against candidates as perceived lack of communication skills. These candidates likely have perfectly suitable communication skills, just not according to a white supremacist rubric.

Enthusiasm

Similar to having a "bad attitude," some candidates of Color may not be considered for a faculty or staff position because they are thought to lack enthusiasm for the job. In addition to favoring extroversion, the use of *enthusiasm* as a criterion for hiring decisions can also be racist. As previously articulated in this chapter, the whiteness of higher education presents a hostile environment for People of Color. Thus, it is understandable that candidates of Color often express concern or weariness about working in an environment dominated by whiteness. In fact, hiring committees dedicated to racial justice might anticipate these feelings of trepidation and proactively work to identify the ways in which the institution is or is not addressing systemic racism. Sadly, however, some hiring committees might see any emotion other than excitement as evidence that the candidate does not *really* want the job. Prioritizing enthusiasm can benefit white candidates who do not experience the racial hostility and emotional exhaustion that People of Color face when working at a predominantly white institution.

MOVING BEYOND HIRING PRACTICES

While it is crucial to interrogate the inherent white supremacy that lives in college and university hiring practices, it is also necessary to evaluate how whiteness permeates the entire landscape of higher education. Much of the responsibility to transform campus cultures lies with institutional leadership. When college and university leaders begin the process of change, it "must be systemic and of a magnitude that affects *all* aspects of institutional functioning, rather than a single part or a few parts of the institution" (Gabbard & Singleton, 2012, p. 193). Without this systemic evaluation of white supremacy, the efforts to change smaller components of operation within higher education, like hiring practices, will struggle to gain traction. Indeed, for true racial justice to actualize in higher education, everyone must begin to dissect the ways in which whiteness impacts "underlying assumptions and deeply embedded values and meanings attached to what institutional members do and believe about their institution" (Gabbard & Singleton, 2012, p. 193). When whiteness and white supremacy are identified and eliminated in all the practices of higher education, college and university campuses can truly become diverse and racially just.

Transforming the Landscape of Higher Education

A month after Marybeth Gasman (2016, September) wrote an article on why colleges don't hire more faculty and staff of Color, she received more than 6,000 e-mails from people in higher education who resonated with her message. In a follow-up article, Gasman (2016, October) shared some of the thoughts that these staff and faculty had about the troubling racist hiring process in higher education. A large majority of these messages expressed gratitude for naming a truth that never gets acknowledged in a field that prides itself on being welcoming and inclusive. Others shared their perspective as white people who have either seen or been guilty of perpetuating the racism in search processes that Gasman discussed. Even so, others defended the way things are done, attempting to justify the establishment of racism as a criterion for who is selected to work at colleges and universities.

Several of the People of Color who reached out to Gasman about their experiences with racism in higher education hiring processes "wrote about the many times they were 'told privately that [they] didn't fit in by a member of a search committee'" (Gasman, 2016, October). These sentiments are further evidence of the pervasive reliance on the term *fit* as a mechanism to perpetuate racism and white supremacy at colleges and universities. Too often this idiom, and others like it, goes unnoticed and unexamined. While these words are not the sole reason why higher education is dominated by white people and white culture, they reflect a part of the habitus of whiteness (Bonilla-Silva et al., 2006) in our field.

My experience job searching at a prestigious Ivy league institution and being told that I would "fit right in" with the overwhelmingly white alumni was a wake-up call to the ways in which I have and continue to benefit from the automatic preference given to white people in higher education hiring practices. These practices and preferences for whiteness undoubtedly have a negative impact on communities of Color, the fulfillment of diversity goals in higher education, and the overall learning environment at colleges and universities. Moreover, the covert and subtle nature of words like *fit* that determine who is and who is not hired for staff and faculty positions reveal just how insidious white supremacy can be.

If the hiring of faculty and staff is to change in a manner that does not favor white people, but rather prioritizes racial justice, professionals must begin naming where and when white supremacy rears its ugly head. For too long this responsibility of identifying racism in higher education has fallen on the shoulders of People of Color, a burden that only adds to the weight of systemic racism they already experience. For real change to occur, white people must take on the task of acknowledging white supremacy in higher education hiring practices. Additionally, white people must embrace the personal self-work that is required to combat their own contributions to racism in higher education, including the defensive resistance that is all too commonly exhibited from white people when confronted with the realities of racism. Moving away from fit toward racial cognizance (Reason & Evans, 2007) will require honesty, humility, and persistence. Embracing these values in hiring practices, however, might just be the first step in transforming the racial landscape of higher education.

NOTE

1. Contrary to tradition and the APA style guide, which states that "[r]acial and ethnic groups are designated by proper nouns and are capitalized" (American Psychological Association, 2010, p. 75), the author has intentionally chosen not to capitalize the word *white* throughout this chapter. This choice is an act of political resistance intended to challenge the assumed power and dominance that is embedded in whiteness and white supremacy.

REFERENCES

American College Personnel Association & National Association of Student Personnel Administrators. (2015). *Professional competency areas for student affairs educators*. Professional Competencies Task Force. Washington DC: Authors. Retrieved from https://www.naspa.org/images/uploads/main/ACPA_NASPA_Professional_Competencies_FINAL.pdf

American Psychological Association. (2010). *Publication Manual of the American Psychological Association* (6th ed.). Washington DC: Author.

Ancis, J., Sedlacek, W., & Mohr, J. (2000). Student perceptions of campus cultural climate by race. *Journal of Counseling and Development, 78*(2), 180–185.

Antwi-Boasiako, K. (2008). The dilemma of hiring minorities and conservative resistance: The diversity game. *Journal of Instructional Psychology, 35*(3), 225–231.

Association of American Colleges & Universities. (2007). *College learning for the new global century*. Washington DC: Author.

Bell, D. (1987). *And we are not saved: The elusive quest for racial justice*. New York, NY: Basic Books.

Black, L. (2004). Ivory towers? The academy and racism. In I. Law, D. Phillips, & L. Turney (Eds.), *Institutional racism in higher education* (pp. 1–6). Sterling, VA: Trentham Books.

Bonilla-Silva, E. (2003). *Racism without racists: Color-blind racism and the persistence of racial inequality in the United States*. Lanham, MD: Rowman & Littlefield.

Bonilla-Silva, E., Goar, C., & Embrick, D. G. (2006). When whites flock together: The social psychology of white habitus. *Critical Sociology, 32*(2), 229–253. doi:10.1163/156916306777835268

Bourdieu, P. (1984). *Distinction*. Cambridge, MA: Harvard University Press.

Collins, P. H. (2004). Toward a new vision: Race, class, and gender as categories of analysis and connection. In L. Heldke & P. O'Connor (Eds.), *Oppression, privilege, and resistance* (pp. 529–543). Boston, MA: McGraw Hill.

Cooke, D. Y. (2002). *Racial discrimination and well-being among African American students*. (Unpublished doctoral dissertation). University of Michigan, Ann Arbor, MI.

Crenshaw, K. W. (1989). Demarginalizing the intersection of race and sex: A Black feminist critique of antidiscrimination doctrine, feminist theory, and antiracist politics. *University of Chicago Legal Forum, 139*, 139–167.

Criminal Justice Information Service Division. (2009, November). Uniform Crime Report. Washington DC: U.S. Department of Justice, https://www.fbi.gov/services/cjis

Delgado, R., & Stephancic, J. (1997). *Critical White studies: Looking behind the mirror*. Philadelphia, PA: Temple University Press.

Delgado, R., & Stefancic, J. (2001). *Critical race theory: An introduction*. New York, NY: New York University Press.

DiAngelo, R. (2011). White fragility. *International Journal of Critical Pedagogy, 3*(3), 54–70.

Dovidio, J. (1997, July 25). "Aversive" racism and the need for affirmative action. *The Chronicle of Higher Education*. Retrieved from http://www.chronicle.com/article/Aversive-Racismthe-Need/77077

Flagg, B. J. (1993). "Was blind, but now I see": White race consciousness and the requirement of discriminatory intent. *Michigan Law Review, 91*(5), 953–1017.

Flowers, L. A., & Jones, L. (2003). Exploring the status of Black male faculty utilizing data from the national study of postsecondary faculty. *Journal of Men's Studies, 12*, 3–13.

Fouad, N. A., & Byars-Winston, A. M. (2005). Cultural context of career choice: Meta-analysis of race/ethnicity differences. *The Career Development Quarterly, 53*(3), 223–233.

Frankenberg, R. (1993). Growing up White: Feminism, racism, and the social geography of childhood. *Thinking Through Ethnicities, 45*, 51–84.

Fries-Britt, S., & Turner, B. (2002). Uneven stories: Successful Black collegians at a Black and a White campus. *Review of Higher Education, 25*(3), 315–330.

Gabbard, G., & Singleton, S. (2012). Cultivating campus cultures that support racially diverse and other underserved students. In S. Museus & U. M. Jayakumar (Eds.), *Creating campus cultures: Fostering success among racially diverse student populations* (pp. 190–209). New York, NY: Routledge.

Gasman, M. (2016, September 26). An Ivy League professor on why colleges don't hire more faculty of color: "We don't want them." *The Washington Post.* Retrieved from https://www.washingtonpost.com/news/grade-point/wp/2016/09/26/an-ivy-league-professor-on-why-colleges-dont-hire-more-faculty-of-color-we-dont-want-them/

Gasman, M. (2016, October 11). What people did when an Ivy League professor wrote faculty of color don't get jobs because "we don't want them." *The Washington Post.* Retrieved from https://www.washingtonpost.com/news/grade-point/wp/2016/10/11/how-people-responded-when-an-ivy-league-professor-wrote-nonwhite-faculty-dont-get-jobs-because-we-dont-want-them/

Ginder, S. A., Kelly-Reid, J. E., & Mann, F. B. (2014). Enrollment in postsecondary institutions, fall 2013; financial statistics, fiscal year 2013; and employees in postsecondary institutions, fall 2013. *First Look (Provisional Data) (NCES 2015-012). U.S. Department of Education.* Washington DC: National Center for Education Statistics.

Greenwald, A., & Banaji, M. (2013). *Blindspot: Hidden biases of good people.* New York, NY: Random House.

Griffin, K. A., Pérez II, D., Holmes, A. P. E., & Mayo, C. E. P. (2010). Investing in the future: The importance of faculty mentoring in the development of students of color in STEM. *New Directions for Institutional Research, 148*, 95–103. doi:10.1002/ir.365

Gusa, D. L. (2010). White institutional presence: The impact of whiteness on campus climate. *Harvard Educational Review, 80*(4), 464–586. doi:10.17763/haer.80.4.p5j483825u110002

Harper, S. R., & Hurtado, S. (2007). Nine themes in campus racial climates and implications for institutional transformation. *New Directions for Student Services, 120*, 7–24.

Harris III, F., & Bensimon, E. M. (2007). The equity scorecard: A collaborative approach to assess and respond to racial/ethnic disparities in student outcomes. *New Directions for Student Services, 120*, 41–53.

Harvey-Smith, A. (2002). An examination of the retention literature and application in student success. *Center for Community College Student Engagement.* Retrieved from https://www.ccsse.org/center/resources/docs/research/harvey-smith.pdf

Hernández, E. (2016). Utilizing critical race theory to examine race/ethnicity, racism, and power in student development theory and research. *Journal of College Student Development, 57*(6), 168–180.

HigherEdJobs. (2016). Audience demographics. [Data file]. Retrieved from https://www.higheredjobs.com/popup/myHEJDemographics.cfm

Holland, J. L. (1959). A theory of vocational choice. *Journal of Counseling Psychology, 6*, 35–45.

Holland, J. L. (1966). *The psychology of vocational choice: A theory of personality type and model environments.* Waltham, MA: Blaisdell.

Holland, J. L. (1973). *Making vocational choices.* Englewood Cliffs, NJ: Prentice-Hall.

Holland, J. L. (1985). *Making vocational choices: A theory of vocational personalities and work environments* (2nd ed.). Englewood Cliffs, NJ: Prentice Hall.

Holland, J. L. (1997). *Making vocational choices: A theory of vocational personalities and work environments* (3rd Ed.). Odessa, FL: Psychological Assessment Resources.

Jackson, J. F. L. (2008). Race segregation across the academic workforce: Exploring factors that may contribute to the disparate representation of African American men. *American Behavioral Scientist, 51*(7), 1004–1029.

Jayakumar, U. M., & Museus, S. D. (2012). Mapping the intersection of campus cultures and equitable outcomes among racially diverse student populations. In S. D. Museus & U. M. Jayakumar (Eds.) *Creating campus cultures: Fostering success among racially diverse student populations* (pp. 1–27). New York, NY: Routledge.

Kayes, P. E. (2006). New paradigms for diversifying faculty and staff in higher education: Uncovering cultural biases in the search and hiring process. *Multicultural Education, 14*(2), 65–69.

Kivel, P. (1996). *Uprooting racism: How white people can work for racial justice.* Gabriola Island, BC: New Society.

Knapp, L. G., Kelly-Reid, J. E., & Ginder, S. A. (2010). Employees in postsecondary institutions, fall 2010, and salaries of full-time instructional staff, 2009–10. *First Look (Provisional Data) (NCES 2015-012). U.S. Department of Education.* Washington DC: National Center for Education Statistics. Retrieved from http://nces.ed.gov/pubs2012/2012276.pdf

Ladson-Billings, G. (1998). Just what is critical race theory and what's it doing in a nice field like education? *International Journal of Qualitative Studies in Education, 11*(1), 7–24. http://doi.org/10.1080/095183998236863

Lareau, A., & Weininger, E. (2003). Cultural capital in educational research: A critical assessment. *Theory and Society, 32,* 567–606.

Matias, C. E. (2015). I ain't your doc student. In K. Fasching-Varner, K. Albert, R. Mitchell, & C. Allen (Eds.), *Racial battle fatigue in higher education: Exposing the myth of post-racial America* (pp. 59–68). Lanham, MD: Rowman & Littlefield.

Matias, C. E., & Mackey, J. (2016). Breakin' down Whiteness in antiracist teaching: Introducing critical Whiteness pedagogy. *Urban Review, 48*(1), 32–50. doi:10.1007/s11256-015-0344-7

Miller, M. H., Anderson, R., Cannon, J. G., Pérez, E., & Moore, H. A. (1998). Campus racial climate polices: The view from the bottom up. *Race, Gender, and Class, 5*(2), 139–157.

Mills, C. (2007). White ignorance. In S. Sullivan & N. Tuana (Eds.), *Race and epistemologies of ignorance* (pp. 13–38). Albany, NY: State University of New York Press.

Mohammed, I. (2013). *The relationship between perceptions of fit and job satisfaction among administrative staff in a Midwestern university* (Unpublished doctoral dissertation). Bowling Green State University, Bowling Green, OH.

Moore, L.W. (2008). *Reproducing racism: White space, elite law schools, and racial inequality.* Lanham, MD: Rowman and Littlefield Publishers, Inc.

Museus, S. D., & Iftikar, J. (2013). An Asian critical theory (AsianCrit) framework. In S. Museus (Ed.), *Asian American Students in Higher Education* (pp. 18–29). New York, NY: Routledge.

Nauta, M. M. (2010). The development, evolution, and status of Holland's theory of vocational personalities: Reflections and future directions for counseling psychology. *Journal of Counseling Psychology, 57*(1), 11–22. doi:10.1037/a0018213

Pérez Huber, L. (2010). Using Latina/o critical race theory (LatCrit) and racist nativism to explore intersectionality in the educational experiences of undocumented Chicana college students. *Educational Foundations, 24*(1–2), 77–97.

Rankin, S. R., & Reason, R. D. (2005). Differing perceptions: How students of color and white students perceive campus climate for underrepresented group. *Journal of College Student Development, 46*(1), 43–61.

Reason, R. D., & Evans, N. J. (2007). The complicated realities of whiteness: From color blind to racially cognizant. *New Directions for Student Services, 120,* 67–75. doi:10.1002/ss.258

Reid, L., & Radhakrishnan, P. (2003). Race matters: The relation between race and general campus climate. *Cultural Diversity and Ethnic Minority Psychology, 9*(3), 263–275.

Reynolds, A. L., & Rivera, L. M. (2012). The relationship between personal characteristics, multicultural attitudes, and self-reported multicultural competence of graduate students. *Training and Education in Professional Psychology, 6*(3), 167–173. doi:10.1037/a0029774

Sagaria, M. A. D. (2002). An exploratory model of filtering in administrative searches: Toward counter-hegemonic discourse. *Journal of Higher Education, 73,* 676–710.

Stovall, A. J. (2005). Why Black cultural centers? The philosophical bases for Black cultural centers. In F. Hord (Ed.), *Black cultural centers: Politics of survival and identity* (pp. 102–112). Chicago, IL: Third World Press and Association for Black Cultural Centers.

Turner, C. S. V. (2002). *Diversifying the faculty: A guidebook for search committees.* Washington DC: Association of American Colleges & Universities.

Waldman, J. D., Kelly, F., Arora, S., & Smith, H. L. (2004). The shocking cost of turnover in healthcare. *Health Care Management Review, 29*(1), 2–7.

Watson, L. W., Terrell, M. C., Wright, D. J., Bonner, F. A., Cuyjet, M., Gold, J., Rudy, D., & Person, D. R. (2002). *How minority students experience college: Implications for planning and policy.* Sterling, VA: Stylus.

Williams, B. N., & Williams, S. M. (2006). Perceptions of African American male junior faculty on promotion and tenure: Implications for community building and social capital. *Teachers College Record, 108,* 287–315.

Zinn, H. (1995). *A people's history of the United States.* New York, NY: Harper Collins.

10

(Re)Viewing and (Re)Moving the Mystique Surrounding "Fit" in Student Affairs

A Challenge to Our Field

Walter P. Parrish III

"For whom is it dark and dangerous? For years many in student affairs have rested comfortably with the idea that we are a nice and safe profession, which couldn't be further from the truth. If the [Student Affairs Professionals Facebook] page is such 'a dark and dangerous place' then seasoned professionals like you should be attempting to address the issues that created these conditions, rather than exiting as you did. But that's just it, . . . you get the luxury of abandoning dark and dangerous places without realizing that your privileges are the primary reason for why such places exist."

–Lori Patton Davis, personal communication, December 5, 2016

Lori Patton Davis, in the quote that opens this chapter, sheds light on the discourses surrounding the tensions concerning who fits in and who is granted access to our profession. Patton Davis was responding to a White, female senior student affairs officer (SSAO) who diminished and relegated the presence of student affairs and higher education professionals belonging to marginalized communities in a blog post and then later deleted that same post. The removal of the post by a White SSAO reinforces Patton Davis's argument that privileged professionals in our field can easily withdraw from spaces or even the field itself without many consequences. Yet, the

217

damage done to the most vulnerable communities lingers and continues to be part of the very essence and culture of our field.

As a practitioner and scholar who studies the higher education workforce and workplace experiences of administrators and faculty, I was enthused to see the call for proposals on a book that illuminates issues related to the student affairs job search process and the evaluation of professionals. In this book, my colleagues have specifically addressed an ambiguous, yet heavily used word—*fit*—that permeates departments and search committees across the country. What is even more enticing is the opportunity to discuss, learn about, and share experiences of job fit as it relates to race, gender, class, and other minoritized identities and grounded in critical theories. Despite its stated intentions to advance the principles of social justice and inclusion, student affairs is not exempt from discrimination and marginalization. In other words, as thoughtful, intentional, and well-meaning as many student affairs administrators proclaim to be, conscious and unconscious bias still exist. Moreover, as the preceding chapters illuminated, these biases can be found among colleagues who have a high amount of social capital, as well as among those who are not as privileged.

Therefore, I write this chapter with a few goals in mind. First, I wish to share my personal experiences with job searching and screening processes—as both an applicant and as a search committee member. The second goal is to encapsulate the earlier chapters written by my colleagues and add to their discourse around the behaviors, policies, and culture that oppresses professionals with one or more minoritized identities. The last goal is to provide recommendations for search committees and hiring managers, graduate faculty and advisers, and job candidates.

Several chapters in this volume consider the racism that is embedded in the fabric of our country. In the current context of our historical and current political and racial climate, many practitioners, regardless of political affiliation, may feel the need to speak out against covert and overt discriminatory practices. The field of student affairs appears to be caring, considerate, and conscientious of the needs of students, but we often overlook, or simply ignore, how we treat each other, particularly how we treat our colleagues of minoritized identities, for example, people of color (POC); poor and working class individuals; and those with physical, developmental, or hidden impairments. As a Black, first-generation, college student who was raised in a low socioeconomic status by a single mother, I have experienced and witnessed toxic behaviors in the job search process that oppress and place a glass ceiling on minoritized people, even before professionals are offered an interview. I have also witnessed and experienced how my cis male identity has afforded me advantages in the job search processes and within student affairs workplace and professional environments.

Many things jumped out at me after reading the preceding chapters, but one main point came across clearly—*job fit* is a vague term, which leaves much room for free interpretation. In a society dominated by one culture (i.e., Whiteness), it makes sense that the most vulnerable identity groups are typically the applicants and employees who experience the consequences of not fitting in. Many POC do not receive interviews, campus visits, or job offers because the dominant culture considers them to be inappropriate, ill-prepared, or even disconcerting. The word *fit* provides a mask or a code for describing these assumptions and biases without referring to them directly. Thus, a word so abstract has been given the power to significantly impact the trajectory of a professional's career.

In my experience as an administrator who has served on search committees, colleagues commonly state that candidates would not be a good fit without explaining what they mean, often simply based on a résumé or phone interview. For one particular search where I served as the committee chair, I recall the hiring manager adamantly professing how the first of two finalists was ideal for the position while the second was not a good fit for the office and institutional culture. However, the search committee, campus partners, and students felt completely the opposite. In this case, the hiring manager and two finalists were all White, but the first finalist had a previous working relationship with the manager. Although *job fit* can often be a mechanism to weed out prospective or current employees, it is also a term that promotes social closure. In a tight and very conflicting predicament, I remained steadfast in my decision, supporting the committee, and was prepared to continue the conversation with the human resources department if needed. After many conversations between the hiring manager and myself, they decided hire the more qualified second finalist.

Another important observation made throughout a number of chapters is that the culture of a dominant identity can still dominate even through those who are not a part of that identity group. Although White supremacy is the root of racism, colonialism, patriarchy, and imperialism, like-minded behaviors still occur within spaces predominantly filled with POC. White supremacy is a drug or "the Kool-Aid" that many have digested, and all people are caught up in using words like *fit* as coded language that signals a person is disliked for reasons that are simultaneously assumed to be obvious yet completely unclear.

I recall graduating with my bachelor's degree, applying to a historically Black college or university (HBCU) for my first student affairs job, and securing an interview. On the interview day, I met with a series of administrators, faculty, and students. At my first interview, with all Black administrators and one White professor, I was asked, "Where are you from again?" In my mind, I wondered if the question was a joke as my résumé was printed and placed in front of everyone. But I replied simply with, "West Philly," only to be asked as a follow-up, "Where in West Philly?" While I could visibly see that my résumé was placed in front of everyone with my mailing address atop, what I did not know at the time was that my Blackness was being tested because I did not attend an HBCU. I later did not receive a job offer because it was "not a good fit."

Another important lesson for readers that emerged from these chapters is that while the student affairs profession is perceived to be a field of good intentions, meaningful work, and holistic development of students, this is not ubiquitous, and the treatment of employees often differs from the treatment of students. The incongruent and inconsistent behaviors of personnel toward each other is alarming, disappointing, and often extremely problematic.

Across various platforms—personal conversations, social media, Internet blogs, and empirical research—I have gained invaluable insight into and understanding of the experiences of other racially minoritized and marginalized groups in higher education. More specifically, spaces that are dedicated for "all" student affairs professionals have also proven to be harmful and oppressive to these groups. For instance, there is a Facebook group called Student Affairs Professionals. Created in 2006, just 2 years after the social media platform's inception, the Student Affairs Professionals group has reached a membership of roughly 30,000. Unfortunately, this social network has not been inclusive of many racially and sexually minoritized groups. A space that was created to be for all student affairs professionals to share knowledge, jobs, and news spiraled into one of hurtful comments, micro- and macroaggressions, and misinformed statements.

As a result, numerous groups have been created that provide a safer and more inclusive space for underrepresented groups and those who have been pushed to the margins of the profession. These are spaces where venting, mentorship, and comfort abound and where individuals can feel a sense of community—that their experiences are not anomalies. As a member of one of the groups that is specifically dedicated to colleagues interested in uplifting and supporting Black student affairs professionals, I have seen the hurt and disappointment as well as the significant impact a collaborative and communal space can have on a group of people—even on social media.

RECOMMENDATIONS FOR PRAXIS

Reading the scholarly narratives of the preceding chapters, reflecting on my own personal experiences, and reviewing best practices have led to the following recommendations for search committees and hiring managers, faculty and advisers, and job seekers. I provide three recommendations for each group that can help to mitigate and rebel against systems of oppression within student affairs on a broader scale. These recommendations are not a comprehensive list of strategies to cease the harms of the term *job fit* or to ensure successful employment, but they are helpful tactics and practices that can lead to a more inclusive and equitable hiring process and workplace.

Search Committees and Hiring Managers

Search committees and hiring managers are gatekeepers. Professionals in academe are likely to believe that they assess applicants and employees objectively, judging people solely on their credentials, experience, and performance. However, a generous amount of research (Bertrand, Chugh, & Mullainathan, 2005; Biernat & Manis, 1994; Ginther et al., 2011; Steinpreis, Anders, & Ritzke, 1999; Trix & Psenka, 2003) has indicated that everyone has a substantial amount of unconscious bias that shapes the review process. This is why an array of perspectives and walks of life are needed on search, screening, and hiring committees. Search committees and hiring managers also have an obligation to find the most qualified candidate for the position. Therefore, before joining a search committee, there should be adequate training and review of policies to minimize biases and assumptions. I offer the following recommendations.

Recommendation #1: Increase Diverse Representation on Committees

When considering campus partners to include on the search committee for your next open position, review your list of names to ensure representation from POC, women, and colleagues who openly identify as lesbian, gay, bisexual, trans, or queer. Depending on the diversity of the institution, this can be a fairly easy task. However, many hiring managers will need to think broadly outside of their immediate scope of colleagues and friends, as many institutions across the country still struggle with employing a diverse workplace. If your campus has majority White, full-time student affairs professionals, think creatively—seek faculty in relevant disciplines, graduate students, and administrative/clerical staff. This practice has potential to shift conversations about the recruitment methods and review of applicants based on the background and perspectives of those committee members. By broadening the *type* of committee members on your committee, this approach can also help alleviate those of minoritized identities from being overused or perceived as the only promoters for diversity on the committee.

Recommendation #2: Do the Work to Find Diverse Candidates

According to the National Center for Educational Statistics (U.S. Department of Education, 2014), there are 3.6 million full- and part-time staff members (excluding faculty) in higher education. Of this total population, 69% are White, 10% Black, 8% Hispanic, 6% Asian, 2% "nonresident," 1% Bi/Multiracial, and less than 1% are Native American or Hawaiian/Pacific Islander. Does the higher education enterprise have difficulty attracting racially underrepresented populations? Or, is academia successfully masking discrimination toward minoritized communities? Building a diverse pool of candidates takes a conscious effort. As a search committee member, you should seek outlets and job boards that support and advocate for diversity in higher education to reach a broad range of talent. Interrupt ill-informed rhetoric, including statements such as, "We want to hire the best candidate," "Would this candidate want to come here? We're not very diverse and they may feel isolated," and "I do not want to dilute the quality of the pool for the sake of diversity." These assertions are excuses for not being willing to put in the effort to conduct an active and aggressive search process. If you cast your search widely to associations and subcommittees that target marginalized groups, candidates of those groups will have greater access to apply.

Recommendation #3: Institute Meaningful Training to Reduce Bias

As previously stated, everyone has biases and no one is exempt from the potential that they might act on them. Therefore, before evaluating candidates, the entire committee, regardless of experience, should engage in training to review institutional, state, and federal policies and to reveal and mitigate their implicit biases. Inviting your institution's general counsel, human resources department, and institutional diversity office to facilitate training can help prevent discriminatory practices despite your best intentions. Moreover, search committee members should review the research on unconscious and implicit bias, as well as take assessments to measure their own biases—such as the Implicit Association Test (https://implicit.harvard .edu). Additionally, during this process of training and reflection, the search committee can also carefully review the evaluation process itself to eliminate as much prejudice as possible in the criteria used to select and hire candidates. Assembling clear criteria for job applicants can help to eliminate assumptions and favoritism and to redirect focus toward the merits and capital that candidates bring to the pool.

Faculty and Advisers

Preparing graduate students for successful careers in student affairs is a central goal for many student affairs programs. The faculty in these programs may include adjuncts who work full time in administration, former administrators who are now professors, and professors who have no previous full-time student affairs work experience. The type of support that graduate students receive is typically based on the concentration of the program (e.g., student affairs, leadership and administration, policy, and counseling) and the experiences of the program faculty. Regardless of one's access to training and preparation, the following recommendations can assist faculty and advisers in helping students successfully navigate the job search process.

Recommendation #1: Provide Understanding of the Full Higher Education Landscape

The higher education enterprise is layered and expansive. Job opportunities can vary from student affairs and general higher education administrative roles to international higher education, policy, access programs, and more. Affording students the opportunity to understand the breadth of options in the field helps facilitate better congruence between the job seeker's values and the values of the organization. A method to achieve this objective is requiring students to conduct informational interviews with various professionals in the student affairs and higher education profession. Exposure to and in-depth dialogue with seasoned and entry-level colleagues about their roles, qualifications, and career trajectories can be insightful and offer clarity for budding professionals. Another method for advancing students' understanding is to require intentional practicum experiences. Many student affairs graduate programs recommend or require assistantships within a college or university's student affairs division to ensure graduate students are able to operationalize theory to practice. Another method beyond academic-year assistantships is to encourage summer internship opportunities such as those offered through the Association of College and University Housing Officers-International and the Association for Orientation, Transition, and Retention in Higher Education.

Recommendation #2: Encourage Conference Meeting Attendance and Participation

One of the most useful aspects of the job search process is having a strong network of colleagues. Many students, particularly those who are novices in the student affairs realm, do not understand the complexity and importance of attending annual conferences. These annual meetings are where networks can be created, strengthened, and enlarged. By building a professional "village," one also gains the chance to learn more about various institutions, functional areas, and the culture attached. If your program does not offer financial assistance to attend conferences, make this a priority to help even the playing field for students from lower socioeconomic backgrounds. Additionally, in this digital age, there are many ways to maintain involvement in professional associations that don't require an expensive plane ticket, registration fee, and hotel reservation. Help your students navigate these complex associations and point them toward affinity groups if they express an interest. Leaning on and gaining insight from a solid network of colleagues can help demystify the job search and interview process.

Recommendation #3: Review Materials and Practice

While the primary focus of any graduate program should be on developing expertise and skill in a content area, graduate students should also be building the skills they need to navigate the job search process so that they can put the skills they learn into practice—and financially support themselves and their families. While some students already possess the skills needed to succeed in the job market, this is not true of all students and is especially often not true of the most marginalized. Looking back, for example, I recall the mistakes I made on job applications, such as writing the wrong institution's name, including redundancies, and not noticing formatting issues.

It is also essential for graduate program faculty and advisers to review common practices within student affairs. Résumés, curriculum vitae (CVs), and cover letters look very different in higher education than in other professions. Including summer internships, conference presentations, professional service, publications, and technological skills on one's résumé is common in student affairs, but students searching the Internet for samples will likely find one-page templates that do not fit the norm of this field.

In addition to getting help with application materials, students should be prepared for navigating interviews and campus visits. The interview process for student affairs is daunting, often including several rounds of interviews and culminating with a one- to two-day on-campus visit. Hosting seminars or special office hours to review materials and practice interview skills for the job search process is not only worthwhile—it will likely make the difference between success and failure on the job market.

Job Seekers

I often tell colleagues that the student affairs search process is the equivalent of a part-time job. The amount of work and energy one must pour into it can be draining and intimidating, but it can also be quite an exciting time if you are prepared. During the last semester of my master's program, I applied for approximately 80 positions across the nation. I was organized, well-informed by talking to colleagues in my network, and had been preparing my materials much earlier than the month I began completing applications. As a person of color, I knew that I needed to prepare as early as possible and that one way to help mitigate discriminatory behaviors during the interview process was to be exceptional—though it is not a sure way to reduce potential racism, classism, and microaggressions. As I have transitioned to and from various positions and organizations within higher education, I have kept close to me the habits and behaviors that I have found to be most effective. Through my personal experience on searches, as an applicant, reviewer, and hiring manager, I offer the following recommendations.

Recommendation #1: "If You Stay Ready, You Don't Have to Get Ready"

One of the most stressful moments of the job search process is rushing to submit a complete application for a position with only a few days or weeks until the deadline. "If you stay ready, you don't have to get ready" is a saying that constantly resonates with me, especially when preparing to job search.

I encourage readers to stay ready, and how this is applied varies. Being organized looks very different depending on learning styles, needs, access, and personality. Some fundamental exercises that may help you include using an Excel spreadsheet to keep track of applications, organizing folders on your computer according to the institution, and using your network to help you prepare.

Additionally, be sure to prime your résumé or CV even before you start sifting through job boards. The activity of updating a résumé may be perceived as a slow, painful exercise, but starting early will help save time. I often found myself spending nights critiquing my résumé. I examined the content, formatting and whitespace, font sizes and types, and headings. Don't be afraid to ask your friends and colleagues for permission to use their résumés or CVs as examples as you create and revise your own. Many student affairs administrators, particularly those who are generalists or who have a broad range of experiences, also create multiple versions of their résumés. The purpose of the résumé is to depict professional work history and activities in hopes that a search committee or hiring manager will find those qualities to be congruent with those of the position and the needs of the unit. Having multiple résumés (e.g., social justice-, student activities-, or housing-related) or a tailored CV in your professional arsenal can afford you the ability to curate a desirable yet factual narrative.

Recommendation #2: Stay Attentive and Observe

Once you have received an interview, it is important to remain observant of what is happening and being said during the interview process. This can be best described as organizational culture, which is a great determinant of job fit for the job seeker. Based on the preceding chapters, *culture* can be defined as a ubiquitous phenomenon that is constantly created and manipulated by interactions with others and shaped by the behavior of leaders within an organization, and a set of standards, routines, and norms that guide members' behavior within the organization. Being alert to and cognizant of visible and tangible aspects of the environment; the espoused beliefs of the staff, unit, and institution as a whole; and what is being said or perhaps avoided in dialogue can provide significant insight on whether or not the position or organization is an ideal match.

For those who belong to a minoritized identity, it is especially important that you pay close attention. Ask yourself: Is this institution window-dressing diversity and inclusion or is it authentic? Did a potential colleague or manager make suggestions on how I should wear my hair or clothing or commit other microaggressions? Will I have to dilute my [insert identity] in order to make people feel comfortable or for me to feel welcomed? Organizational cues are often overlooked as job seekers are typically focused on one task—obtaining the job. I urge readers to take a deep breath, assess the totality of the interview process, and move forward with an informed decision. For many functional areas, student affairs professionals spend most of the day at work, so ensuring that a potential workplace environment is consistent with personal values and meets your identity-specific needs is essential.

Recommendation #3: Know When Your Time Is Up

It may be difficult to fully grasp the culture of a department or organization during the search process. Interviews are typically when employers smile the most and present their best display of teamwork and the ideal work environment—at least one would hope. It is not until you transition from candidate to employee that the veil is lifted, exposing all of the secrets about the culture that may have been withheld during the interview sessions. If what was hidden about the organization is incongruent with your personal values, I believe you should carefully assess the concerns, take action in attempting to correct or mitigate the issues, and evaluate personal needs and obligations to determine if departure is necessary and feasible. As I stated earlier, employees spend most of their time during the day at work, often far more than 8 hours a day and 40 hours a week in this profession. Thus, I firmly believe staying in a workplace that makes you unhappy is a waste of your time and will ultimately affect your motivation and job performance. In turn, these consequences have effects on your students as well.

There are varying opinions on how long one should stay in a role before departing. The common feedback that I have heard is, "Just stay for a year; you can do anything for a year." While this suggestion seems sensible, some may find themselves in situations that are, indeed, untenable. Personally, I have left a position under a year due to incompatible practices and values. My supervisor was not helpful when I needed it and did not invest in my growth and success. While in that position, I was expected to sit with front desk student employees to converse on Friday nights. On one occasion, a student leader walked me to my car at 11:00 pm to discuss programming, even after I politely dismissed the conversation as I was heading out to enjoy time with friends. Because these experiences did not align with my own professional expectations or values and were vastly different from my prior institution, I could have easily decided for myself that the expectations and behaviors were wrong. But I remembered the words of a former professor, adviser, and mentor: "It's not right or wrong. It is what it is, and if is not for you, then leave." So I left after seven months, luckily with another position lined up.

I share personal stories and recommendations to help dispel the belief that leaving a position after a short time will end in disaster. Understandably, my scenario will not be the same for all, but having a strong network of colleagues who care about your development, adequate preparation, and an understanding of how to communicate transferable skills can help make it possible. I encourage you to think about what is needed to do your best work in student affairs. Find spaces that are congruent with your own personal values and people who respect you being your authentic self.

CONCLUSION

As many authors have stated through this book, the word *fit* is very ambiguous. Because of such uncertainty, many job seekers and employees may find it to be an intimidating word. Being told "you're not a good fit" can leave one pondering an array of questions on what exactly *fit* means, how it is assessed, and the consequences that follow. Educators, scholars, and practitioners should be at the forefront of creating diverse, equitable, and inclusive spaces and practices. The future of this country is dependent on the education system, which provides students with the necessary knowledge, skills, and competencies to be successful in various industries. As student affairs professionals, we should effectively prepare students to face a pluralistic society and to be leaders in creating a more socially just world.

I argue that this begins with the perspectives of varying identities within student affairs—those of us teaching and making decisions that directly affect students. By increasing and maintaining a robust and diverse student affairs workforce, particularly at predominantly White institutions, feelings of isolation, tokenism, loneliness, and alienation among our student affairs colleagues (as well as students) have potential to greatly decrease. Therefore, minoritized practitioners will experience less stress associated with their identities on campuses and be able to do their best work for their students. The satisfaction and retention of minoritized practitioners can also increase when institutions appreciate them and their respective identities, provide opportunities to work with other minoritized faculty and staff, and, have an increased sense of belonging to their institution. As faculty and advisers you have an obligation to prepare minoritized graduate students to face a workforce that was not created for them and teach them how to thrive in it. As job seekers you have the right to work in places where you are valued for who you are and treated equitably and with respect. As hiring managers and search committees, you have an opportunity to dismantle systemic oppression for marginalized groups and those who have been made to feel invisible. Our students are depending on all of us to act with integrity and with their best interests in mind.

REFERENCES

Bertrand, M., Chugh, D., & Mullainathan, S. (2005). Implicit discrimination. *American Economic Review, 95*(2), 94–98.

Biernat, M., & Manis, M. (1994). Shifting standards and stereotype-based judgments. *Journal of Personality and Social Psychology, 66*(1), 5.

Ginther, D. K., Schaffer, W. T., Schnell, J., Masimore, B., Liu, F., Haak, L. L., & Kington, R. (2011). Race, ethnicity, and NIH research awards. *Science, 333*(6045), 1015–1019.

Steinpreis, R. E., Anders, K. A., & Ritzke, D. (1999). The impact of gender on the review of the curricula vitae of job applicants and tenure candidates: A national empirical study. *Sex Roles, 41*(7), 509–528.

Trix, F., & Psenka, C. (2003). Exploring the color of glass: Letters of recommendation for female and male medical faculty. *Discourse & Society, 14*(2), 191–220.

U.S. Department of Education, National Center for Education Statistics, Integrated Postsecondary Education Data System (IPEDS). (Spring 2014). Table 314.40. Employees in degree granting postsecondary institutions, by race/ethnicity, sex, employment status, control and level of institution, and primary occupation: Fall 2013. *Digest of Education Statistics: 2014.* (Table prepared March 2015.) Washington DC: Author.

EDITORS AND CONTRIBUTORS

EDITORS

Elliott N. DeVore is a PhD student in the Department of Psychology at the University of Tennessee, studying counseling psychology. After completing his MEd in student affairs and a graduate certificate in social justice in higher education at Iowa State University, he worked as a residence director at the University of San Francisco, where he also conducted workshops with the Gender and Sexuality and Intercultural Center and campus ministry, advised the Queer Student Alliance, and taught a course on peer assistance and education. His current program of research includes both quantitative and qualitative projects, including the role of adult attachment style in participants' experiences of group climate process and outcome variables in intergroup dialogue, sexual orientation beliefs, and the influence of homonegative attitudes on mental health care professionals' attitudes toward and willingness to provide clients information about PrEP Truvada. In his free time DeVore loves experiencing the beauty of his birthplace in the Appalachian Mountains of East Tennessee, exploring his own gender through drag, and singing with the Knoxville Gay Men's Chorus.

Gabby Porcaro is currently serving as the assistant director for queer and trans student initiatives in the Intercultural Center at Roger Williams University. Prior to this role, Porcaro served as the student affairs case manager, the bystander intervention program coordinator, the interim safe zone program coordinator, and as an instructor for the first-year academic success program at the University of North Carolina at Asheville. Porcaro received her MA in higher education and student affairs from Virginia Tech. Porcaro has taught leadership development and academic success courses and has presented on topics such as the evolution of hate in society, the intersection of faith and queer identities, the effects of race and gender on economic stratification, supporting LGBTQIA communities on college campuses, and communicating across lines of difference. Porcaro spent one year serving the ACPA Commission for Social Justice Education as the intern for the scholarship team.

Brian J. Reece is the associate director of residential life at Colgate University in Hamilton, New York, where he also serves on the institution's Diversity, Equity, and Inclusion Task Force. Reece is also a PhD student in the Department of Learning and Instruction at the University at Buffalo, studying curriculum, instruction, and the science of learning. Previously, he was the associate director of the Toppel Career Center and lecturer in mental health counseling in the Department of Educational and Psychology Studies at the University of Miami in Coral Gables, Florida. Reece earned MAs in higher education administration from the University of Delaware and counseling, family, and human services with a specialization in prevention science from the University of Oregon. He has taught career counseling, women's studies, queer studies, and leadership courses and has published and presented on topics such as LGBTQ history, supporting LGBTQ students, the relationship between racism and homophobia, antioppressive approaches to student affairs work, and the future of social justice in the profession of student affairs. He has spent six years on the directorate body of the ACPA—College Student Educators International Commission for Social Justice Education, where he cofounded the Commission for Social Justice Education (CSJE) blog and recently became chair-elect. He is also a reviewer for the *Journal of Critical Scholarship in Higher Education and Student Affairs*.

Vu T. Tran currently serves as an assistant director of residence education at Michigan State University. As a graduate of The Ohio State University's higher education and student affairs PhD program, Tran's research focuses qualitatively on issues of age and adult identity, adultism, and social justice education in the context of colleges and universities. He has been involved in various forms of social justice education work throughout his career, including the Asian American Cultural Center at the University of Connecticut, the Program on Intergroup Relations at the University of Michigan, and the Next Step Social Justice Retreat at the University of Vermont. He has also been involved in numerous capacities with the Social Justice Training Institute, as well as ACPA's Commission for Social Justice Education. Tran identifies as 30-something, Asian American, college-educated, currently able-bodied, English-speaking, heterosexual, man, male, middle-class, raised Catholic, and Vietnamese.

CONTRIBUTORS

Sonja Ardoin is a leader, educator, facilitator, and author. From a working-class community in "Cajun country," she is proud of her first-generation college student to PhD educational journey. Ardoin's career path includes experience in student activities, leadership development, community engagement, fraternity and sorority life, student conduct, and academic advising. She made the move from full-time practitioner to full-time faculty member in 2015 but continues to view her professional role as that of a scholar-practitioner. Ardoin studies social class identity in higher education; college access and success for first generation college students and rural students; student and women's leadership; and career preparation and pathways in higher education and student affairs. Ardoin authored *The Strategic Guide to Shaping Your Student Affairs Career* (Stylus, 2014) and *College Aspirations and Access in Working-Class Rural Communities: The Mixed Signals, Challenges, and New Language First-Generation Students Encounter* (Lexington Books, 2017). She also stays engaged in the field through presenting, facilitating, and volunteering with national organizations such as ASHE, NASPA, ACPA, LeaderShape, Zeta Tau Alpha, Delta Gamma, and College Summit. Ardoin enjoys traveling, dancing and listening to music, reading, writing, sports, laughing, and spending time with people she loves.

Kyle C. Ashlee is a PhD candidate in the student affairs in higher education program at Miami University. His research interests include critical approaches to student affairs graduate preparation, critical Whiteness studies in higher education, as well as critical perspectives on college men and masculinities. Ashlee's career in student affairs includes experience in housing and residence life, new student orientation, leadership programs, health promotion, and gender centers, both in the United States and abroad. In addition to contributing to the field of student affairs through his professional involvement in both ACPA and NASPA, Ashlee is the founder of the Ohio Consortium on Men and Masculinities in Higher Education. He has been involved in authoring many publications, including *Reconceptualizing Student Success in Higher Education: Reflections From Graduate Student Affairs Educators Using Anti-Deficit Achievement Framework* (2017), *Positioning Privileged White Men in Social Justice: Exploring Barriers and Strategies for Privileged White Men and Those Who Work With Them* (2016), and *VITAL: A Torch for Your Social Justice Journey* (Brave Space Publishing, 2016). Ashlee is also the cofounder of Ashlee Consulting, a firm focusing on building critically engaged communities that strive to dismantle systems of oppression. Ashlee has a passion for all things that connect him with humanity including travel, cooking, baking, coffee, writing, music, yoga, and mindfulness.

Van Bailey is a student affairs educator, international speaker, and diversity consultant. Bailey's speeches and workshops relate to LGBTQ+ student leadership, pedagogical practice, and intersectionality. He was listed in LGBTQ Nation's Top 50 Successful Transgender People You Should Know, the Trans 100, and the 100 to Watch LBGTQ/SGL Emerging Leaders noting his work in higher education. Currently, he is cochair for the Consortium of Higher Education LGBT Resource Professionals. His published work has been featured on NPR, the *Boston Globe*, *Huffington Post*, the Feminist Wire, and Buzzfeed. As a diversity specialist, Bailey has worked with constituents internationally in addressing LGBTQ inclusion on college campuses. Bailey is currently the inaugural director of the LGBTQ Student Center at the University of Miami. He has also served as the inaugural director of BGLTQ Student Life at Harvard College. In that role, he established a college-wide resource center for LGBTQ+ students. Outside of higher education, Bailey is a member of bklyn boihood, the collective who released the award-winning *Outside the XY: Queer Black and Brown Masculinities* (Riverdale Avenue Books, 2016). Bailey received an EdD in educational leadership from California State University-Northridge, an MA from Ohio State University in higher education and student affairs, and a BA in Black studies and English from Denison University.

Jessica Bennett received a PhD in higher education from the University of Maryland, an MA in higher education and student affairs from The Ohio State University, and a BA in cognitive science from the University of Virginia. She has worked in judicial affairs, residence life, fraternity and sorority life, and sexual assault prevention education roles in student affairs. She is interested in how organizational cultures affect the experiences of minoritized participants in higher education, particularly women and people of color. Her scholarship focuses on the intersectional experiences of women throughout their higher education careers: as undergraduates, graduate students, faculty, and administrators.

Heather O. Browning is an educator and thought leader in institutional diversity and inclusion. She earned a BA in international studies from California State University, Long Beach, and an MA in college counseling and student development from Azusa Pacific University. Browning has over nine years of experience as a student affairs practitioner working with marginalized and underrepresented student populations. She has particular interest in helping others understand how their identities intersect and impact their experiences and successes within higher education. Browning contributes to the larger profession, having held regional positions within NASPA and by publishing and presenting on the experiences of staff of color in student affairs. Outside of the profession, Browning enjoys global travel, focusing on her holistic health, and spoiling her beloved canine.

Léna Kavaliauskas Crain is associate dean of students at Denison University. Additionally, she serves as primary investigator for the National Study of the Student Affairs Job Search (NSSAJS), a role she has held since 2011. The NSSAJS team studies employers' and candidates' behaviors and experiences through hiring processes, particularly at the entry level. Her other research interests include links between national culture, pedagogy, and cognition, and how these shape student development theory and practice. She received her PhD from the higher education, student affairs, and international education program at the University of Maryland.

Stacey D. Garrett is an assistant professor of higher education in the Department of Leadership and Educational Studies at Appalachian State University. With six years of experience as a practitioner in housing and fraternity/sorority life, Garrett has served on search committees for professional, graduate, and undergraduate staff members and served on and chaired department training committees for graduate and undergraduate students. Identifying as a Black female scholar, the theme of her research agenda is the diversification of higher education. Her current research focuses on the experiences of women of color faculty, the development of graduate students as scholar-activists, and the development of African American engineering majors through noncurricular activities.

Marshall Habermann-Guthrie serves at the director of the Student Enrichment Program, partially funded by a TRIO-SSS grant, at Western Oregon University. One of Habermann-Gurthri's current priorities is conducting a comprehensive first-year experience curriculum for students who are first-generation, low-income, or who have documented disabilities. Habermann-Gurthri has previously held elected office and is currently active in local politics around issues of advocacy for the underrepresented. Habermann-Guthrie enjoys distance recumbent cycling and the tech side of home entertainment.

Luis Jimenez Inoa serves as the assistant vice president of student affairs at Skidmore College. He is a PhD candidate in the educational policy and leadership program at the University at Albany, SUNY. His research focuses on Latino students and the impact of sports participation. He is the founding director of a four-year program supporting first-generation, low income, and undocumented students at Vassar College. Inoa is the son of Maria and Jose Jimenez and identifies as a 40-something, 2.5 generation English-speaking Latino, middle-class, grandfather, father, husband, and lover of life.

Kyle Inselman is a career adviser at the University of Denver. He graduated from the University of Utah with an MEd in educational leadership and policy, emphasis in student affairs. His master's thesis was a mixed-methods study of in-group diversity among trans students in higher education. He holds a BA in linguistics, BFA in film studies, and a certificate in LGBT studies from the University of Colorado Boulder. Outside of work he enjoys exploring the Rocky Mountain region, practicing meditation and yoga, and spending time with his adorable rescue cat.

becky martinez is a consultant and trainer with an emphasis on social justice, leadership, and organizational change. Her work focuses on dismantling systems of oppression through critical dialogue and reflection intertwined with theoretical foundations. martinez's career portfolio includes being a business owner as an organization development consultant and working as an administrator at both public and private institutions. She is a faculty member for the Social Justice Training Institute, a colead facilitator for the LeaderShape Institute, a certified trainer for the Gay, Lesbian, & Straight Educational Network, and works with a Title I elementary school in California focused on preparing students for college. While she values her work and recognizes its importance, her greatest responsibility is raising two awesome, spirited nephews who are truly her smartest teachers.

David Hòa Khoa Nguyễn is an assistant professor of urban education leadership and policy studies at the Indiana University School of Education at Indiana University - Purdue University Indianapolis (IUPUI) and an adjunct professor of law at the Indiana University Robert H. McKinney School of Law. He teaches courses on education law, policy, politics, and administration, generally. Nguyễn's research focuses on the intersection of law and policy with education to examine the policies and practices that address inequities of access to education for marginalized populations. Nguyễn has a BSEd in secondary education, an MBA, a JD, and a PhD in education policy studies, all from Indiana University. He also has an LLM Adv from Leiden University in the Netherlands. Nguyễn is admitted to practice in the state and federal bars of Indiana, Texas, and North Dakota.

Patrice M. Palmer currently serves as a faculty academic adviser for the College of Business at Colorado State University as well as an instructor under the management department. sHE is also the adviser for Business Diversity Leadership Alliance (BDLA), a student-led organization that bridges the gap between business and diversity within the college. Palmer earned both HEr BA in social science with emphasis in sociology and HEr MA in social justice with emphasis in educational equity from Marygrove College in Detroit, Michigan. Palmer will be pursuing a PhD in applied developmental science in the upcoming year. Palmer has over eight years of experience working with and for communities of color within predominantly White institutions. Understanding the complexities of intersectional learning and living that occur in communities of color, while simultaneously learning and living in predominantly White spaces, has given Palmer a platform to advocate for students, faculty, and staff of color that inhabit these communities. Palmer uses the pronouns sHE, Hym and tHEY along with the title Mx.

Walter P. Parrish III is director of multicultural affairs at The University of Chicago Pritzker School of Medicine, and he is pursuing his PhD in educational leadership and policy analysis with a graduate minor in management and human resources at the University of Wisconsin-Madison. Parrish has served as a researcher in Wisconsin's Equity and Inclusion Laboratory within the Wisconsin Center for Education Research and in the Center for Policy and Research Strategy within the American Council on Education. His primary scholarly interests are workforce diversity, workplace and labor issues, and organizational behavior in higher education as well as their effects on marginalized faculty and administrators. He has previously served as directorate member for both the ACPA Commission for Multicultural Affairs and the Pan African Network. Parrish is a native of Philadelphia, Pennsylvania, and holds an MA from Old Dominion University and a BA from Millersville University of Pennsylvania.

Stephen John Quaye is an associate professor in the student affairs in higher education program at Miami University and past president of American College Personnel Association (ACPA): College Student Educators International. His research focuses on strategies for engaging in difficult dialogues; student and scholar activism; and how Black student affairs educators navigate racial battle fatigue. His work is published in different venues, including the *Journal of College Student Development,* the *Journal of Diversity in Higher Education,* and *Teachers College Record.* He is also a coauthor on the third edition of *Student Development in College: Theory, Research, and Practice* (Wiley, 2016). His PhD is from Pennsylvania State University, his MA is from Miami University, and he holds a BA from James Madison University.

Mathew J.L. Shepard is the coordinator for non-academic misconduct in the Office of Student Conduct at the University of Maryland, College Park. He currently serves as the president of the Maryland College Personnel Association, a state division of ACPA. He earned a BA in economics and environmental studies at the University of Kansas and an MEd in higher education and student affairs administration at the University of Vermont.

Nick Thuot is a White, trans*, nonbinary, and disabled killjoy committed to envisioning and enacting a different world. Thuot's favorite things are their partner, their cat, spicy food, and Fiona the hippo. Thuot earned a degree in Spanish from the University of Wisconsin-La Crosse and an MSEd in Student Affairs and Administration from the same institution. Thuot's research interests are in critical trans politics and critical liberation theory and their application to higher education. To pay bills, Thuot works as a hall director at Iowa State University.

Natasha T. Turman is a visiting assistant professor in the student affairs in higher education program at Miami University. For four years prior to this role, Turman served as the project manager for the Multi-Institutional Study of Leadership (MSL), an international quantitative research study measuring socially responsible leadership. As a critical scholar, Turman's research interests cut across two distinct yet complementary areas: gender and diversity in higher education and critical leadership education. These targeted foci allow her to examine who is excluded from the dominant narratives of leadership and postsecondary education, what systemic processes maintain this exclusion, and how institutions of higher education can better position themselves as viable environments for healthy social identity development and sustainable leadership development for social change. Turman has worked in the field of higher education student affairs for nine years in a variety of functional areas including leadership studies, student activities, residential life, and multicultural affairs. Turman has a PhD in higher education from Loyola University Chicago, an MSEd in educational leadership and policy from Old Dominion University, and a BS in chemistry from Spelman College.

C. J. Venable is a fat, White, queer, genderqueer killjoy who serves as an academic adviser in the College of Communication and Information at Kent State University. They hold undergraduate degrees in mathematics and secondary education from Webster University, an MA in college student personnel from Bowling Green State University, and began coursework for the PhD in cultural foundations of education at Kent State University in 2016. Venable's scholarly interests include Whiteness, critical theory, philosophy of education, social justice education, and academic advising. Outside of higher education, Venable enjoys cooking, fa(t)shion, and learning to play the baroque recorder.

LaWanda W.M. Ward is an assistant professor in the higher education program and a research associate in the Center for the Study of Higher Education at The Pennsylvania State University. She teaches courses about legal issues in higher education, equity and inclusion, and critical methodologies. Ward's scholarly interests include critically exploring legal issues in higher education, including race-conscious admissions, academic freedom, and free speech. Ward holds a law degree from Indiana University McKinney School of Law and a PhD in higher education and student affairs from Indiana University.

Meghan Gaffney Wells is a small business owner living in Philadelphia. As a former higher education administrator, she feeds her love of education as a colead facilitator for The LeaderShape Institute. Wells is a two-time graduate from The Pennsylvania State University, earning both her BA in journalism and her MEd in college student affairs at University Park. When she's not exploring next steps in her professional life, Wells loves to craft, teach workshops, complete projects around her house with her partner, travel, and spend time with her large extended family.

Akiko Yamaguchi serves as the senior associate director in the Office of Student Engagement at New York University Stern School of Business where she oversees the social and leadership development programs, implements diversity and inclusion initiatives, and teaches a first-year innovations course. Prior to joining NYU Stern, Yamaguchi worked at NYU School of Medicine where she oversaw professional and social programming along with new student orientation. Her background in higher education began in residence life, and she has served in various residence life capacities at Vassar College and the University of Southern California. Yamaguchi graduated from the University of California, Irvine, with a BA in international studies and holds an MEd in postsecondary administration and student affairs from the University of Southern California.

Travis T. York is the director of student success, research, and policy at the Association of Public and Land-grant Universities (APLU). His research centers on issues of college student access, success, and educational equity. York's work has focused on examining pathways into and through postsecondary environments for low-income and first-generation students. Currently, York is the project director and co-PI of APLU INCLUDES: a collective impact approach to broaden participation among the STEM Professoriate, an National Science Foundation-funded project, and a lead researcher and co-PI on the U.S. Department of Education-funded completion grant project—a joint project with APLU and Temple University's HOPE Center for College, Community, and Justice. York also coordinates APLU's Project Degree Completion—a collaborative effort with AASCU in which nearly 500 institutions have committed to award an additional 3.8 million BAs by 2025. York has authored several peer-reviewed articles and book chapters and is currently the lead editor of the 2018 volume of the *Advances in Service Learning Research* (Information Age Publishing) series. York earned his BA and MA in higher education from Geneva College, where he worked in student affairs, and his PhD in higher education administration from The Pennsylvania State University. York is active within several professional associations, serves on the editorial review board of the *Journal of Diversity in Higher Education* and *Journal of International Research on Service Learning and Community Engagement*, and serves a representative within several organizations including the Postsecondary Data Collaborative.

Index

Abes, E. S., 14, 69, 78
academic affairs, 51, 77, 121
Acker, J., 70-71
ACPA Commission for Social Justice
    Education, 3
ACPA/NASPA Professional
    Competencies, 4, 27, 29, 30, 41
advisors, 63-64
Age Discrimination in Employment Act
    of 1967, 27, 45
agency, 15, 26, 29, 67-70, 72, 93, 101
Ahmed, S., 137, 180, 184
alumni, 194-98, 200, 202-204, 210
ambiguity, 56-57
American Council on Education
    (ACE), 102, 237
Anzaldua, G., 14, 131
appearance, professional, 123-124, 131,
    157, 169, 179-80, 186
application, job, 130-31
aspiration window, 135
attitude, 84, 123, 203, 208-209
authenticity, 123-24, 140, 147-49,
    156-58, 160-61
  authentic selves, 67, 70, 75-76,
    83-86, 152-53
  inauthentic, 44, 104, 106, 142, 153

Beemyn, G., 176
Bell, D. A., 52, 197, 206
benefits, 106
best practices, 84, 183-84, 187, 221
bias,
  conscious, 218
  cultural, 10
  education about, 42-43, 138
  fit as, 219

implicit, 44, 129, 131, 138,
    222-23
incident, 25
individual, 62, 198
inherent, 62
racial, 198-99, 202, 206
subconscious, 62
unconscious, 8, 9, 43, 123, 193,
    218, 221
Bickerstaff v. Vassar College (1999), 39
bklyn boihood, 90
Bohman, J., 51-52
bona fide occupational qualification, 33
Bondi, S., 181
Bourdieu, P., 60, 97, 100-102, 201,
    203
Bronfenbrenner, U., 14, 149, 151-53
Brown, B., 1, 149
Brown Boi Project, 90
Budge, S. L., 171
Butler, J., 153-54

capital, 105, 223
  academic, 97, 104
  aspirational, 101, 126, 134-36, 141
  class, 98, 115
  community cultural wealth. *See*
    Community Cultural Wealth,
    Model of
  cultural, 100-101, 135, 157-58
  economic, 97, 99, 100, 103-4
  familial, 101, 111
  financial, 126
  linguistic, 101-2, 109-10
  navigational, 101, 104, 106, 126,
    134-35, 140
  professional, 126

resistant, 101, 106, 110, 126, 134-35, 139-40
scholastic, 104
social, 97, 100-101, 114, 126, 140
Carnaghi, J. E., 4
case studies, 19-26
Cheatham, H. E., 4
Chickering, A. W., 128
cisgender
cisgenderism, xii
cisgenderism, institutional, 167-73, 176-77, 179-84, 186-89
cisnormative, 174-76, 184, 186
Civil Rights Act of 1964, 27-28, 30-33, 36, 43-44
class
attributed class, 99
blue collar, 102
class of origin, 97, 99, 103-4, 110
current class, 99
felt class, 99, 103, 110
middle-class, 108
stereotypes, 108
straddler, 98, 100
working-class, 74, 81, 97-115
climate
campus, 41-43, 63, 92, 150, 152, 182-83
cultural, 137
political climate, 218
working conditions, 43, 141
code-switching, 104, 124, 155
Collins, P. H., 8, 121-22, 132, 135, 206
collusion, 172, 175
communication skills, 202, 208-9
community
connection to, 57, 83-84, 90, 128
role of, 49-50
values of, 58-59
Community Cultural Wealth, Model of, 101, 119, 124-26, 135, 140-41, 158
covering, 63, 172-76
Crenshaw, K., 8, 14, 69, 121, 125-26, 187, 206

critical theories, 3-5, 14, 40, 134, 171
Critical Race Feminism, 119, 124-25
Critical Race Theory, 29, 31, 52, 125, 149, 171, 206-7
Critical Trans Politics, 171, 238
Feminist, 40
as a framework for fit, 3-5, 51-53
latCrit, 40
Queer, 40
tribalCrit, 40
CRT. See critical theories: Critical Race Theory
culture
aesthetic, 81
backgrounds, 60, 153, 200-201
campus, 9, 29, 41-43, 88-89
departmental, 133-35, 140-41, 153, 227
divisional, 68-71
dominant, 28, 52, 60, 131, 153, 219
of higher education, 172, 201-2
Indigenous, 151
institutional, 11, 13, 124, 131-33, 160
marginalized, 60
middle-class, 108
organizational, 43, 50, 101-2, 138, 226-227, 234
of professionalism, 4
racially oppressive, 201
of student affairs, 4, 81
subcultures, 70, 86
university, 168
of Whiteness, 194, 201, 205, 207-8, 210
working-class, 115
workplace, 43, 148, 150
cultural awareness, 39-40
cultural competence, 39
cycle of diversification, 142

Dartmouth College, 151
Delgado, R., 38, 206
Delgado Bernal, D., 52, 126, 130
discrimination

age, 36
  antidiscrimination law, 43, 44
  class, 108
  direct, 38
  in employment, 27-45, 174, 222
  employment discrimination law,
    27-45
  in hiring, 29, 41, 45, 60-62
  intentional, 32, 36-37, 41
  national origin, 36-38
  overt, 176
  pregnancy, 32
  race, 36-38, 52, 197
  sex, 28
  sexual orientation, 27
  transphobia, 173-74, 176, 182
  unintentional, 40
disparate impact, 33
disparate treatment, 33
display rules, 159
diversity
  commitment, 136-37, 198
  compositional, 134
  goals, 38, 210
  hiring, 102
  institutional, 162, 223
  office of, 182
  perspectives, 56-57, 61-63
  proportional, 62
  quota, 148, 162
  representative, 62, 137
  responsibility, 158
  statements, 123, 138, 161, 176, 198
  structural, 129
  as a value, 98, 127
dominant group, 38, 133
DuBois, W. E. B., 135

Ecological Theory, 14, 149, 151-53
emotional labor, 158-59
emotional management, 159-60
Employment Non-Discrimination Act
  of 2009, 43
Equal Employment Opportunity
  Commission, 33-35

Eurocentric, 37, 116, 126, 130, 201
evaluation
  candidate, 58-59
  performance, 27
  personnel, 39
  standards, 37, 137, 223
  systemic, 209
Evans, N. J., 205, 211
evidence, 30, 37-38, 131, 198,
  209-10
  circumstantial, 36
  definitive, 72
  direct, 36, 39
extravert, 71

faculty
  advisors, 11, 87
  case study, 36-40
  hiring process, 129-30, 193, 202
  job search, 85
  representation, 199-201, 204
  research, 134
  statistics, 121-22
  student affairs, 6, 186
  target hiring, 129
  tips for, 63-64, 223-25
  training, 88-89, 205-6
Family Medical Leave Act of 2006, 32
fit
  as ambiguous, 56-57, 60
  as comprehensive, 58-60
  as connected, 57-58, 60
  definition of, general, 6-7
  definitions of, employers', 56-59
  as euphemism, xii, 64, 107,
    193-94, 197, 202-4
  hegemonic notions of, 42
  incongruence, 122, 136, 195
  individual, 68-69
  institutional, 6, 68-69
  mismatch, 127
  ongoing, 69
  organizational, 30
  rhetoric of, 2, 4-6, 9, 11-12,
    161, 222

sense of, 87
formal equality, 37
Fouad, N. A., 203

gender, 71, 121, 125, 167-89
    binary, 148-49, 156, 168, 177
    conformity, 175
    discrimination, 32
    dysphoria, 170
    exclusion, 52
    expectations, 170, 179
    expression. *See* gender expression.
    genderism, 15, 185
    gender-normative, 37, 176
    genderqueer, 169
    gender-variant, 43
    history, 173
    identity. *See* gender identity.
    misgender, xii, 10, 173, 177-78
    non-binary, 170
    non-conforming, 167-68, 176
    norms, 121, 173
    perceived, 179
    roles, 179
    studies, 129
gender expression, 156, 175-76, 188
gender identity, 168, 180, 186, 188
gendered organization, theory of, 70
Genetic Information
    Nondiscrimination Act of 2008,
    27
Girma v. Skidmore College (2001),
    36-40
graduate preparation programs, 186-87
graduate students, 2, 20, 134, 222-24,
    229
greed, 71

habitus, 100
    of Whiteness, 200-203, 210
hair, 32, 67, 106, 132, 152, 159, 182,
    227
happy hour, 112-13
Harding, S., 8
Harper, S. R., 41, 202

health insurance, 21, 25, 168, 175
hegemony, 102
hidden curriculum, xii, 120, 133, 140
Higher Education Research Institute
    (HERI), 105
hiring
    authorities or managers, 5, 14, 58,
        61-62, 102, 127, 137-38, 142,
        221-23
    behaviors, 64
    bias, 8, 10
    case study, 20-22
    committees. *See* search committees
    decisions, 56, 60, 62, 68, 199
    discrimination. *See* discrimination
    laws. *See* legislation
    mechanisms, 53, 54
    methods, 49
    needs, 56
    outcome, 62
    pool, 194
    practices, 50, 53-55, 62, 64, 102,
        193-94, 197-200, 207-11
    preferences, 200-205
    preventing mismatch, 127, 129, 142
    process, 49-51, 53-59, 61-64,
        127-32, 137-38, 204-6
    seasons, 51
    targeted hire, 129
    teams, 14, 56, 138
    timelines, 50, 55
    values, 162
Hirt, J. B., 4
Hodges, J. P., 82
Holland, J. L., 8, 223
Holland's Vocational Theory, 203
holograms, 70, 75, 77-80, 84-85, 87,
    92-93
    hologram projection, 78, 84, 92
homophily, 123
hooks, b., 97, 103, 108, 134

Implicit Association Test, 223
imposter syndrome, 102-3, 128
impression management, 124, 131-32

in media res, 69
inclusion
    competency, 4, 29, 44, 82, 107
    dynamics of, 42–43, 174, 176
    inclusive environment, 43, 127
    tokenizing, 158, 185
inequality, 3
    class, 126
    gender, 126
    race, 36, 126
    social class, 71
    systems of, 125
inequality regimes, 70-72, 86, 91-93
intersectionality, 8, 14, 28, 125-26,
        171, 206
interview
    behavior-based questions, 42
    case studies, 19-26
    informational, 223
    notes, 25
    on-campus, 24-25, 71, 83, 193
    phone, 20-21, 57, 193, 219
    process, 8-9, 59, 106, 141-42, 156,
        224-27
    protocols, 43, 55
    race and, 131-32, 141, 155-57,
        208-9
    responses, 12
    skills, 225
    strategies, 41-44, 87

Jansen, K. J., 69-70
job description, 43, 58-59
    departmental mission and values, 33,
        128, 137
    educational background, 130
    experience (responsibilities), 3-4, 72,
        111, 153
    experience (years), 111, 204
    qualifications, 127
job satisfaction, 138, 203
job seekers
    affirmative action, 41
    bias, 8
    career pathways, 51

career stages, 5
case study on, 23-26
professionalism, 105-6
recommendations for, 63-64, 225-28
rejection, 11-12
self-awareness, 41-42
Johnson, A., 188
Jones, S. R., 69, 72, 124

killjoy, 180-81
Kristof-Brown, A. L., 68, 70
Kumashiro, K., 14

labor
    division of, 71
    emotional, 158-59, 162
    invisible, 84-85, 153, 163
    productive, 172
Ladson-Billings, G., 31, 52, 119, 149,
        206
language
    coded, 123, 127, 153
    inclusive, 137
    word choice, 102, 104, 107-9
legislation
    Age Discrimination in Employment
        Act of 1967, 27, 45
    Civil Rights Act of 1964, 27-28,
        30-33, 36, 43-45
    Family Medical Leave Act of 2006,
        32
    Genetic Information
        Nondiscrimination Act of 2008,
        27
    Girma v. Skidmore College (2001),
        36-40
    Lilly Ledbetter Fair Pay Act of 2009,
        32
    Pregnancy Discrimination Act of
        1978, 32
    Public Facilities Privacy & Security
        Act, 182
    Rehabilitation Act of 1973, 27
    Tenn H.R. 2248 2016, 182
    Title IX, 27

Lewin, K., 30
Lilly Ledbetter Fair Pay Act of 2009, 32
Lorde, A., 125, 131, 135, 140
Lynn v. Regents of the University of
    California (1981), 33

Magolda, P., 4
marginality
    marginalized identities, 40, 76
    marginalized people, 30
McEwen, M. K., 69
men, White, 102, 200, 203, 233
mentors, role of, 11, 76, 135, 140, 155
microaggressions, 37, 39, 77
    racist, 37, 171
    transphobic, 169
misfit, 70, 75, 77, 80, 85, 87, 89, 93
mission statements, 199
Multiple Dimensions of Identities,
    Model of, 69

narratives, 76, 80, 82, 86, 91-92
    narrative agency, 72
    self-narratives, 69
National Study of the Student Affairs
    Job Search (NSSAJS), 49, 53-54,
    63
Native Americans, 151
neoliberalism, 180
networks
    professional, 5, 90, 114, 224, 228
    social capital, 126, 135, 139-41
    support, 182, 188
Nicolazzo, Z., 172
Nordmarken, S., 169
normativity, 27
    cisnormativity, 42
    heteronormativity, 42

onboarding, 132, 138-39, 142
oppositional positions, 134-36, 140
oppression, 5-6, 8, 14, 125, 131, 151
    experiences, 206
    gender, 189
    historical, 150

institutionalized, 120, 150
intersectional, 182
professionalism, 104
racial, 125, 198, 200
structural, 171
systemic, xii, 2, 52, 61, 134-35, 139,
    167, 186
organizational change, 41

Parsons, F., 30
Patton, L. D., 29, 31, 37, 217
people of color, 147, 208-11, 221
    exclusion of, 122, 150
    experience and knowledge of, 158
    job searching, 196, 219
    trans people of color, 182
    underrepresentation, 199-201
performativity, 153-54
person-environment fit, 203
poor, 15, 74, 76, 97-115, 182
Pope, R. L., 4
positionality, 69, 92
power
    intersections within, 69
    structures, 69
Predominantly White Institutions, 120,
    149, 159
    culture, 162
    definition, 15
    experiences of Black women, 122,
        132-33, 140
    fit in the context of, 123
    tokenization, 157
Pregnancy Discrimination Act of 1978,
    32
preparation, 63-64
privilege, 168, 170, 186, 197
professional associations and
    organizations, 113, 184
professional development, 186
professionalism, 185
    attire and professional dress,
        105-6, 179
pronouns
    misgendering. See under gender

they, 169-70, 178
third person, 168
usage, 170, 177-79, 183
professionalism, ethics of, 81
Pryor, J. T., 172, 187
PWI. *See* Predominantly White
Institutions

race
aversive racism, 199
racial identity, 77
racism, 30
systemic racism, 39, 42, 68
racial justice, 134, 194, 209-10
racial stratification, 150
Rankin, S. R., 202
Reason, R. D., 202, 205, 211
recruitment, 72, 120, 127, 137, 138,
142, 222
Rehabilitation Act of 1973, 27
Reisser, L., 128
relationships, 80, 136
mentoring. *See* mentors, role of
professional, 11, 72, 133
supervisory, 86, 107, 109
Renn, K. A., 82
resistance, 68, 136, 179, 183-84, 186,
188, 201, 211
acts of resistance, 177, 181
definition, 176
resistant capital, 134
retention, 138, 142, 228
Reynolds, A. L., 4, 202-3

salary, 24, 106-7, 196
scholar-practitioner, 72, 73, 134, 233
search committees, 68, 85, 129-31,
193-94
case study on, 20-22
evaluation standards, 137, 219
expectations of, 137, 208-10
recommendations for, 61-62, 221-23
representation on, 62
Seelman, K. L., 174, 189
self-care, 81

sensemaking, 69
situating, 69
smoking gun, 38
social capital, 140
social justice, 27-28
social justice competency, 42
social location, 70
social media, 138, 220-21
social networking. *See* social media
socialization, 13, 107, 115, 128,
138-40, 147, 159, 200
cultural socialization, 155
gender socialization, 154
model, 160
professional socialization, 63, 160
Spade, D., 168, 171, 178, 182
stereotype, xii, 32, 119, 132,
158, 205
Stryker, S., 182
student services, 77
subordinated groups, 29, 31
Sue, D. W., 93, 169
supervision, 71, 86, 89
supervisory relationship, 31
systemic oppression, xii, 52, 229

Tatum, B. D., 60
tenure, 37
tenure process, 39
tenure-track faculty, 37, 39, 85
theoretical frame, 70, 72, 75
thriving, 151-53
Title IX, 27
tokenization, 157-60
training, 32, 81, 137, 139,
160, 172, 193, 198-99, 205,
221-23
job expectations, 38, 102,
129, 133
orientation, 4, 138
search committees. *See* search
committees
trans, 167-89
transgender, 8, 28, 41, 168, 186
transformation agents, 42

University of Tennessee, 182

values, 11-13
    departmental, 69
    espoused, 90
violence, administrative, 168

Whiteness, 29, 52-53
    critical Whiteness studies, 206-7
    culture of, 28, 52
    habitus of, 200-203, 210

White patriarchy, 132
White privilege, 201
White supremacy, 29, 149-51
women of color, 120, 173, 182, 185
worldview, 69, 70

Yin, R. K., 53, 55
Yoshino, K., 63, 172, 175
Yosso, T. J., 60, 98, 101-2, 104-6,
    109-15, 124-27, 134-35,
    150, 158